EUROPEAN STUDIES SERIES

General Editors   Colin Jones
                  Richard Overy
Series Advisers   Joe Bergin
                  John Breuilly
                  Ruth Harris

...is series marks a major initiative in European history publishing aimed primarily, though not exclusively, at an undergraduate audience. It will encompass a wide variety of books on aspects of European history since 1500, with particular emphasis on France and Germany, although no country will be excluded and a special effort will be made to cover previously neglected areas, such as Scandinavia, Eastern Europe and Southern Europe.

The series will include political accounts and broad thematic treatments, both of a comparative kind and studies of a single country, and will lay particular emphasis on social and cultural history where this opens up fruitful new ways of examining the past. The aim of the series is to make available a wide range of titles in areas where there is now an obvious gap or where the existing historical literature is out of date or narrowly focused. The series will also include translations of important books published elsewhere in Europe.

Interest in European affairs and history has never been greater; *European Studies* will help make that European heritage closer, richer and more comprehensible.

EUROPEAN STUDIES SERIES

Published

Forthcoming

More titles are in preparation

France, 1934–1970

RICHARD VINEN

First published 1996 by
MACMILLAN PRESS LTD
Houndmills, Basingstoke, Hampshire RG21 6XS
and London
Companies and representatives
throughout the world

ISBN 0–333–61359–7
ISBN 0–333–61360–0

A catalogue record for this book is available
from the British Library.

10 9 8 7 6 5 4 3 2 1
05 04 03 02 01 00 99 98 97 96

Printed in Malaysia

To Giles Ockenden

Contents

Acknowledgements

I am grateful to Richard Overy and Colin Jones for inviting me to write this book and for their help and encouragement while I was doing so. Janet and Stella Bell, Graham Goodlad, Richard Henwood, Claudia Muller, Kevin Passmore and Julian Sherwood made helpful remarks on all or part of the typescript. Judy Marshall copy-edited with great care and patience.

Since French history has been at the centre of my working life for the last ten years, this book is also associated with three more general debts. The first is to all those who afforded me hospitality in France, especially David Baker, Dagmar Braun, Patrick Chesnot, Christine Darrieu, and Joel Felix. Their friendship has made me like France much more and understand it a little better. The second general debt is to all the students at King's College London who have taken my second year course on modern French history. I am particularly endebted to Ekbe Attah and Thomas Collinson who endured my many obsessions and punctured a few of my more outlandish theories. Thirdly, I am grateful to Alison Henwood – for everything.

Abbreviations

AD	*Alliance Démocratique*
CFLN	*Comité Français de Libération Nationale*
CFTC	*Confédération Française des Travailleurs Chrétiens*
CGPF	*Confédération Générale du Patronat Français*
CGT	*Confédération Générale du Travail*
CGTU	*Confédération Générale du Travail Unitaire*
CJP	*Centre des Jeunes Patrons*
CNIP	*Centre National des Indépendants et Paysans*
CNPF	*Conseil National du Patronat Français*
CNR	*Conseil National de la Résistance*
CRS	*Compagnies Républicaines de Sécurité*
EDC	European Defence Community
EDF	*Electricité de France*
ENA	*Ecole Nationale d'Administration*
ENS	*Ecole Normale Supérieure*
FFI	*Forces Françaises de l'Intérieur*
FGDS	*Fédération de la Gauche Démocratique et Socialiste*
FLN	*Front de Libération Nationale*
FNSEA	*Fédération Nationale des Syndicats d'Exploitants Agricoles*
FO	*Force Ouvrière*
FR	*Fédération Républicaine*
FTP	*Franc-Tireurs et Partisans*
HLM	*Habitation à Loyer Modéré*
JAC	*Jeunesse Agricole Chrétienne*
MLN	*Mouvement de Libération Nationale*
MRP	*Mouvement Républicain Populaire*
MSR	*Mouvement Social Révolutionnaire*
NATO	North Atlantic Treaty Organization
OAS	*Organisation de l'Armée Secrète*
OCRPI	*Office Central de Répartition des Produits Industriels*
ORTF	*Office de la Radio-Télévision Française*
OS	*Organisation Secrète*
PCF	*Parti Communiste Français*
PPF	*Parti Populaire Français*

PRL	*Parti Républicain de la Liberté*
PSF	*Parti Social Français*
PSU	*Parti Socialiste Unifié*
RGR	*Rassemblement des Gauches Républicaines*
RNP	*Rassemblement National Populaire*
RPF	*Rassemblement du Peuple Français*
SAS	*Sections d'Administration Spéciaux*
SFIO	*Section Française de l'Internationale Ouvrière*
SOL	*Service d'Ordre Légionnaire*
STO	*Service du Travail Obligatoire*
UDCA	*Union de Défense des Commerçants et Artisans*
UDSR	*Union Démocratique et Socialiste de la Résistance*
UFF	*Union de Fraternité Française*
UNC	*Union Nationale des Combattants*
UNEF	*Union Nationale des Etudiants de France*
UNIR	*Union des Nationaux et Indépendants Républicains*
UNR	*Union pour la Nouvelle République*

Introduction

This book begins with a bang and ends with a whimper. The bang occurred on 6 February 1934 when fourteen of the demonstrators attacking parliament were shot dead by police. The whimper occurred on 9 November 1970 when de Gaulle, who had survived numerous assassination attempts, died peacefully at home. Between these two dates, France was transformed in three ways. Firstly, the level of political violence dropped. France was never as violent as, say, Weimar Germany, but throughout the period from 1934 until at least 1962 some Frenchmen believed that killing their fellow countrymen was a legitimate way to achieve their political ends. Furthermore, each act of violence fed off the memories of earlier acts: conflict in Vichy France was seen through the prism of events that had happened in the 1930s, or even earlier, and the dispute over *Algérie Française* was seen through the prism of Vichy. Some historians have argued that modern France has been in a state of virtual civil war. Charles de Gaulle, who rose against Vichy and was recalled to power to deal with Algeria, was a product of France's political violence. The mythology that surrounded his person was associated with a series of conflicts and many of his enemies came to believe that he encapsulated the wrongs that had been done to them. Indeed it might be argued that de Gaulle drew the poison of French animosities by focusing hatred, which had formerly been directed against whole groups of people, on one man. De Gaulle's departure from power was associated with the end of violence: his successor had been a non-combatant under Vichy who had appealed for amnesty after the Algerian war and who had sought to avoid bloodshed during the student riots of 1968. Since 1969 it has been inconceivable that a British cabinet should discuss, as it did in 1961, whether to send troops to support the French government against its own people, or that a French president should fly to Germany, as de Gaulle did in 1968, to check on the loyalty of the army before confronting rioters on the streets of Paris.

There are two other respects in which France was transformed between 1934 and 1970. In constitutional terms, the domination of the legislature that had characterized French politics since the early Third Republic came to an end. France acquired a strong president, stable government, and more structured political parties. In economic terms, France in 1934 was a weak and declining power that was finding it particularly hard to escape from the consequences of the great depression; in 1970 she had experienced 'thirty glorious years' of growth and seemed poised to outstrip the economic growth of Germany and Japan.

This book attempts to describe and explain these changes, but it is not meant to be the first or the last word on the subject. Those who intend to read only one book on twentieth-century France should look elsewhere. I have neither tried to write a straight narrative account of events nor to write a comprehensive synthesis of all previous historical interpretations. Rather I have tried to write a series of interpretative essays on particular subjects. It might help readers to decide how to approach this book, and indeed whether to approach it all, if I outline what I believe to be the peculiarities of my own approach. Firstly, I have given particular attention to the centre and right of the political spectrum. This is partly because the right has been in power for most of the time between 1934 and 1970. It is also because I believe that historians, especially those from Britain and America, have been led astray by a fruitless search for a reformist or social democratic left that would correspond to their own political sympathies. In reality, the parties of the French left remained fixated on a Jacobin revolutionary past or a Bolshevik revolutionary future. If such parties worked within the capitalist system at all, they did so by suspending their revolutionary intentions altogether and becoming functional conservatives. The French right, on the other hand, has been influential precisely because of its lack of a clearly defined ideology: this made it flexible and innovative.

The second peculiarity of this book relates to Vichy France. Many historians regard much of post-war French history as an extension of the struggle between Pétainists and the Resistance. I believe that neither Vichy nor the Resistance attracted the active support of more than a small proportion of the population. Much of the impact of the Vichy period came from the general effects of war and occupation rather than the policies of the government. By contrast, I am more inclined than most historians to emphasize the importance for French society of departure from Algeria; indeed I would argue that the fact that this event attracted so little explicit discussion after 1962 is a sign that it had helped to bring about such transformations that all events before it came to seem irrelevant.

The third peculiarity of my approach relates to post-war economic growth. Most historians have emphasized the role of state planning in this growth, and some seem to believe that a small group of heroic individuals gathered around Jean Monnet managed to transform the French economy simply by the exercise of their will and intelligence. I am sceptical about such interpretations for two reasons. Firstly, state planning was not simply a technocratic instrument of economic management: it had political roots in the threat that the French bourgeoisie felt themselves to be under in the late 1940s. Secondly, the failure of other countries to imitate France's planning success and the failure of the French to sustain their economic success beyond the mid 1970s suggests that processes – such as immigration, technological change, and the development of consumerism – outside the control of government played a large part in economic growth.

Map 1   Departments of France

MAP   XV

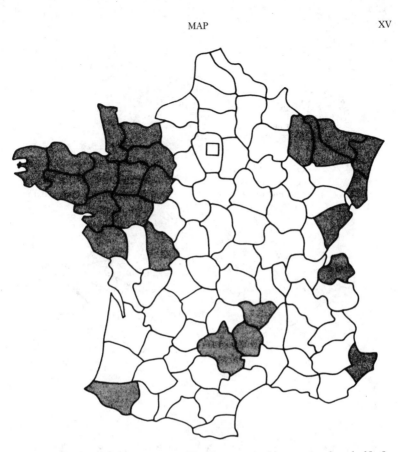

Map 2   The Political Geography of France: areas where more than half of
votes were cast for the right in 1936 are marked in black

Zone attached
to the German
Command in Brussels

Arras

Amiens
Prohibited
zone
Laon
Mézières

German zone of
occupation
PARIS
Reims
Metz

St-Dizier   Bar le Duc
Chaumont
Tours   Reserved
Bourges Langres   zone
Poitiers   Dijon   Belfort   Annexed
Châteauroux   Moulins   Dôle   zone
Angoulême
Charolles
Demarcation   Vichy   Nantua
line
Langon   Vienne
Périgeux
Mt-de-Marsan   Free zone   (after the
Valence   Italian   Armistice)
German occupation   zone of
(after Nov 1942)   occupation
(after
Avignon   Nov 1942)
Aix   Menton

FRENCH NORTH AFRICA
(Vichy until liberated by the Americans
in November 1942)

0   100 Miles
0   100 km

Map 3 Vichy France

1 Background: France in 1934

Third Republic France often seems to offer the geographer more than the historian. Regional differences were considerable. Everyone was aware of the contrast between Paris and quiet provincial towns such as Neuvic d'Ussel or Dol de Bretagne. Indeed for much of the nineteenth century the provinces had been literally behind Paris because France did not have a unified time system. Even within the capital city there were geographical differences. The Left Bank of the Seine was the centre of intellectual life. This area contained the medieval university of the Sorbonne as well as the elite *École Normale Supérieure*. French historians such as Marc Bloch and Fernand Braudel might talk about the need for regional or international perspectives, but both men were obsessed by the need to return to the Latin Quarter; when Simone de Beauvoir was given a teaching job in Rouen, she rented a room by the station so that she could get back to Paris quickly. The western *beaux quartiers* were home to the French bourgeoisie and the headquarters of large companies. Northern and eastern Paris were the centres of working-class and immigrant life. The city itself had been kept free of industry for much of the nineteenth century, for political reasons, but in the twentieth century it came to be surrounded by a belt of industrial *banlieues* where the metallurgical, automobile and aircraft industries employed around 180,000 people. As the inhabitants of the wealthy areas were uncomfortably aware, these *banlieues* provided the left with a new source of strength.

Regional variations affected economic life. The average wage of Parisian workers was 50 per cent higher than that of provincial ones, and in 1936 unemployment varied from 3.5 to 12 per cent of the male population according to the area. Large-scale industry was focused in the Nord and Pas-de-Calais, greater Paris, the Rhône basin and the Meurthe and Moselle. Politics were also subject to regional variation. The right was strong in Brittany, the Vendée, Alsace-Lorraine and the Massif Central (see Map 2). This strength corresponded with areas of religious devotion as well as with patterns of land tenure and settlement that had, at least until the advent of a genuinely secret ballot, given landlords great power. The left was

1

strong in the 'midi rouge' and the dechristianized south-west. Certain areas were associated with particular tendencies. Brittany and the Vendée harboured the traditions of the counter-revolutionary right that dated back to their rebellions against the French Revolution. The culture of the Nord and Pas-de-Calais was rooted in its heavy industrial landscape and bore some resemblances to that of northern England (complete with black pudding, rugby league and pigeon racing). Alsace and Lorraine were influenced by the fact that they had been ruled by Germany between 1870 and 1919. Much of their population spoke German, they had been spared the separation of church and state, the influence of the German Centre party meant that they were the only part of France with an important Christian Democratic tradition, and the experience of invasion meant that they were particularly nationalistic.

Regional differences in France may surprise British observers more than continental ones. However, the extent of continuity over time in Third Republic France was striking by any standards. Stability in France was reflected in demography. Her population hovered between 36 million and 39 million throughout the lifetime of the Third Republic. While other countries were transformed by migration from the country, the growth of large cities, and emigration to the new world, France remained a country of quiet small towns. This demographic stability was partially due to laws that land be divided equally among heirs. This forced peasants to limit their family size if they wished to maintain a farm of a workable size.

The precise nature of social and economic stability in the Third Republic is the subject of heated debates. 'Pessimists' see the period 1870 to 1940 as one of economic retardation (briefly broken by an uncharacteristic burst of growth between 1906 and 1929); 'optimists' see the period from 1906 to 1973 as one of economic growth (briefly broken by a period of stagnation between 1929 and 1947). The differences between the two schools are partly rooted in the difference between sectors: those who study the French automobile industry paint a picture of dynamic and innovative entrepreneurs; those who study the textile industry see backward family firms. Some historians argue that French industry as a whole experienced growth for most of the twentieth century but has been held back by an inefficient agricultural sector. Two points are to be borne in mind when reading the work of both schools. Firstly, industrial statistics can be deceptive. Economies starting from a low base often experience a period of rapid, but unsustainable, growth. Secondly, understanding whether or not the French growth of 1906 to 1929 really anticipated that which was to occur after the Second World War means taking into account its nature as well as its extent.

Those who adopt a pessimistic interpretation of the French economy tend to emphasize the social restraints on economic change. This interpretation, most famously expressed by Stanley Hoffmann,[1] presents France as a 'stalemate society' dominated by a 'republican synthesis' between the bourgeoisie, peasants, shopkeepers and small producers who made up much of the population. This arrangement spared the *haute bourgeoisie* from the social threat which a powerful working class presented to their counterparts in other European countries, and it spared the peasants and the *petite bourgeoisie* from the economic threat that rapid industrialization presented to their counterparts in other countries. The republican synthesis is seen to have been underwritten by a common acceptance of certain values: thrift, prudence, conservatism. The key institution for the propagation of such values in industry was the family firm which placed status and security above growth and the maximization of profits. The concept of the republican synthesis raises awkward questions. Some historians point out that those who claimed to represent the *petite bourgeoisie* and the peasantry often had rather tenuous relations with their supposed constituency, and that social arrangements of the Third Republic may have been based on manipulation as much as compromise and on economic necessity as much as the internalization of a common ideology.

There are also problems with the economic implications of the 'stalemate society' interpretation. It assumes that economic progress is a straight and one way street leading from 'tradition' to 'modernity'. It fails to allow for the possibility that there may be different varieties of modernity depending on whether the structure of firms, their relationship with the market or their use of technology is taken into account. The full complexity of these possibilities is revealed by looking at two sectors: automobile manufacture and coal mining. In terms of management structure, the French coal industry was 'modern'. It was run by a highly trained and professionally conscious core of managers rather than by owners. However, in technological terms, the coal industry was backward. The automobile industry, by contrast, was archaic in its managerial structure. It was run by proud authoritarian entrepreneurs (Renault, Citroën, Peugeot) who hoped to pass on their firms to their descendants. However, in terms of openness to technological innovation the automobile industry was highly 'modern'. Finally, in terms of their relations to the market, both the automobile and the coal industry were 'backward'. Both depended largely on state markets and, in the case of the automobile industry, on luxury consumption. Neither made much attempt to find a mass market for their produce.

It might be argued that the real weakness of the French economy lay not in social arrangements, but in France's natural resources. France lacked coal reserves. She was always obliged to import around a third of her needs and much of her industry was clustered around the coal fields in the north and in the Loire. France was also affected by her agricultural resources. The very fertility of her land meant that people were not forced into cities to seek industrial employment and the consequent shortage of labour was exacerbated by the low birthrate described above. The obsession with the acquisition of land in France, which dated back to the sale of noble estates after the revolution, also diverted wealth that might normally have gone into industrial production.

The politics of Third Republic France does not, at first glance, seem to fit into the pattern of stability outlined above. Governments changed with a regularity that makes it almost impossible to write a narrative history of political events. However, continuity was hidden under the changes. Successive cabinets often contained the same ministers and pursued the same policies. Furthermore the regime itself survived for 70 years, outliving the Weimar Republic in Germany by 56 years, and the Second Republic in Spain by 65 years. The most characteristic party of the Third Republic was the Radical party (founded in 1898), which mobilized between 70,000 and 120,000 members in the 1930s (membership figures were notoriously inaccurate), and gained around 160 seats in the 1932 elections. The Radicals emerged out of the need to organize and rally political forces that was felt in the wake of the Dreyfus affair (the debate over the fate of a Jewish army officer unfairly convicted of spying for the Germans in 1894). They were republicans who looked back to the Revolution of 1789 as the origin of all political virtue. They were also anti-clericals who wished to maintain the separation of church and state enacted in 1905. However, though the Radicals were 'left-wing' in terms of their attitude to clericalism and the constitution, they were often conservative in their attitude to social matters. They did not believe in state intervention in the economy or in the redistribution of wealth. Most of their electorate was composed of peasants, shopkeepers, small businessmen, members of the liberal professions, and lower level state employees.

The Radical party was pragmatic. When the leading philosopher of the party 'Alain' (Emile Chartier) sent his *Elements of a Radical Doctrine* to all Radical ministers, one of them sent back the withering reply: 'If we had a doctrine I am sure that we would be the first to know about it.' Radical politicians spent much time seeking to secure advantages for their constituencies or jobs for their supporters and their position as a central hinge party, the support of which was essential for the formation of any cabinet, facilitated these functions. Radicals attracted scorn from commentators who regarded them as unprincipled, corrupt and responsible for the economic decline of the Third Republic. However, there was also a strong case to be made in favour of the Radicals. They had a general attachment to the principles of democracy and, unlike more idealistic and ambitious groups, they also had the political skill to defend those principles effectively. The Radicals did much to see off the threat of fascism in France during the 1930s just as they were to head off the threats of Stalinism and Gaullism after the Second World War. Their action during the 1930s was particularly effective because their electorate included many of the groups that turned to fascism in other European countries.

Action Française was in many ways a photo-negative of the Radical party. It too had been founded, in 1901, in the aftermath of the Dreyfus case. But *Action Française*'s presiding genius, Charles Maurras, asserted the guilt of Dreyfus. His movement was monarchist and clerical (though it had stormy relations with the French royal family and laboured under the official disapproval of the Vatican from 1926 until 1939). Where the Radical party was an electoral machine, *Action Française* only contested elections once in its history (in 1919). It sought to diffuse what Maurras called a 'conquering idea' through a daily newspaper and the publications of leading supporters such as Bainville and Daudet. The influence of *Action Française* extended over the whole of the Catholic bourgeoisie and touched men like Mauriac and Charles de Gaulle, who were never royalists. The style as well as the policies of *Action Française* was diametrically opposed to that of the Radical party. Radicals were seen, indeed often saw themselves, as old, provincial and prudent. The students who flocked to join the *Action Française* youth movement, the *Camelots du Roi*, saw themselves as representing hot-headed idealism and Parisian chic. For all their disagreements, *Action Française* and the Radical party had some things in common. Both saw the French Revolution and the Dreyfus case as the centre of political debate. Neither had very much to do with the modern industrial world. Both received funds from industrialists and made sentimental noises about the working classes, but both were led by lawyers and journalists who had rarely set foot in a factory.

Between the Radical party and *Action Française* stood the parties of the parliamentary right, although such parties rarely admitted to being right-wing and preferred the title 'moderate'. These parties defended bourgeois interests while pledging loyalty to the republic. The two most important parties in this group were Louis Marin's *Fédération Republicaine* (FR) and Pierre-Etienne Flandin's *Alliance Démocratique* (AD). The FR had been founded in 1903. It was intensely nationalistic and generally sought to defend the interests of the church. It grouped around 10,000 active members and mobilized something between 60 and 100 deputies in parliament throughout the 1930s. Many of its supporters were wealthy and observers, wrongly, believed that the Lorraine ironmaster François de Wendel exercised great power over the party. The party's leaders also tended to be old, the average age of its deputies in 1935 was over 58, and many of them came from political 'dynasties' that controlled particular constituencies. The *Alliance Démocratique* had been founded in 1901. It bore many resemblances to the Radical party since it was traditionally hostile to clerical influence (though this hostility had begun to diminish by the 1930s). Its supporters were generally bourgeois.

Throughout the interwar period certain individuals on the parliamentary right, such as André Tardieu or Georges Mandel, sought to reform the French political system. They wanted to see a stronger presidency and more disciplined parties on the right that might resemble the British Conservative party. However, efforts to create disciplined parties on the right were hampered by three things. Firstly, religion continued to play a role among the parliamentary right: in particular it divided the clerical FR from the *laïque* AD. Secondly, the eccentricities and obvious ambition of some of the right's leaders – notably Marin, Reynaud, Tardieu, and Mandel – guaranteed that they would always be condemned to quarrels. Thirdly, the frontiers between the parliamentary right and more extreme organizations were never clearly defined. Many conservatives maintained links with a variety of extra-parliamentary leagues. Such leagues were funded by André Tardieu with government secret service money, and by the FR industrialist François de Wendel from his own resources. The FR recruited a number of former members of extra-parliamentary leagues, such as Taittinger, and a number of its members, such as Xavier Vallat and Philippe Henriot, were later to become prominent in undemocratic politics. The leagues also provided guards for meetings of parliamentary right-wing parties. It was never clear that all leaders of the right would remain committed to democracy and some events, such as Tardieu's decision to address himself directly to the country after his defeat in the parliamentary arena, suggested that they would not.

The parties mentioned above were preoccupied with clerical and constitutional issues that had come to the fore during the aftermath of the Dreyfus case. However, there were also issues emerging from the growth of an industrial working class which came to the fore in the aftermath of the Russian Revolution. Achieving unity among the French socialists had always been complicated by the regional diversity of French industry and by the persistence of the non-class issues described above, but in 1905 a variety of socialist factions had come together to form the *Section Française de l'Internationale Ouvrière* (SFIO). In the aftermath of the Russian Revolution this unity broke down again. Those socialists who wished to join the Moscow-based Third International broke away from the SFIO at the congress of Tours (1920) and formed the *Parti Communiste Français* (PCF). This split was mirrored in the trade union confederation as the Communist *Confédération Générale du Travail Unitaire* split away from the *Confédération Générale du Travail.* Both the SFIO and the PCF continued to describe themselves as Marxist and revolutionary parties. In practice the SFIO combined a defence of the working class with anti-clericalism and a defence of republicanism that sometimes facilitated alliance with the bourgeois Radical party. The SFIO had around 110,000 members in 1934 and 97 deputies in parliament. The Communist party was different. Its leaders were almost all men of working-class background who owed their promotion exclusively to the patronage of the party. Often such men had been educated in Moscow, and of all the Communist parties in western Europe, the PCF was generally the most disciplined and the most loyal to the line defined in Moscow. In 1928 Moscow ordered the adoption of a 'class against class' strategy that involved the denunciation of the SFIO leadership as 'social fascists' and the refusal to ally with any other formation. This policy was badly adapted to French circumstances. Unlike the German Social Democrats, the French SFIO was not a party of government and had never been involved in the repression of communism. Some PCF leaders tried to resist class against class tactics: when such tactics were adopted the party's membership dropped to around 87,000, and in the 1932 election the party gained only ten seats in parliament.

2 'Inaction française'

When the fascist Lucien Rebatet wrote his memoirs in 1941 he entitled the chapter dealing with the 1930s '*Inaction française*'.[1] Rebatet was referring to the passivity of *Action Française*, the royalist movement to which he himself had once belonged, but his words might be taken as a more general comment on the nature of the Third Republic in the late 1930s. During this period French society and politics remained much as they had been during the previous six decades of the Third Republic. But what had formerly been seen as stability was now seen as stagnation – no one felt inclined to describe France on the eve of the Second World War as a *belle époque*. The problem was that while France changed little the world around her had changed much. International events induced a sense of crisis among some French intellectuals and politicians. Some of them embraced dramatic solutions to such crisis and put their faith in the fascism preached by Doriot or Déat, the technocratic modernization preached by Ernest Mercier's *Redressement Français* or the Christian humanism preached by the *Esprit* group gathered around Emmanuel Mounier.

It is sometimes suggested that these men were isolated outsiders in a political system that was complacently attached to the status quo. In fact, it is striking how many mainstream politicians during the 1930s believed that France ought to undergo radical change. The 1930s saw a government of national unity, under Doumergue, that contained many such people; two years later, the first Socialist prime minister was invested in the first government of France to have Communist support. Even the Radical Daladier, who was prime minister at the beginning and the end of the period described in this chapter, had been seen as a reformer within his own party. However, the various groups that were dissatisfied with the state of France seemed unable to translate their dissatisfaction into change: the closer that they came to power the less radical their intentions became. This chapter will suggest that the caution of French politicians during the 1930s did not just spring from their own personalities or from the political traditions from which they came. Rather it was a result of constraints, imposed by public opinion, the economy and international events, that limited the freedom of manoeuvre that any government could hope to exercise.

The first of these constraints sprang from the Great War of 1914 to 1918. The war had a double effect. On the one hand, it showed the importance of technology and economic organization. Some French industries responded well to the challenges of war production. Industrial concentration increased so that the number of firms employing more than 5000 people doubled (from 17 to 35) during the war. Furthermore, collaboration between industrialists and the state increased. Some Frenchmen, such as the minister of armaments Louis Loucheur, hoped that the lessons of the war would be translated into peacetime. This did not happen. The *Confédération Générale de la Production Française* was formed to group French employers in 1919, but it exercised little influence. A few industrialists became fascinated by American techniques and by the production line organization of work pioneered by the American Frederick Winslow Taylor, though they often misunderstood and misapplied these lessons. However, in agriculture the war had very different effects. In France, as everywhere else, the peasantry benefited from wartime inflation to pay off debt. But, whereas in many countries this surplus was invested in mechanization, in France the peasantry simply bought more land. During the 1920s a striking disparity arose between increasing industrial production and stagnant agricultural production and by the late 1930s the average French farmer fed only 5.1 people while his American counterpart fed 14.8 people.

The war also left a psychological legacy; the lesson that the majority of Frenchmen drew from the First World War was exactly the opposite of that drawn by those who wished to change French society. Peasants were the largest single element in the French army, and victory was often interpreted as a vindication of their way of life. The war memorials to these men dominated every small town in France during the 1930s. The great battle at Verdun became a part of France's collective memory and contributed much to the cult of marshal Pétain who had commanded French forces there. Furthermore, the organizations of veterans, known colloquially as *poilus*, grouped around 3.5 million men in interwar France. The mythology that grew up around these men blended in with the republican tradition of the 'nation in arms' that dated back to the French Revolution. It stressed their ordinariness and their roots in rural or small town France. In short it glorified the pre-1914 social structure of France. This mythology outlived the men who had served in the war. In 1954 the small business leader Pierre Poujade (born in 1920) attacked the self-consciously modern prime minister Pierre Mendès-France (born in 1907) in these terms: 'Our fathers were at Verdun ... and you were not.'[2]

The Great War had more straightforward material effects on France. The casualties of the First World War exacerbated the problems caused by France's low birthrate. In addition to the 1,300,000 men killed during the war, France lacked the people who might normally have been born during the war, when birthrates had dropped to one half of their normal level. The demographic shadow of the First World War was especially important because men born between 1914 and 1918 would normally have become available for military service in the years leading up to the Second World War. The war also left an economic legacy. Inflation had ruined many rentiers. In practical terms this meant that fewer French people lived off fixed incomes, but in psychological terms it increased the attachment of the French bourgeoisie to sound money. There were 600,000 widows and 750,000 orphans left by the war; of every 10 men who had been aged between 20 and 45 in 1914, 3 were invalided for some time and one ended up entirely dependent on the state. In the late 1930s, half of all French government spending went on war pensions and interest on loans. The economic legacy, which was made worse by France's inability to secure from Germany the reparations that had been promised in the treaty of Versailles, impeded both investment in industrial modernization and rearmament against Germany.

The second constraint that affected France was the result of the great depression that was sparked off by the Wall Street crash of 1929. At first it seemed that the world economic crisis would spare France. Banks in France had been notoriously reluctant to take risks with industrial lending, and this protected her from the spate of bank failures that afflicted America and Germany. Indeed French gold reserves increased from 46 billion francs in 1929 to 83 billion francs in 1932, and the fact that the Bank of England was obliged to borrow on the Paris markets made some French financiers hope that Paris might replace London as the financial centre of Europe. During this optimistic period French politicians embarked on two major projects for increased public spending which were to have heavy consequences. In December 1929 parliament voted credits for the construction of the Maginot Line: a series of fortifications along France's eastern frontier. In April 1930 parliament voted to create universal pensions for veterans of the First World War. However, from 1931 the French economy went into noticeable decline. Industrial production dropped by 17.5 per cent in this year. By 1935 production had dropped by 20 per cent (from its 1929 level), share prices had dropped by 33 per cent and dividends had dropped by 52 per cent.

Having arrived late, the French depression also stayed late. France did not recover her 1929 levels of production until after the Second World War. This had particularly severe consequences because it meant that France remained economically weak at a time when her military rival Germany was reviving. However, the consequences of the French depression for her internal politics often seemed less severe than those experienced by other European countries. Official unemployment figures never exceeded half a million. The static population of the Third Republic meant that the French industrial labour force had always been tightly stretched, and that it had always contained a large proportion of immigrants and women. During the economic crisis it was relatively easy to push both these groups out of the labour force. Women were sometimes encouraged to 'return' to being housewives while immigrants were encouraged to return to their countries of origin. In 1932 the government introduced a quota to restrict immigration and in 1935 married women were excluded from some civil service jobs. The fact that neither immigrants nor women had the vote left them with few means to resist such a fate. French leaders never had to confront the huge pool of despairing unemployed male proletarians that their counterparts in Germany, Great Britain and America faced.

It might be argued that the economic crisis helped France to break away from her past. It is true that the worst hit areas of the economy were those that are normally seen as backward: agriculture and small business. By contrast, standards of living for workers, or at least those who remained in work, increased because wages fell by only 15 per cent while prices fell by 20 per cent. The economy was also restructured by the depression. The state intervened in certain respects (most notably in the foundation of French national railways in 1937). In some areas, production was concentrated as industrialists snatched the opportunity to buy up competitors or suppliers. However, industrial concentration was not synonymous with mechanization or investment in plant. Many large-scale heavy industries relied on ruthless labour discipline rather than new technology to sustain production levels, and the depression encouraged some firms to turn away from the free market towards the 'sheltered

sector' of sales to the state. Furthermore, the fact that small businesses and agriculture did badly does not mean that they ceased to
exist or even that they diminished in importance. The number of
self-employed in the French economy actually increased as men who
had been laid off resorted to setting up insecure and often itinerant
small enterprises. Similarly some industrial workers returned to
family farms where at least they could obtain regular food. The
state's intervention also protected the politically powerful independent and agricultural sectors. Agricultural subsidies and tariffs were
increased and laws were passed to protect certain sectors against
competition (such as the *loi Pullen* designed to prevent the international Bata shoe company from driving French shoemakers out of
business).

The third constraint faced by France during the 1930s was that
generated by the rise of international fascism. There were a number
of extra-parliamentary leagues in France. The oldest of these was
Action Française but after the First World War a number of other
bodies had been founded. The *Jeunesses Patriotes*, set up by the cham-
pagne magnate Taittinger in 1924, claimed to have a membership of
300,000 by 1929. *Solidarité Française* was founded in 1933 by Marcel
Bucard; it received subsidies from the perfume manufacturer Coty
and from Mussolini. The most important of the interwar leagues was
the *Croix de Feu*. Founded in 1927, the *Croix de Feu* began to reach a
large audience after 1931 when colonel de la Rocque became its
leader. The *Croix de Feu* appealed to veterans of the First World
War, its membership was initially confined to those who had been
decorated with the *Croix de Feu*, though it subsequently widened its
audience by establishing a youth wing.

Some commentators have suggested that these movements were a
French version of fascism. This interpretation has been unpopular
among French historians who have generally followed René Rémond
in arguing that the leagues merely represented traditional French
'Bonapartism'. Rémond suggests that France was kept safe from
fascism by her victory in the First World War, by the comparatively
low levels of unemployment experienced during the economic crisis,
by her long experience of democracy and by the fact that an aged
population had little sympathy for a movement that based its appeal
on youth.[3] Rémond would argue that French fascism was a comparatively marginal movement. He would suggest that its most prominent
representatives in France were either regional nationalists, such as
the Alsatian Nazi Karl Roos, or men with left-wing origins who

became disgusted with their original party during the 1930s. Jacques Doriot (who moved from the Communist party to found the *Parti Populaire Française* in 1936), Simon Sabiani (a Communist from Marseilles who also joined the PPF), and Marcel Déat (who moved from the Socialist party to found the *Rassemblement National Populaire*) all fitted into the second category.

Rémond's arguments are open to question. Countries that had gained from the First World War, such as Romania, did give birth to substantial fascist movements, and the electorate of fascism, if not its leaders, was often drawn from the old. Other historians argue that the links between fascism and conservatism in the 1930s were closer than Rémond allows. They would argue that the violence and para-military style of a movement such as the *Croix de Feu* were fascist. Perhaps it is dangerous to attempt to define the word fascist with too much precision. It might be argued that the most important charac-teristics of fascism were precisely its lack of intellectual coherence and an ability to adjust to national circumstances. Furthermore, many right-wingers did regard fascism with favour, whether or not they thought of themselves as fascists, and many left-wingers believed that their most dangerous opponents were fascists. The struggle between these two groups was to dominate much of French political life between 1934 and 1940.

Economic discontent and the growing power of the leagues found a focus in January 1934 when Serge Alexandre Stavisky was found dead at a chalet in the Alps. Stavisky was a professional swindler who appears to have committed suicide after being exposed. As an East European Jew who seemed to have been protected from prosecution in the past by political links, he could have been tailormade for the demonology of the extreme right. *Action Française* hinted that Stavisky had links with members of the government and that he had been murdered to prevent him from revealing these links. Such alle-gations helped to bring down the government of Camille Chautemps and to bring in his fellow Radical Edouard Daladier as prime minister. Daladier was regarded as being a strong leader and he sought to create a broadly based government that would take in both right and left. Possibly in a bid to win over the left, he ordered the transfer of the Paris prefect of police Chiappe. Chiappe had been implicated in the Stavisky affair, but he was also seen to have been excessively lenient with right-wing demonstrations and the right resented his removal. On 6 February 1934, a variety of organ-izations combined in a demonstration in Paris. The demonstration

turned into a riot and then into an attack on parliament. In repuls-
ing this attack police and *gardes mobiles* killed 14 demonstrators and
caused numerous casualties.

Some, such as the Socialist leader Léon Blum, presented these
events as an attempted coup d'état that anticipated the Vichy regime
of 1940. In reality the men who demonstrated in February had little
in common with each other. Some of these demonstrators came
from the veterans' leagues and the *Croix de Feu*, which were republican and patriotic. However, the events also involved *Action Française*,
which was patriotic but emphatically anti-republican, and some
Communists who were internationalist in outlook. The various
groups involved in the riots did not even coordinate their action.
They met at different places and only came together in the course of
the riots. Furthermore, there was never much unity of purpose or
determination among the rioters. Colonel de la Rocque, the leader
of the *Croix de Feu*, held his own supporters back at a crucial moment
and there is evidence that de la Rocque himself had been involved in
negotiations with government representatives before February 6.
Indeed in some respects the prospect of a coup d'état was a night-
mare for the *Croix de Feu* leadership which had always combined
violent rhetoric and occasional paramilitary operations against
Communists with a respect for the republic and for legality. De la
Rocque may well have hoped that growing chaos or the menace of
Bolshevism would force the government to offer him power, but he
had no intention of seizing it. The movement that bore the brunt of
the fighting on the night of February 6 was *Action Française*. 4 out of
14 of those killed and 42 per cent of the wounded came from it.
However, the leaders of *Action Française* did not plan the violence in
which they were involved and they had no techniques to follow up or
exploit such violence. The leaders of the movement remained preoccupied with words even when their followers were seeking to
change France by deeds. Robert Brasillach, one of the movement's
intellectual supporters, was attending a performance in his capacity
as a theatre critic and when he emerged to see the riots in the streets
he viewed them as just another form of 'spectacle'. The movement's
other leaders decided that the best thing to be done in the aftermath of the riots was to return to their office and bring out the next
edition of their newspaper. Maurras himself subsequently retired to
his study and spent the rest of the night writing poetry.

After the riots, Daladier resigned and Gaston Doumergue (a
former president of the republic) was persuaded to form a new gov-

ernment. Doumergue's regime was described by Trotsky as 'senile bonapartism'; it governed by decree law and it took in several men, such as marshal Pétain the victor of Verdun, from outside the world of formal politics. Furthermore, Doumergue, at the instigation of Tardieu, sought to introduce constitutional reform that would strengthen the powers of the president of the republic and weaken those of parliament. However, Doumergue's government contained Herriot, the veteran Radical, and it depended on the support of the Radicals as well as that of the right. In November Herriot withdrew his support rather than allow Doumergue to introduce constitutional change and the government fell.

The events of 6 February 1934 also had consequences on the left. Immediately after the riots, Socialists and Communists had demonstrated together. Their rapprochement was rooted partly in the spontaneous distaste of the two parties' supporters for fascism. More importantly it sprang from the fact that the men in Moscow, who exercised such influence over the French Communist party, had decided that the major threat to the Soviet Union came from Nazi Germany. This made them encourage European Communist parties to abandon 'class against class' tactics and ally with democratic parties to present a united front against fascism. On 3 March a *comité de vigilance des intellectuels anti-fascistes* was established. It contained thinkers ranging from the Communist sympathizer Romain Rolland to the Radical Emile Chartier (Alain). On 27 July 1934 the Socialists and Communists signed a pact for joint action which helped them make gains in the municipal elections of May the following year. Eventually the majority of Radicals also came to join a left-wing *Rassemblement Populaire* which issued its manifesto on 12 January 1936. The unification of the left was reflected in the trade unions when the Communist *Confédération Générale du Travail Unitaire* merged with the Socialist *Confédération Générale du Travail* in March 1936. In May 1936 the new left-wing alliance gained a spectacular victory in the general elections. It won around 380 seats against its opponents' 237 seats.

At first glance the Popular Front election looked like a sharp move of French politics to the left. The Communists had increased their representation in parliament from 10 to 72. The Socialists had increased their representation from 97 to 146. The Radicals, by contrast, had seen their strength in parliament fall from 159 to 116. In reality the policies advocated by the successful candidates in this election were less radical (and more Radical) than they first appeared. The Socialists and the Communists did not wish to restructure French society; they both believed that such real change would be impossible without the destruction of capitalism and that in the circumstances such a destruction was impossible. Both Socialists and Communists wished to bring together the widest coalition of Frenchmen to unite against fascism. These involved ostentatious moderation and the policy of the 'outstretched hand' towards groups – such as Catholics and small businessmen – that had traditionally been hostile to the left. They also wished to rearm France and this meant avoiding measures that might disturb industrial production. Consequently Blum stressed that he wished to 'govern within the capitalist framework', while Popular Front manifestos studiously avoided any commitment to social change.

The reassuring moderation of the Popular Front government was reinforced by two things. The first of these was the decision of the Communist party not to accept ministerial office in the government. The second was the personality of the Socialist leader and Popular Front prime minister elect: Léon Blum. Blum was an unlikely leader of a proletarian party. He had been an intellectual dandy and friend of Marcel Proust in his youth. As a Jew, a Dreyfusard and a supporter (in his 1908 book *On Marriage*) of sexual equality for women, Blum attracted the dislike of the extreme right. Maurras was particularly venomous and once compared Blum to a camel fourteen times in a single article. However, Blum's background was impeccably bourgeois. He had been at school with the head of France's largest merchant bank, and he had served in the *conseil d'état* with the president of the *Comité des Forges* (the association of French ironmasters). He had even, like many Dreyfusard Jews, proved his credentials as a gentleman by fighting duels. In 1936 his concern for constitutional propriety was so great that he refused to take office immediately after the elections but insisted on waiting until his official inauguration. Such gestures won the Popular Front some sympathy from representatives of the property-owning classes. The Lyon chamber of commerce expressed support for the Popular Front slogan of 'peace, bread and liberty'. After the Communists declared that they would not take ministerial office, Claude Gignoux, editor of *Le Figaro* and soon to be elected as leader of the main employers' association, wrote an article entitled 'The bourgeoisie breathes again'.

The bourgeoisie breathed too soon. If the leaders of the Popular Front had turned away from demands for social change, those who voted for them had not done so. Throughout 1936 the Paris metal-working industry had been affected by strikes. Between the Popular Front electoral victory and Blum's assumption of office these strikes spread. Workers at three aircraft factories in Courbevoie, Toulouse and Le Havre occupied their workplaces (a practice that had rarely been seen in France). By June 1936, 1,800,000 workers from 12,142 factories were on strike; 8441 factories had been occupied. The strikes exposed the gulf between the left-wing leaders and the working class. This gulf sprang partly from the bourgeois background of men like Blum and Daladier, partly from the fact that both the Radicals and the Socialists were often absorbed by a rhetoric that stressed the defence of the republic and of individual rights rather than class interests, and partly from the fact that Communist strategy was dictated by Moscow's international interests rather than by a response to events within France.

The gulf also sprang partly from the nature of the French working class. This can be illustrated by a brief international comparison. The German working classes had, at least up until 1933, a long tradition of trade union and political organization and a working-class 'subculture' that embraced much of their leisure lives. The English working classes had benefited from their country's relative prosperity during the late nineteenth and early twentieth centuries. Suburbanization, restriction of working hours, the birth of the weekend and of a commercialized popular culture had shifted the focus of their attention away from the workplace towards the neighbourhood, and the wider society, in which they lived. These stabilizing experiences had affected the French working class much less. French workers were an isolated group in a country dominated by the peasantry and the *petite bourgeoisie*. Many of them were immigrants or recent migrants from the countryside who had come to industrial areas to take jobs in the metallurgical industries that had sprung up during the First World War. They lacked the culture, tradition and political organization that had grown up with the more established working classes. They often lived in grim industrial *banlieues* in which they had little possibility of leisure activities and little contact with other classes. The lives of the workers often centred on the workplace itself because working hours were long and free time, such as it was, often occurred within the working day in the form of a long lunch-break. The results of these conditions can be seen in the events of 1936. The spontaneity of the strikes was characteristic of a working class that had few traditions of organization and the occupation of the factories reflected lives that revolved around the workplace.

What the workers hoped to gain from the strikes is unclear. Trotskyite writers regarded the Popular Front as a *révolution manquée* in which an opportunity to arm the workers and overthrow capitalism had been missed. However, if the working classes rejected the non-revolutionary strategy of the Popular Front leaders, there is no proof that they had any revolutionary strategy of their own. Some argued that the aim of the strikers was to assert the workers' control over production: such an interpretation is partially supported by the fact that some workers took care to maintain their equipment and even set machines running again. Many commentators argued that the key to their strikes was their non-rational nature. Simone Weil, an intellectual who had taken a job on a production line, talked of an attitude of 'kermesse' or festival. Workers who had taken over factories put on pantomimes and fancy dress parades. Some strikers seemed more concerned with celebrating their temporary liberation from the stopwatch and the factory whistle than with any political demand or labour regulation. The truth is probably that all three of the interpretations given above are partially correct. The strikes affected widely differing kinds of workers – ranging from certain highly skilled craftsmen in repair workshops at the Renault factory, to the unskilled immigrant workers in many other plants, to the female workers in textile factories and department stores. It is possible that skilled workers sought to control work in a manner that harked back to the radical artisans of the nineteenth century, while unskilled workers rebelled against work in a manner that recalled the festivals of the countryside from which so many of them had recently emerged. Many workers were also probably influenced by a mixture of motives: the confusion and burst of utopian hope that emerged from 1936 may not have been conducive to the kind of clear distinctions that historians have attempted to draw.

Employers' leaders decided that the strikes could only be ended by negotiation and on 7 June 1936 four employers' leaders met union representatives at the prime minister's residence (the Matignon Palace). They signed an agreement, known as the Matignon accords, under the terms of which wages were raised between 7 and 15 per cent, and union recognition and workers' delegates were instituted in factories employing more than 10 people. Government legislation also imposed a 40-hour week, the recognition of collective contracts between employers and workers, and paid holidays. The problem with the accords was that the leaders of neither side were in a position to impose it on their own 'followers'.

The leaders of the government and the CGT could not persuade the workers to return to work. Thorez sternly remarked that 'it is necessary to know how to stop a strike', but it was conspicuously obvious that he did not, and the strikes were ended only in July 1936 when the French working class migrated to the country and the seaside in order to benefit from their first paid holidays. Similarly, the four business leaders who had signed the Matignon accords lacked authority over employers. One of them died soon after the signing, and two of them were deposed. Only Lambert-Ribot, veteran secretary of the *Comité des Forges*, survived. Once the immediate crisis of the strikes was over, the employers elected more aggressive leaders. Men who claimed to represent small business alleged that the accords had been signed by representatives of large-scale industries which were insulated from market forces by their dependence on state markets. In fact the small business leaders were often highly dependent on the same large-scale industries that had always controlled the employers' movement, but their agitation created the impression of a new current in the business world.

The strikes and their aftermath undermined the strategy of the Popular Front leaders. Where they had set out to unite France, they now divided her. Businessmen railed against the Matignon accords. Far from being won over by the government's *main tendue*, Catholics were suspicious of what now seemed to be a dangerously revolutionary government. Their suspicions, and those of many other bourgeois conservatives, were exacerbated by events in Spain. Of all the democratic countries, France was most affected by the Spanish Civil War. The government of republican Spain was also an alliance of left-wing parties, and many Frenchmen, especially European inhabitants of Algeria, had relatives in Spain. Bombs dropped by Spanish aircraft fell on French soil four times in 1938. The French government refused to intervene to help the republicans in Spain, but the belief that the Popular Front in Spain had led to violent anticlericalism made Catholics unsympathetic to Blum. Even Francisque Gay, later to be seen as the eminence gris of left-wing Christian Democracy, wrote a lurid pamphlet entitled 'In Blood and Flames' about the alleged atrocities perpetrated against churchmen in Spain.[4]

The government's failure was reflected most clearly in the history of the right-wing leagues. These leagues were now banned, but the most significant of them – the *Croix de Feu* – constituted itself as a regular political party: the *Parti Social Français* (PSF). The apparent respectability of the PSF and the fear that was induced in much of the middle class by the Popular Front meant that the PSF achieved levels of support that exceeded anything that the leagues had ever dreamed of. By 1939 the PSF claimed a membership of 3 million and had support from 12 deputies, 3000 mayors, and 1000 municipal councillors. Some believed that had elections been held in 1940 the PSF would have obtained 100 seats in parliament. The failure of the Popular Front was also reflected in economic policy. The Popular Front leaders started with very conventional economic ideas. They did not believe in the *planisme* that was being promoted by the Belgian Socialist Henri de Mann. On the contrary Blum thought that there was no middle way between overthrowing capitalism entirely and running the economy within capitalist lines. However, conventional economics were difficult to apply after the Matignon settlement when the government was burdened by new social costs and by the hostility of much of the capitalist class. In September 1936, Blum was obliged to break his pledge not to devalue the currency, and on 13 February 1937, he announced a 'pause' during which the government would halt costly social measures. The Popular Front also initiated a period of conflict in labour relations. The most obvious of these conflicts was generated by the efforts of employers to regain control of the factory floor. They sought to restore the authority of foremen and to undermine that of union delegates. There were frequent clashes over the speed of work, and the imposition of discipline. The conflict did not just pit workers against managers. The strikes of 1936 had also illustrated the possibility of conflict between workers and their official leaders. After the strikes, the CGT expanded its membership enormously: total union membership, which had stood at 755,000 workers in 1934, reached almost 4 million in 1937. However, trade unions did not always exercise much authority over their new members. The CGT was keen to maintain production in line with the Popular Front strategy and its leaders often disapproved of workers' absenteeism and laboured, without much success, to contain wildcat strikes. The Communist party put forward a vision of productivist work based on the Soviet 'hero of labour' Aleksei Stakhanov, while the employers put forward a productivist vision based on the American engineer Taylor, but many workers felt unenthusiastic about both models.

Curiously juxtaposed with the Popular Front's drive for production was its interest in the organization of leisure. Much was made of attempts to provide workers with theatres, sporting grounds and holiday activities. Léon Blum was to look back on the working-class couple cycling off to spend a weekend in the country as the most enduring symbol of his government's success. This preoccupation with leisure was partly due to the expansion of working-class leisure time that sprang from the Matignon accords; it was also partly due to the fact that Hitler's 'strength through joy' programme and Mussolini's Dopolavoro had shown the political importance of leisure. Perhaps there was also an element of control in the organization of leisure. The strikes of 1936 had shown how workers whose lives centred on the workplace could remain outside the control of left-wing and trade union leaders. Might not the organization of leisure have been a means to reassert that control? Like the 'rational recreationalists' of nineteenth-century England, the Popular Front leaders presented a vision of leisure that was organized, respectable and clearly separated from work: they opposed this vision to a leisure that was rough, spontaneous and liable to be enjoyed at the expense of work.

Labour conflict and the legacy of the Matignon accords undermined the Popular Front's attempts to increase arms production. Employers claimed that the 40-hour week made it impossible to increase production. Such arguments deserve to be regarded with scepticism. The Matignon accords contained provision for numerous industries to be exempted from the 40-hour week. Furthermore, it proved impossible to enforce labour regulations in many small enterprises. Indeed, in spite of claims on the part of employers that small business had been the principal victim of Matignon, the number of such firms increased in the aftermath of the accords as big business subcontracted work to employers who were small enough to evade the 40-hour week. However, in two respects the Matignon accords did damage French industry. Firstly, they exacerbated a shortage of certain skilled workers: it was not easy to replace aircraft engineers from France's pool of unemployed. Secondly, the wildcat strikes that followed the accords frequently interrupted production.

The Popular Front also began to suffer from internal tensions. It would have been difficult to hold such a heterogeneous coalition together under the best of conditions and in 1936 and 1937 it was often the worst of conditions that prevailed. Failure to intervene in Spain alienated the left of the alliance while the effects of the Matignon accords alienated some of the right. The Radicals were subject to particular pressure. Employers' organizations were working hard to mobilize small businessmen: the *Petites et Moyennes Entreprises* section of the CGPF was founded in 1936. The expanding PSF was also taking some of its support from among the *petite bourgeoisie*. It was, of course, these very groups who composed the electoral bedrock of the Radical party. In June 1937 the Senate refused to ratify various special financial powers. Although it was a comparatively trivial matter, Blum resigned. He may have had personal reasons for this decision (his wife was ill), but he may also have been motivated by the feeling that it was no longer possible to hold together the Popular Front coalition.

Blum was replaced by the Radical Chautemps who held office, except for a short interlude when Blum returned, until April 1938. Chautemps was replaced by his fellow Radical Daladier who was invested with the almost unanimous support of the Chamber. Daladier's first finance minister, Marchandeau, sought to implement a mildly *dirigiste* policy. However, the right of the coalition supporting Daladier defeated this proposal and a new finance minister from the right, Paul Reynaud, was installed. Reynaud believed that the key to France's economic strength lay in the reversal of the concessions given to labour in 1936. He talked of the need to abolish the 'week with two Sundays' and linked this to France's ability to rearm. Labour regulations were relaxed in industries seen as essential to armament, and on 30 November 1938 the CGT called a general strike to resist these measures. The strike was ruthlessly crushed: public sector workers were put under military discipline while troops and policemen were deployed against strikers.

It is easy to see the suppression of the strike of 30 November 1938 as marking the defeat of the Popular Front. Indeed in some respects the Daladier government anticipated the authoritarian regime that was to be established by marshal Pétain in 1940. Daladier by-passed parliament and governed by decree law. He also flirted with a proto-corporatist 'labour code', and enacted a 'family code' that tightened regulations on birth control yet further. However, it might also be argued that Daladier came closer than his predecessors to enacting the policies that had been set out in the Popular Front manifestos of 1936. Daladier did speed up arms production and he did weaken the extreme right within France, indeed business finance for the extreme right seems to have dropped off after the government showed that it was capable of crushing labour agitation. Daladier also succeeded in uniting the country, or at least the property-owning majority of the French population, more than his predecessor had done. Particularly notable was the fact that, in spite of the traditional hostility between the Radical party and the church, Daladier's government was supported by the leading French church-man (Cardinal Verdier).

Conclusion

Politics in the late 1930s had a curiously archaic quality. Far from changing in order to adjust to the new world that was presented by international crisis, French politics seemed to be pushed back into the past. The struggle between fascism and democracy was widely interpreted in terms of previous conflicts over the defence of the republic and the Dreyfus case. Even the symbols around which demonstrations congregated reflected this preoccupation. The left's icons were provided by the Place de la Bastille and the Père Lachaise cemetery in Paris, where those killed after defending the Commune of 1870 were buried. The right's icons were provided by the Place d'Etoile in Paris or by the statue of Louis XIV in Lyon. Industrial areas were rarely touched by political displays, except when their workers were on strike. Perhaps the very persistence of the street demonstrations reflects the archaic nature of politics in 1930s France. This was a country that contained at least 400,000 radio sets at a time when Hitler, Mussolini and Roosevelt had all shown how important radio broadcasts could be to politics, yet none of the movements of the 1930s ever sought to control a radio station, the epicentre of modern revolutions.

Not only did both sides seem to be looking to the past in the 1930s, but increasingly they seemed to be looking to the same kind of past. At the beginning of the decade France was a country of polit-ical extremes. The revolutionary Communist party and the anti-republican right both attacked the political centre with vigour. By the end of the decade it seemed that both these extremes were seeking to occupy the centre ground themselves. This change was most evident in the Communist party which embraced the republi-can tradition with enthusiasm. Communist militants juxtaposed the 'Marseillaise' and the 'Internationale', and campaigned to have a metro station named after Robespierre. More significantly they also adopted the patriotism and the sentimentalization of 'traditional' homelife (i.e. large families and non-working mothers) that they had rejected in earlier years. Some of the changes on the left were mir-

rored on the extreme right. Increasingly, right-wing parties emphasized union. The PPF launched a *Front de la Liberté* with a variety of
other groups, notably the *Fédération Républicaine*. The PSF became
hostile to other right-wing parties, perhaps because its own increasingly electoral appeal brought it into conflict with such parties, but it
also sought to present itself as a centre for moderate conservatives to
rally around, and it signed an agreement with the veterans' organization (the UNC). Maurras mocked the enthusiasm with which some
of his own admirers sought to outdo the republicanism of the left. It
was no coincidence that the one hundred and fiftieth anniversary of
the French Revolution was celebrated with such fervour in parades
that attracted one and a half million people in Paris alone. The tricolour flag was a symbol for both sides. The left abandoned its inter-
nationalism and the right abandoned its anti-republicanism to rally
around this symbol. In this context of patriotic republican consensus
it may not be entirely surprising that the same parliament voted for
both Blum in 1936 and Daladier in 1938, or that it would go on to
vote for Pétain in 1940.

3 Strange Defeat

On 3 September 1939 France declared war on Germany, and after ten months of 'phoney war' Germany invaded France. The French army was routed and the government of marshal Pétain sought an armistice after only six weeks of fighting. The nation of Napoleon held out against Hitler's armies for less time than the island of Crete. Explanations for this defeat had important implications for France's subsequent politics. Marshal Pétain's Vichy government that ruled France from 1940 to 1944 was concerned to demonstrate that the defeat should not be blamed on the army. It argued that the defeat could be attributed to the general weakness of French society, and to the particular mistakes of Popular Front politicians. It put this latter group, and the soldier most closely linked to them (general Gamelin), on trial at Riom in 1941. The post-war government also established its own enquiry into 'events in France between 1933 and 1945'. Some of the witnesses called by this enquiry presented the defeat as the product of a conspiracy by a group of politicians who deliberately took advantage of France's crisis to install themselves in power.

Mythologies arose around the political roots of defeat. Left-wingers gleefully quoted Maurras' reference to the 'divine surprise'. They failed to mention that this remark referred not to defeat but to the advent of Pétain's government after defeat or that Maurras himself remained fervently anti-German and many Maurrassians joined the Resistance. Right-wingers drew attention to the Hitler–Stalin pact and to the approach that French Communist leaders made to the German authorities after the defeat to obtain permission to resume publication of *Humanité*. They failed to mention the fact that most Communist deputies voted in favour of war credits even after the Hitler–Stalin pact. Numerous commentators attribute the words 'sooner Hitler than Blum' to 'the French bourgeoisie', though no one has identified a particular individual who said any such thing. In fact few Frenchmen wanted defeat in 1940. It is true that much of the right feared communism more than nazism and that some had become hostile to the conduct of French foreign policy at the time when sanctions were imposed on Italy after the invasion of Abyssinia (in 1935). However, war itself was still seen in traditional terms of nationalist unity. The *Fédération Républicaine* deputy Henri de Kérillis probably spoke for most of the right when he said, in December 1936, that he and his colleagues would fight for France even under a Popular Front government.

At the other end of the political spectrum, there were those on the left who had reservations about the war. In the SFIO, Paul Faure and Marcel Pivert both led pacifist factions. The Communists were the one major political group that clearly opposed the war. The German–Soviet non-aggression pact of August 1939 reversed Communist policy. On 20 September 1939, the Comintern ordered the *Parti Communiste Français* to oppose the war and soon after Thorez deserted from the army. However, many Communists were confused and unhappy in the aftermath of this *volte face*: 21 deputies resigned from the party and many Communist sympathizers drifted away. Most importantly, there is little evidence that ordinary Communists were tempted to mutiny or sabotage production.

The pacifism, which many claimed to identify in the French population on the eve of war, was more complicated than it appeared at first glance. There was a difference between a general desire for peace and specific hostility to the French war effort. Indeed, while French public opinion as a whole was favourable to peace, it seems to have reconciled itself to the necessity for war faster than some of its political representatives. The Munich accords, which received the support of 87 per cent of French parliamentarians, were supported by only 57 per cent of the French population; a few months later opinion polls showed that 70 per cent of the public favoured resistance to Hitler. On the eve of war, France was characterized not by defeatism but by a sober realism.

The political divisions of France did contribute to defeat. This was not because significant numbers worked for defeat, but because some were convinced that their political opponents were working towards such a goal or seeking to benefit from it. The government began to attack the Communist party even before it had turned against the war. The party was dissolved on 26 September and 40 Communist deputies were arrested two weeks later. Sometimes the scope of such attacks spread to include whichever left-wingers happened to have attracted the disapproval of local authorities. Often accusations of defeatism had more to do with the people making the accusations than with those against whom they were directed. Raoul Dautry, the minister of armaments, illustrates this. A graduate of the

École Polytechnique, Dautry had great faith in technology and organization. He was also prone to hysterical confusion when such techniques failed to work. Dautry blamed low production first on Communist saboteurs and later on obstruction by defeatist capitalists. He contrasted the mood of 1940 with the enthusiasm that he, wrongly, believed to have accompanied the outbreak of war in 1914. Political divisions may also have exacerbated conflicts in the armed forces. French commanders depended on political patronage, and this did not improve relations between general Gamelin, a republican protégé of Daladier who commanded French forces after 1935, and Weygand, his predecessor and successor, who was a right-winger. The sense of political division may also have heightened the conflicts between officers and men which seems to have contributed to the collapse in morale after the German invasion.

Alongside the explanations for defeat that stress the lack of political will to fight are those that stress the lack of resources to do so. In his first broadcast from London, de Gaulle remarked 'Much more than by their number, it was by their tanks, their planes and their tactics that the Germans beat us.' The French economy was certainly weak in the late 1930s. France remained in depression long after other countries, particularly Germany, had begun to recover. Problems were made still worse by the economic consequences of the First World War (see chapter 1). In spite of these weaknesses, France's military resources in 1940 were surprisingly good. Gamelin was a skilled administrator and political operator. He had handled relations with politicians well and the army had been given most of what it asked for. Thanks to the efforts of the Popular Front minister Pierre Cot, France had a good stock of aeroplanes (though they were often in the wrong place). She also had more tanks than Germany (4188 against 3862). What undermined French defence was not lack of resources, but the use to which those resources were put.

France's strategy in the Second World War hinged on the Maginot Line, a set of defensive fortifications along the eastern frontier. The strategy failed. German forces by-passed the Maginot Line by going through Belgium and cutting through the forest of the Ardennes. Not surprisingly, the Maginot Line has become the byword for military inflexibility and conservatism. However, the men who devised the Maginot Line in 1930, Tardieu and Maginot himself, were not fools. Of course military realities changed in the time between 1930 and 1940, as technology made more mobile warfare possible, and some commentators have been harsh in their condemnation of French commanders who had failed to appreciate the significance of these changes. In fact there were good reasons to be sceptical about the changes that the large-scale use of tanks would bring to warfare. Experienced soldiers knew that machines often worked better on the drawing board than on the battlefield, and the Spanish Civil War, which ended in 1939, had been a slow conventional war with little recourse to new techniques.

Even if the full implications of military innovation had been grasped, it is not clear that the French would have been able to change their strategy much. The most obvious flaw in the Maginot Line was that it failed to defend the Franco-Belgian border, through which the Germans eventually came. A few Frenchmen were as naïve as president Albert Lebrun, who believed Hitler's promise to respect Belgian neutrality as late as 8 September 1939. But even those who appreciated the weakness of the Belgian frontier could do little about it. Building fortifications between France and Belgium would alienate an ally and make it painfully clear that France was unable to provide aid to anyone outside her own frontiers. It would also have been technically difficult to construct deep fortifications in the flat and wet ground around the Belgian frontier. The most realistic alternative was to help Belgium to fortify her own frontier with Germany, but this was an expensive and politically delicate operation; it had not been achieved by 1940.

Other considerations encouraged the French to stick with the Maginot Line. Well-fortified defences can compensate for small numbers of troops, and small numbers of troops were always a problem for France because of her low population. Furthermore this problem was made worse by the demographic shadow of the First World War. In 1916 and 1917, birth rates had dropped to half their normal level; this meant that France experienced 'empty years' in the late 1930s when the number of young men eligible for military service was unusually low. France's capacity to pursue anything other than defensive warfare was also limited by her empire. The French high command had to devote resources to Corsica, Algeria and Indo-China as well as to mainland France. When the Germans invaded, there were 1000 French fighter planes in North Africa and only 500 in north-eastern France. Economics also made it difficult to abandon the Maginot Line. It had been extremely expensive. Furthermore this expense had been contracted shortly before the impact of the world depression had been felt in France. In the late

1930s the effects of this depression were very obvious. Under these circumstances, it was hard for the French government to accept that the Maginot Line was redundant and to embark on a whole new range of arms spending. Politics also made the tactics of the Maginot Line seem attractive. The French working classes were largely concentrated in the northern and eastern areas on any likely German invasion route. Many soldiers and politicians believed that war on French soil might spark a revolution. This made it all the more essential that the German invader should be prevented by an inflexible defensive line from posing such a threat.

The Maginot Line was also important because of the regions immediately behind it. Much of France's heavy industry and many of her natural resources were located in the area adjacent to her northern and eastern frontiers: Alsace-Lorraine alone produced 42 per cent of French iron ore, 36 per cent of her pig iron, 33 per cent of her steel and 100 per cent of her potash. In the First World War many of these areas had been occupied by the Germans. The French expected the Second World War to be a long war of attrition which would be decided by economic endurance. They hoped that the autarkic German economy would be worn down by Britain and France supported by their economic links with America. This expectation made the French unenthusiastic to risk a war of movement that might lose them their most economically valuable regions. The east of France was of political as well as economic importance. Alsace-Lorraine had only been restored to French rule in 1919. It was seen as essential that this area should be adequately protected. Furthermore, the construction of the Maginot Line, which provided jobs as well as military reassurance, was welcomed by the inhabitants of the area.

The most coherent alternative to the strategy embodied in the Maginot Line was one based on mobile warfare using concentrated forces of heavy battle tanks. This was the strategy advocated in England by captain Liddell Hart, in Germany by general Guderian and in France by colonel Charles de Gaulle. De Gaulle's ideas attracted the interest of politicians in France. Paul Reynaud made himself their champion in parliament and Léon Blum arranged an interview with de Gaulle. However, military strategy in France was rarely separable from politics and the political associations of de Gaulle's ideas were unfortunate. Tanks were seen as intrinsically offensive weapons. This aroused the concern of even some of their most enthusiastic advocates, such as Liddell Hart. It aroused special

concern in France where defensive warfare was seen to be associated
with democratic republican ideas. Furthermore, de Gaulle linked his
ideas about tank warfare with the demand for a more professional
army. This was an anathema to most politicians, especially on the
left. They saw a conscript 'people's army' as part of the legacy of the
revolution of 1789. They believed that such an army was an indis-
pensable defender of democracy from enemies at home as well as
abroad. Jean Léon Jaurès, the hero of French socialism, had written
of the need to create a true citizens' army, and as late as 1936 two
Communist deputies had called for the replacement of the army by a
citizen's militia. Under the circumstances, de Gaulle did his cause no
good by calling for a professional army and made matters even worse
by going out of his way to draw attention to the possible use of professional troops for internal counter-revolutionary activity. De
Gaulle's personal awkwardness and that of his patron Reynaud also
weakened his case.

Once the Germans broke through the French lines of defence,
everything changed. The French army had a surfeit of strategy, but a
shortage of tactics. French leaders had planned to manage resources
and organize the economy during a long war; they could not adapt
to rally soldiers at short notice in an apparently hopeless position.
Gamelin had been a good peacetime commander, but, like many
good peacetime soldiers, he was bad at fighting battles. In March
1934 Pétain had judged that it would be impossible for the German
forces to come through the heavily wooded area of the Ardennes.
Consequently the majority of troops were sent to Holland and
Belgium, where they were outflanked by the Germans. In most of
the army, and especially among reserve troops, morale collapsed.
Civilians were also gripped by panic. Many inhabitants of the north
took to the road to escape the invader; refugees blocked the road
and confusion was so great that, at one point, 90,000 children were
reported missing. Some British leaders, notably Winston Churchill,
tried to stiffen French resolve during the battle of France and British
authors were later to be very sanctimonious about the alleged moral
roots of French failings. However, the British Expeditionary Force
sent to France was very small (only nine divisions), and the British
kept their best fighter planes to protect their own cities. In June the
British government offered an Anglo-French union, but one French
minister dismissed the proposal as 'union with a corpse'.

Even after the military debacle, the French government still had
choices. Other governments, such as those of Belgium, Holland and

Poland, refused to treat with the enemy and withdrew to pursue the struggle from overseas. In some ways, France was well placed to pursue such a course. She still had a large overseas empire to which she might have withdrawn her navy, airforce and at least part of her army. Some ministers did join a ship, the *Massila,* in an attempt to reach North Africa, but their colleagues prevented them from reaching their destination. Curiously, measures that had been taken to increase France's capacity to fight the war, at a time when military victory still seemed possible, undermined her political capacity to continue the war after military defeat on the mainland. Paul Reynaud, who had replaced Daladier as prime minister in March 1940, might have changed French military strategy if he had been appointed earlier: he plucked de Gaulle out of the army to serve as his undersecretary of state for war. However, it was too late to change France's strategy, and the qualities necessary to avoid disaster were different from those required to survive disaster once it had happened. Reynaud was unpopular. The bourgeoisie remembered his campaign in favour of devaluation in the early 1930s; the working class remembered his role in the suppression of strikes in the late 1930s. Reynaud's brusque manner did not increase his chances of rallying the nation: Sartre recorded the complaints of his fellow conscripts that Reynaud, unlike Daladier, failed to mention 'our valiant soldiers' in his radio broadcasts.[1]

Reynaud dismissed Gamelin as commander-in-chief, and brought back Weygand on 19 May 1940. Reynaud was motivated partly by political resentment against Daladier's protégé and partly by the belief that Weygand would be a better commander in the thick of battle. This belief may have been correct; however, Weygand's appointment, like that of Reynaud, came too late to do any good. Weygand might have had the military competence to defend France, but he did not have the political conviction to defend the republic once France had been defeated. He despised the Third Republic and feared communism. It was Weygand's claim that the Communist party had seized power in Paris and hoisted the red flag over the prime minister's residence that finally convinced the cabinet that it should seek an armistice with Germany. It was seen as essential to leave an army intact to defend order. Most importantly, those who wished to keep France in the war were weakened by the appointment of marshal Philippe Pétain as deputy prime minister on 18 May. It had been hoped that this appointment would gain the government popularity and perhaps even increase resolve to fight on. In fact Pétain provided a rallying point for those in the cabinet who were hostile to the continuation of the war. On 16 June he replaced Reynaud as prime minister and on 17 June he approached the Germans to enquire about the conditions under which an armistice might be possible.

The problem of French strategy in 1940 was not one of blindness or simple mindedness. If anything, it was a product of the excessive clarity with which French commanders saw a complicated situation. They understood the full range of political and economic problems that beset France. Far from hoping to counter Germany by any single means, they tried to devise a strategy that would involve the full range of their strengths. It was this hope that made them so enthusiastic to defend French reserves of natural resources on the eastern frontier. It was also this hope that made them try to maintain their links with their own empire and with their Anglo-Saxon allies. In the long run their analysis was right. The Second World War was a long struggle which involved the mobilization of considerable resources across the globe and it was one in which allied economic strength ultimately ground down Germany. Unfortunately, the attention with which France prepared for the long-term world war contributed to her defeat in the short-term battle for France.

4 Vichy

During the defeat of 1940, the government of France was on the run. The last cabinet of the Third Republic took refuge in Bordeaux. Subsequently, Pétain's government established itself at Vichy, a small spa town in the Auvergne. The new government concluded an armistice with the Germans on 22 June at Rethondes. Under this arrangement, the French army was restricted to 100,000 men; the Germans were to occupy the north and west of France; France was to pay Germany's occupation costs and hand over German refugees. Meanwhile Pétain and his new deputy prime minister, Pierre Laval, planned reform of France from within. Parliament was convoked at Vichy and on 10 July it voted by 468 to 80 to grant Pétain full powers as head of state. The Third Republic constitution of 1875 was now dead: replaced by the *état français*.

Robert Paxton has stressed that 'Vichy was not a bloc'.[1] It did not mark the triumph of any single party or any ideological canon. Its supporters came from across almost the whole political spectrum ranging from socialists, such as Paul Faure, to extreme right-wingers, such as Xavier Vallat. There was not even much consistency of personnel at Vichy. German disapproval, fear of allied retribution and the struggles between factions meant that Vichy rivalled the Third Republic for ministerial instability: six education ministers were appointed in four years. Some historians have tried to divide Vichy into camps: an honourable Vichy of Pétain against the treacherous Vichy of Laval; a modernizing Vichy of the *jeunes cyclistes* against a traditional Vichy of *the vieux romains*; a 'fascist' Vichy of Déat against a conservative Vichy of Paul Baudouin. None of these divisions work well. Vichy was not divided into two camps, but into a great variety of squabbling factions. These factions were divided by their political views, which differed widely, and also by background, personal associations and rivalry.

Public reactions to Vichy were even more complicated. They varied from one place to another. To the inhabitants of Strasbourg, which was annexed by the Germans in 1940, Vichy meant unconditional surrender; an inhabitant of Oran, in which German troops never set foot, might reasonably have believed that Vichy was a regime of national reconstruction that would ultimately lead to military revenge against Germany. Public opinion changed over time. The growing identification of the regime with the political right began to lose it support as early as January 1941. Thereafter, the growing belief in allied victory, and the increasing burden of German occupation made ever larger sections of the French population hostile to Vichy. Particularly significant events were the American liberation of Algeria, which provided Frenchmen with an alternative focus for their loyalty, the German occupation of all of France at the end of 1942, and the institution of compulsory labour service, which forced young Frenchmen to work in Germany, in 1943.

However, it would be wrong to assume that these changes over time were one-dimensional. France did not slowly transform herself from '40 million Pétainists' in 1940 to a nation of Resistance supporters in 1944. Opinions were always full of ambiguities, reserves and contradictions. The German invasion of Russia made many feel that it would be prudent to distance themselves from the regime, but it also made some keen to join what they saw as a struggle for survival against bolshevism. Some hoped that Vichy would acquire a new importance as a bridge between America and Germany, or even that Germany would be forced by her military reverses to grant France a real peace treaty. One Vichy supporter believed as late as October 1943 that such a settlement 'will soon make Laval appear as the peaceful liberator of the country'. People did not necessarily think in terms of the categories of Resistance, Pétainism and collaboration that are used by historians. Marc Ferro reports that many fighters in his Resistance group continued to regard Pétain with a high degree of personal respect.[2] Peasants who approved of the idea of Resistance might disapprove of the particular Resistance activists in their own area, often ill-disciplined young men who stole food and attracted German reprisals. Many people continued to work within the Vichy state, and perhaps to approve of some of its values, while indulging in countless acts that might be counted as Resistance. François Mitterrand was decorated with a Vichy honour, the Francisque, while working for the Resistance. Gendarmes turned a blind eye to false papers, municipal employees quietly refrained from painting new signs when the government sought to change a street name from 'Avenue Jean Jaurès' to 'Boulevard Foch'. Many actions were intrinsically ambiguous. An industrialist who worked for the Germans might be a 'collaborator' in economic terms, but such men might also persuade their community, and themselves, that their activity was 'Resistance' because it prevented employees from being deported to Germany.

Most importantly, it must be remembered that nothing seemed clear in France between 1940 and 1944. Few people had access to reliable information about the intentions of the Vichy government or the course of the war. Much discussion about such matters had to be conducted in coded form: an article about the American economy might really be about the chances of allied victory, a play about ancient Greece might be about the morality of collaboration, a historical work about the Prussian reform movement might be about the possibility that Vichy would lay the foundations of military revenge against Germany. Rumours of the most bizarre kind swept France, as people relayed information picked up in crackling radio broadcasts or the clandestine press. Rumours of this kind can be found in the diaries of even well-connected and informed people.[3] Charles Rist, an economist and banker, heard in August 1944 that Hitler was being instructed in the ways of a Japanese suicide cult.

Pétain, Pétanism and Laval

All study of Vichy must begin with Pétain. Enemies of the regime might describe it as 'collaboration', 'fascism' or 'reaction', but its supporters almost invariably talked of their attitude in terms of '*Pétainisme*' or '*maréchalisme*'. In October 1940 colonel de la Rocque urged his supporters to rally behind the marshal, but he carefully distinguished between loyalty to Pétain and loyalty to the government. Pétain was treated with a degree of reverence formerly accorded to saints and kings. Busts and pictures of him replaced those of Marianne in town halls, children were taught to sing 'Maréchal nous voilà', eminent industrialists and civil servants squabbled with each other for the honour of sitting next to him at dinner, and peasants sent him clods of earth from their land. An industry of hagiography developed around Pétain. René Benjamin, who produced three biographies of the marshal in as many years,[4] wrote 'one is lucky to be alive in the time of this man who is already destined to exceed history and pass into legend'.[5] The smallest details of the marshal's appearance aroused the enthusiasm of writers who commented on 'his eyes: so pure, so blue'[6] or the whiteness of his moustache 'as immaculate as his virtue'.[7]

To understand the enthusiasm which greeted Pétain's accession to power it is necessary to examine the mythology that had grown around his name in the Third Republic. The Pétain myth was born during the First World War. In 1914 he was a 58-year-old colonel at the end of a mediocre career; in 1919 he was a field marshal known throughout the world and revered in France. This transformation sprang partly from the fact that Pétain's defensive strategic conceptions were suited to trench warfare. It also sprang from a public relations campaign by Pétain's aides who ensured that the press was kept supplied with good stories about the marshal. They were especially successful in manipulating the American newspapers; indeed, many stories about Pétain began life in the USA and were 'reimported' into France. Pétain's name became particularly associated with the defence of Verdun in 1916. This was important because a system of rotating troops meant that much of the French army served at Verdun. Pétain's admirers were later able to claim that a large number of old soldiers had been under his command at some time. Verdun was also important because it gave Pétain the reputation for using guile and patience rather than frontal assault. During the Vichy years many assumed that he would transfer these qualities into the political arena; as late as 1948 a Vichy apologist entitled a book on Pétain's dealings with Hitler *Montoire: Verdun diplomatique*.[8]

After the war, Pétain commanded operations to put down the Rif rebellion in Morocco, where he came across the young general Franco, and served as minister of war in Doumergue's government of national union in 1934. His office became a centre for bright young men, such as Charles de Gaulle, who served as *nègres* or ghost writers for the numerous books and articles that issued under Pétain's name. They were so successful that in 1931 Pétain, who read little and wrote nothing, was elected to the Académie Française. Pétain's profile was also kept high during the 1930s by a series of press campaigns that revolved around his name. A poll of readers of *Le Petit Journal* in 1935 revealed that 38,000 of them believed that Pétain would be the best man to take dictatorial powers in a national emergency, while Hervé, editor of *La Victoire*, argued that the instability of French politics constituted just such an emergency and urged Pétain to run for president. Pétain's name had acquired such resonance partly because of his military reputation, and his capacity to appeal to the veterans' leagues. More importantly, men like Hervé believed that Pétain would be capable of rallying all France, and particularly that he would be capable of appealing to the left. For, though Pétain's personal politics were right-wing, they were not widely advertised. Furthermore, unlike other leading generals (such as Weygand or Foch, whose royalist, Catholic, anti-democratic views were well known), Pétain was seen to be a republican.

The extent to which Pétain had been accepted as a figurehead across the political spectrum was reflected by the protests that came from the left when he was appointed ambassador to Franco's Spain in 1939. Léon Blum complained that 'the most humane of our generals' was too good for Franco, and even the Communist newspaper *Humanité* objected to the appointment. Pétain's image accounts for the ease with which his government obtained the support, or at least the quiescence, of such large numbers of Frenchmen. However, Pétain's position as head of state created new problems. The very fact that he had attracted support from such a wide spectrum of opinion meant that his supporters expected different things of him. Pétain did not manage to satisfy all the hopes that were placed in him, but he did manage to stave off the moment of disappointment. One simple way to do this was to say nothing, or very little. A striking feature about the accounts produced by Pétain's admirers is the emphasis that they put on his silence: 'what is most moving about him is silence' (Romier),[9] 'he has never ceased to master his feeling in silence' (Benjamin),[10] 'this taciturnity which shows energy and firmness' (Laure),[11] 'governed for a century by lawyers, France expects much from this man of few words' (Fabre-Luce).[12] The emphasis on silence fitted in with the image of quiet strength that was associated with the French army, and such habits could be contrasted with the neurotic chattering of Third Republic politics. More importantly, silence allowed Pétain to avoid taking stands that might have alienated some of his supporters. It also allowed Pétainists to imagine that strategies to deceive the Germans and redeem France's future were being devised behind their leader's sphinx-like mask. Jules Roy recalled being told 'trust the old fox, he's going to con Adolf'.[13]

As Vichy became increasingly unpopular and identified with the German occupiers, Pétain's image changed. Sometimes this change involved hostility to the marshal: Resistance fighters 'executed' the oak tree in the Tronçais forest that had been named after Pétain. René Benjamen's 1943 biography of the marshal (*The Great Man Alone*) recognized the new public mood: 'last year most French people ... proclaimed their attachment to the marshal with enthusiasm ... and now they are silent. The marshal is calm and virile ... Public opinion is feminine and nervous.'[14] Even at this stage, however, many people did not turn against the marshal entirely. A report on 47 notables in the Puy de Dome in January 1942 found that only 9 of them were loyal to the government, but that 13 remained loyal to Pétain. Many right-wingers refused to believe that Pétain was a traitor or collaborator. Instead they saw him as a passive sacrificial victim (an image that came easily to the minds of devout Catholics). One writer talked of Pétain/Christ and another biographer wrote 'it took nothing less than marshal Pétain to expiate ... the sins of the Popular Front'.[15] Even those who were now hostile to the Vichy government often regarded Pétain as a confused and well-meaning old man being ruthlessly exploited by the *synarques* of big business or by his duplicitous minister Pierre Laval.

Pétain was surrounded by advisers whom he had known before the war. Most of these men came from the political right and many were soldiers. Until his death in 1943, Lucien Romier, a historian and journalist, was head of the marshal's cabinet. Loustaunau-Lacau, a soldier and former member of the extreme-right *Cagoule,* was a member of Pétain's entourage who eventually joined the Resistance. Pétain's doctor, Ménétrel, dispensed the dictates of the *bien pensant* right along with his medicines. These men took care to cultivate Pétain's image. His every word was carefully scripted: even the 'interview' that he gave to the *New York Times* in 1941 had been written in advance by du Moulin de Labarthète. However, Pétain himself remained in overall control of his entourage and indeed proved ruthless with his subordinates – such as general Laure or Raphael Alibert – who ceased to be useful to him.

The second great figure of the new regime was Pierre Laval. Laval came from a relatively humble background in the Auvergne and had made his fortune as a lawyer and politician. He was the classic Third Republic local boy made good. He had begun life as an undoctrinaire socialist and drifted to the right. His career was not marked by any clear ideology, but it did exhibit certain consistent general themes. He disliked war, though he was not a pacifist: in the First World War he had neither fought nor, unlike some of his Socialist colleagues, opposed the war. He was attached to the interests of the peasant France that was represented by his constituency and birthplace in the Auvergne, and he had a limitless, often unjustified, faith in his capacity to settle any problem through negotiation. During the late 1930s Laval's life had been dominated by his desire to devise a rapprochement between France and Mussolini's Italy and by his hatred of the Popular Front, which he believed had undermined his project. During the phoney war, Laval had plotted to bring down first Daladier and then Reynaud. He had also maintained contact with marshal Pétain. After the defeat, he presented himself to Pétain as the man who would be capable of manipulating and bullying parliament into voting for its own dissolution. Laval failed in his initial quest to be made foreign secretary, but he accepted a ministry without portfolio and, most importantly, he was nominated as Pétain's dauphin: the man who could expect to become head of state after the marshal's death.

Laval's anti-communism and his desire to maintain negotiating channels with the Germans often made him seem like a fanatical supporter of collaboration. This appearance was enhanced by the fact that Laval spent the period between December 1940 and April 1942 in the occupied zone of France where he enjoyed German protection. On 22 June 1942 Laval announced his 'sincere desire for German victory', and later Laval attended the rally in favour of collaboration organized by Paris-based fascists such as Déat, Doriot and Deloncle. In 1940, Laval also seemed to have planned to reshape French internal politics along German lines. He told parliament that France would have to change her institutions to match those of the dictatorships that had defeated her, and he railed against large-scale capitalism in terms that recalled those used by fascists. Vichy's finance minister later wrote that 'Laval wanted a true French fascism' during this period.[16] However, Laval also continued to surround himself with cronies from the Third Republic parliament, and curiously, as his foreign policy became more associated with collaboration, his internal policy seemed increasingly to recall that of the Third Republic. Laval underlined this continuity when he returned to power in April 1942 and remarked that he was forming his 'fifth government'. After 1942 Laval's internal policy seemed to subvert some of the most cherished aspects of Pétain's national revolution. Laval had never had good relations with the First World War veterans who made up the bed-rock of Vichy support, he had cut their pensions in 1935 and he starved the *Légion Française des Combattants* of funds. Laval even allowed prefects to stop swearing an oath of loyalty to marshal Pétain.

Laval seemed everything that Pétain was not. Pétain looked distinguished, and this appearance was carefully cultivated by his refusal to wear glasses in public and his insistence on wearing uniform: the *képi* concealed his bald head. Laval was strikingly ugly and his unappealing appearance was enhanced by the fact that he was invariably seen smoking a cigarette and wearing a grubby white tie. Pétain was France's greatest soldier; Laval had been invalided out of his military service on account of his varicose veins. Pétain stood above politics; Laval seemed to incarnate the most squalid aspects of Third Republic parliamentarianism. Many observers at Vichy, and in subsequent years, distinguished the 'Vichy of Laval' from the 'Vichy of Pétain'. In the short term Pétain's stature was enhanced by comparison with the apparently squalid figure of Laval. Later, when the Vichy government seemed to be discredited, many suggested that the aged but honourable Pétain had been outwitted by the cunning Laval and that aspects of Vichy policy which were disliked, particularly its collaboration with Germany, sprang from the latter's manoeuvres. In reality relations between Laval and Pétain were more complicated. The two men had very different styles and they often quarrelled. On 13 December 1940, Pétain forced Laval to resign from his government and he accepted Laval's return in April 1942 only under German pressure. However, personal tension did not reflect great policy differences between the two men, and Pétain recognized that Laval's help had been useful to him, particularly in subduing parliament. Furthermore, the most notorious symbol of Vichy's collaboration – the meetings between Pétain, Laval and Hitler at Montoire in October 1940 – were engineered by Pétain, not Laval; indeed Laval did not realize that he was about to meet Hitler until hours before the event.

The Nature of the Regime

Pétain and his associates, particularly Alibert, wished to introduce a new constitution. To facilitate the drafting of this document, a National Council of 200 notables was summoned to meet in 1941. The national council contained churchmen, such as pastor Marc Boegner, business leaders, such as Claude Gignoux, and a few conservative politicians from the Third Republic, such as Louis Germain-Martin. However, the disagreements and faction fights to which Vichy was so prone undermined the draft constitution that this body produced. Pétain's immediate associates, Romier, Moysset, Bouthillier and Le Cour Grandmaison, finally produced a new constitution in January 1944, by which time it seemed irrelevant to most French people. The new regime did alter some of the institutions that governed France. Parliament was suspended entirely after its meeting of July 1940, and Pétain governed through decrees that were issued after discussion with his cabinet or advisers. Local government was also changed. The *conseils généraux*, which had been elected in each department, were dissolved on 12 October 1940. Municipal councils continued to exist, but there were no further elections to these bodies. The elected municipal councillors of all urban communes (i.e. those with populations of more than 2000) were replaced by representatives chosen directly by the departmental prefect or the minister of the interior. Certain groups were granted the right to special representation on municipal councils. Each council had to contain delegates from professional associations and at least one father of a large family. More surprisingly, each council had to contain at least one woman (women had been almost completely excluded from political office before 1940).

Some of its enemies denounced the Vichy regime as fascist. Such an interpretation has an obvious plausibility. Vichy worked in parallel with the regimes of Hitler and Mussolini. Like them, it was strongly anti-Communist, and authoritarian. Like fascist regimes, Pétain's government based much of its appeal on the memory of the First World War. However, there were also some notable features that distinguished Pétainism from fascism. The regime was not totalitarian. Marcel Déat proposed in August 1940 that a single party be established to support the regime, but this idea was rejected. Vichy never sought to create an all-powerful state. At his trial in 1945, Pétain claimed to have defended not the *liberty* but the *liberties* of the French people. The distinction between these two words was important (the manifesto of the Pétainist *Service d'Ordre Légionnaire* asked for the support of those who were 'contre la vaine liberté, pour les vrais libertés'). Liberty conjured up the abstract republican notion of individual rights that was associated with the revolutionary tradition. Liberties implied a more complicated network of rights associated with a range of institutions. The Vichy government allowed the church to exercise certain powers, especially over education. It attacked Jacobin centralism and talked of replacing France's numbered departments with the living traditions that were embodied in the regions of the *ancien régime*. It proposed that the professions should be regulated by autonomous corporations.

The Vichy government was also distinguished from fascist regimes by the nature of the people who led it. It was a regime of social elites led by a marshal, not a corporal. Many members of Pétain's entourage were drawn from the officer corps or the senior civil service. Many of them had been wealthy men before they obtained political power and many had been formed in France's peculiar and prestigious *grandes écoles* particularly the *École Polytechnique*. Vichy was also a gerontocracy which contrasted sharply with the fascist movements that laid obsessive emphasis on youth. Pétain himself was old enough to have been a father to both Hitler and Mussolini, and to have been the grandfather of Léon Degrelle (the Belgian fascist). There were some very young ministers in the Vichy government, but these were valued for their perceived technical abilities rather than their youth: no one imagined that the earnest bespectacled Bichelonne represented the animal vitality of the young. Vichy's youth organizations were designed to instil the virtues of experience rather than to liberate the energies of adolescence. Vichy's attitude to violence also distinguished it from fascist movements. The regime revolved around the army and, on occasion, it was responsible for serious violence against its enemies. But there was little attempt to glorify bloodshed in Vichy propaganda. Pétain even preferred to omit the more bloodthirsty parts of the 'Marseillaise'. Hitler and Mussolini came to power to start wars; Pétain came to power to stop one.

Alongside the Vichy regime was a group of men, initially gathering in Paris, who were collaborationists rather than collaborators. They believed that German victory in the Second World War would be a good thing in itself rather than simply a good thing for them or for France. The most prominent individuals among this group were Jacques Doriot, Marcel Déat, Eugene Deloncle, and Alphonse de Châteaubriant. Doriot was a Breton of working-class origin who began his political life as a leader of the Communist party. He quarrelled with his fellow Communists, largely because he urged alliance with democratic parties before the Comintern had embraced a Popular Front strategy, and in 1936 he founded the *Parti Populaire Français* (PPF). Doriot's admirers, such as the novelist Drieu la Rochelle, presented him as a charismatic fascist leader, but it was not until after 1940 that the PPF began to style itself as an unambiguously fascist movement. Marcel Déat was a schoolteacher and First World War captain; he broke with the SFIO and moved to 'neosocialism' in 1933. In occupied France he edited *L'Oeuvre* and in 1941 he founded the *Rassemblement National Populaire* (RNP), which attempted to group all the collaborationists. Deloncle was a naval engineer and former artillery officer. He began political life as a member of *Action Française*, but in the late 1930s had broken with the league to found a right-wing terrorist group: the *Cagoule*. In 1940, Deloncle founded the *Mouvement Social Révolutionnaire* (MSR) which continued many of the traditions established by the *Cagoule*. Alphonse de Châteaubriant was a reactionary Catholic who had admired Nazi Germany since the 1930s. After the defeat, Châteaubriant became editor of a German sponsored newspaper, *La Gerbe*, and in September 1940 he founded *La Groupe Collaboration*.

The Germans, guided by their francophile ambassador Otto Abetz, subsidized the publications and movements of the Paris collaborationists. These men were useful to the Germans because they provided a radical alternative to Vichy which might be used to threaten marshal Pétain if the need arose. Those gathered at Paris scrambled for German favour: the poet Robert Brasillach hastened to reword the pre-war book in which he had described Hitler as a 'sad vegetarian'. However, the collaborationists proved bad at collaborating with each other: even the committee that they established in the autumn of 1940 to campaign for the creation of a single party was soon riven by the conflict between Déat and Doriot. Conflicts sprang from the differences of pre-war backgrounds: hostility between those with origins on the right and left, and between those from the Socialist and Communist parts of the left, persisted after 1940. The behaviour of the different movements after 1940 also varied. Déat was the most passive of the collaborationists and the one most dependent on his relations with Laval; Doriot was more willing to resort to direct action, while Deloncle's MSR continued the violent habits of the *Cagoule* by blowing up synagogues and assassinating enemies. All of the collaborationists had demonstrated their capacity for picking political quarrels by breaking with their various parties of origin and this capacity often led to outright violence after 1940. In Dijon, the Germans banned the *Parti Français National* in November 1940 after its members had been involved in street brawls. Deloncle caused particular problems. In 1941 he was expelled from the RNP because he was suspected of complicity in the attempted assassination of Déat and Laval at a collaborationist meeting. Eventually, Deloncle was forcibly ejected from the offices of his *Mouvement Social Revolutionnaire* by his own rivals in the organization before dying in a shoot-out with Gestapo agents in 1944.

Assessing the extent of popular support for the various fascist leaders and movements in Vichy France is difficult. Bertram Gordon suggests that total membership of all organizations amounted to about 150,000. Lucien Rebatet's fascist book *Les*

Décombres (published in 1941) sold about 60,000 copies, but the letters that Rebatet received suggest that many of his readers did not share all his ideas. The largest collaborationist group was probably that led by Châteaubriant which claimed to have 100,000 members. Local studies have suggested that membership of such groups stood at about 1000 in the Côte d'Or, 263 in Indre et Loire and 299 in the Loiret. In striking contrast to Pétainism, collaborationism's greatest appeal was to urban areas. This was particularly true of Paris, but even in the Côte d'Or 80 per cent of members of collaborationist groups were to be found in Dijon, and attempts to found a *Centre Paysan* in the Loiret failed completely. The Germans were able to protect their clients more easily in cities than in the countryside, and the groups to which the collaborationists appealed – intellectuals, the unemployed, the lumpen proletariat – were mainly found in towns. Collaborationists were also generally younger than Pétainists. With the exception of Châteaubriant, born in 1877, all of the collaborationist leaders were in their early 40s at the beginning of the occupation. Members of the various groups were also relatively young, although the MSR and the RNP seem to have attracted older members than the PPF. The comparative scarcity of militants who had fought in the First World War is particularly striking: only 20 per cent of members of collaborationist groups in the Côte d'Or fell into this category. Fascism in most European countries had been born out of defeat or disappointment in the 1914–1918 war and it seems that such ideas appealed to the Frenchmen who had been defeated in 1940 more than to those who had been victorious in 1918. The youth and poverty of collaborationists sometimes made them very marginal. These figures, portrayed in Louis Malle's 1974 film *Lacombe Lucien*, were motivated by greed, or by the need to survive, not by any ideological kinship with the men who commanded them. In some cases collaborationism spilled over into gangland. The Bonny–Lafont gang in Paris combined Gestapo work with their more regular criminal activities as did the clients of the PPF leader in Marseilles, Simon Sabiani.

Initially, the collaborationists had awkward relations with Vichy. Doriot claimed to be a supporter of the marshal, but did not go to Vichy. Déat was an outspoken critic of what he saw as Vichy's conservatism, and in December 1940 he was briefly arrested on the orders of marshal Pétain. As the war went on relations between Vichy and the Paris collaborationists became closer. The invasion of the Soviet Union gave conservatives and fascists a common cause. Laval publicly expressed his desire for German victory in a speech of September 1942, and the Vichy government aided Doriot's project to establish a 'Legion of Volunteers against Bolshevism', which sent around 3000 men to fight alongside the Germans on the Russian frontier. As the war turned against Germany, Vichy began to rely on more extreme figures to provide it with fighters against the Resistance. The occupation of the southern zone by the Germans at the end of 1942 made it easier for them to exercise influence on behalf of their fascist protégés. Furthermore, in 1943 and 1944, it became increasingly obvious that the upper-class conservatives, who had supported Vichy in its early days, wished to distance themselves from the regime. Pétain himself ceased to exercise his functions in November 1943. Extremists stepped in to fill the gap that was left by these abdications. One of the most well known of these was Philippe Henriot. Henriot was a right-wing Catholic who had been a member of the *Fédération Nationale Catholique* and the *Fédération Républicaine* before the war. He came to feel that nazism was the only alternative to bolshevism. As a journalist in Paris and then, from 6 January 1944, as Vichy's minister of propaganda, Henriot poured abuse on the Resistance, who eventually assassinated him at the end of June 1944. The last significant change in the composition of the Vichy government came in March 1944 when Déat was appointed as minister of labour. However, the collaborationist takeover at Vichy was a hollow victory. The certainty of German defeat was making the collaborationist movements more and more distant from the mass of Frenchmen at the very moment that they began to acquire government office: in the Loiret the collaborationist movements gained only six new recruits after July 1943.

The paramilitary groups established under Vichy shed some light on the changing balance of power between fascism and conservatism under Vichy. The first such organization was the *Légion Française des Combattants*, established on 29 August 1940. Habits of organization among veterans had already been well developed, but the pre-war organizations had been divided and, in some cases, explicitly politicized. The Legion was designed to unite all veterans in patriotic loyalty to marshal Pétain. It did not succeed. Many veterans' associations objected to their forced dissolution and to the transfer of their funds to the Legion. The Legion appealed more to former members of conservative veterans' associations such as the *Union National des Combattants* than to left-wing veterans; war cripples, whose dependence on the state had influenced their politics, were particularly dubious about the Legion. The head of the Legion, François Valentin, was a former member of colonel de la Rocque's *Parti Social Français*. The average age of legionnaires was around 50, and it appealed better to veterans of the 1914–18 war than to those of the 1940 war: in a commune of the Auvergne 80 per cent of veterans from the first category joined while only 10 per cent of those from the second did so. Finally, the Legion appealed to the countryside more than the city: in the Loire 60 per cent of legionnaires were peasants and only 4.5 per cent of them were workers. The Legion was most successful in conservative and rural areas where it blended in with existing social structures. In Haute-Savoie the Legion was presided over by general Cartier, who was also mayor of Annecy, and attracted 20,000 members (77.5 per cent of those eligible). By contrast the left-wing and industrial city of Clermont-Ferrand provided only 2500 legionnaires. In France as a whole the Legion, and some of its associated bodies, claimed to group around one and a half million men at the movement's peak in 1941. As time went on, the Legion began to experience problems. Its leaders sometimes set themselves up as the main pillar of the *Révolution Nationale* and began to interfere in matters, such as the establishment of a corporatist state, that had little to do with them. In Clermont-Ferrand the Legion even began to plan the physical reconstruction of the city. Such interventions brought the Legion into conflict with other authorities (especially mayors and prefects). The Legion also became increasingly, if reluctantly, associated with collaboration. In May 1943 the mayor of a small town in the Loire suggested, perhaps in a bid to embarrass the Legion, that its members might undertake the collection of radios that had been ordered by the Germans. Prudence and patriotism made some legionnaires distance themselves from the movement: in the Loire, membership dropped from 10,000 in 1941 to 4500 in 1944. In the Auvergne, even the peasantry, at whom the Legion had directed so much of its propaganda, began to display hostility towards the organization.

On 12 December 1941, a *Service d'Ordre Légionnaire* (SOL) was created under Joseph Darnand, a hero of both the 1914–18 and the 1940 wars. Darnand was a conservative who had been a member of *Action Française* until 1928, and he was fanatically loyal to marshal Pétain. However, he did not quite fit in with the military elites who obtained power at Vichy – he came from a humble background and he resented the fact that he had not been allowed to become an officer in 1919. Darnand had begun to create a separate group within the Legion in 1941. It began to achieve real prominence when it was given official recognition in January 1942. Although the SOL was not initially armed or linked to collaboration, it was seen as a dangerously radical group by many legionnaires: when Darnand handed over the colours of the new body in Haute-Savoie only a quarter of legionnaires turned up. In January 1943, Laval entrusted Darnand with the creation of yet another body: the *milice*. Although the *milice* shared certain origins with the Legion, the two movements contrasted sharply. Whereas the Legion had been a gerontocratic and rural movement, the *milice* was young – recruits seem to have had an average age of about 30 – and primarily urban. Unlike the Legion, the *milice* explicitly excluded Jews from membership. The contrast between the two movements grew in 1943 and 1944 as the Legion made increasing efforts to return to its conservative and nationalist origins. The *milice*, by contrast, became locked in violent conflict with Resistance organizations and increasingly unpopular with the population in general, which came to associate it with terrorist gestures such as the assassination of the Third Republic politician Mandel. The *milice*'s anti-Resistance activity and its urban youthful support all associated it with the Paris collaborationists. However, it would be wrong to regard it as a slavish imitation of German nazism. The *milice* was initially based in the southern non-occupied zone and its leaders always proclaimed their loyalty to Pétain. Darnand was, like Henriot, a devout Catholic and a French nationalist. Under his influence the *milice* became associated with a pseudo-medieval ritual that recalled the Romanian Iron Guard more than the SS: new recruits spent the night before their initiation on their knees in vigil. However, like Henriot, Darnand decided to throw in his lot with the Germans against communism. Associations between the *milice* and the Germans became increasingly close: in the summer of 1943 Darnand became an officer in the SS and obtained the right to establish military bases in 21 departments of France.

If Vichy was not fascist, what was it? Some described it as a 'reactionary regime' that was seeking to reverse the republican tradition that went back to the revolution of 1789. There is obviously some truth in this analysis. Vichy described itself as an *état*, not a *république*. It put forward its own slogan of '*travail, famille, patrie*' (work, family and fatherland) as an alternative to '*liberté, égalité, fraternité*'. The regime's authoritarianism, regionalism and corporatism all seemed to represent the antithesis of what the Third Republic had stood for.

Furthermore, the most prominent royalist in France, Charles Maurras, influenced many of those who gathered at Vichy. He was treated with respect by the regime and met Pétain who listened sympathetically to his ideas. However, it would be simplistic to suggest that Vichy was a 'Maurrassian regime'. Maurrassianism was a ruthlessly clear and logical doctrine that placed a high priority on the need for political reform above all things. This hardly fitted in with the vague and confused desire to 'rise above politics' that marked Vichy. Pétain himself was far removed from the intellectuals and polemicists of *Action Française* and one of his aides doubted whether the marshal had read 20 pages of Maurras' writings. It is true that the general tone of Vichy – authoritarian, nationalistic, anti-semitic – was derived partly from Maurras. However, Maurras had influenced almost the whole of the French political system and veterans of *Action Française* were as likely to be found among the fascists in Paris or the Gaullists in London as among the Pétainists at Vichy.

Pétain himself was never an outright opponent of the Revolution of 1789. Indeed, as has been suggested above, he owed much of his popularity during the 1930s to the perception that he was a republican general. Even after 1940, Pétain's closest associates such as René Benjamen, himself a royalist, and du Moulin de Labarthète continued to believe that Pétain was a republican if not a democrat. Furthermore, the Vichy regime never sought to destroy all the symbols of the French Revolution. Pétain sang the 'Marseillaise', saluted the tricolour flag and encouraged the celebration of July 14, although this event was presented as a sober homage to the army, not the noisy festival of the left that it had become under the Popular Front. Vichy reacted not against the French Revolution but against Clemenceau's view that the 'revolution was a bloc' which must be accepted or rejected in its entirety. Vichy rejected the violence and egalitarianism of the Revolution, but it embraced the links that had grown up between the revolutionary legacy and military patriotism.

If Vichy did not reject republicanism, it did reject some of the measures taken by the Third Republic. Particularly important were the measures that had been taken against the church in the early twentieth century. Pétain was not a religious man. He believed that listening to organ music on the radio was a good alternative to attendance at mass and his marriage to a divorcée was sanctified by the church in a farcical service when the marshal was 85 years old. Many of his associates, however, were fervent believers in God or the church. Under Vichy the church regained a small amount of the property that had been expropriated at the time of the separation of church and state in 1905. More importantly, the church regained some of the educational role that it had lost in the late nineteenth century. The attempts of Pétain's first education minister, Jacques Chevalier, to restore religious education to schools did not last, but free time was left in the school day for children to attend religious classes and bishops were given state money for educational purposes. Most importantly, there was a change in the tone of church–state relations. Clerics could be seen in many photographs of Pétain's entourage, while men like cardinal Gerlier of Lyon were able to interpret the defeat as God's punishment on France for its secular errors and Vichy as the means by which such secularisation would be reversed.

However, it is easy to overstate the extent to which Vichy reacted against the Third Republic. The regime hardly amounted to a restoration of the moral order that had governed France in the 1870s. Even the legislation relating to the church did not come close to enacting a new concordat. The early days of the Vichy regime were marked by a prurient moralism: Alfred Fabre-Luce recalls signs on the beach at Cannes asking sunbathers to keep their legs together and Roger Peyrefitte was expelled from the diplomatic service after attempting to pick up a boy in a cake shop. However, such attitudes were short-lived. Vichy legislation made little attempt to interfere with sexual morals. The law of 1942 regulating homosexuality, which forbade homosexual relations with persons under 21, only slightly infringed on the tolerance of the Third Republic, while Vichy's legislation on birth control was really a continuation of that enacted under the Third Republic. Such legislation stressed the need to combat *dénatalité* in order to preserve the military strength of the nation rather than the control of sexual activity. Typically, a law of 1942 defined abortion as a 'crime against the safety of the state'.

There were other respects in which Vichy could be seen as carrying on traditions established under the Third Republic. Many Vichy ministers had begun their careers in the Third Republic and some of them were archetypal Third Republic figures. Pierre-Etienne Flandin, who became Vichy's foreign minister in December 1940, had been leader of the *Alliance Démocratique*. Peyrouton, who became Vichy's minister of the interior, had belonged to the classic Third Republic institution, freemasonry. Even Maurice Sarraut, editor of

the *Dépêche de Toulouse* and a godfather of Third Republic radicalism, accepted office in the regime. One of Sarraut's protégés, René
Bousquet, became one of Vichy's most ruthless fighters against the
Resistance. Vichy could not have distanced itself from the Third
Republic even if it had wished to do so. Many members of the
administration, on which Vichy depended, had been appointed
before 1940. The prefectoral corps was particularly important
because prefects took on many of the powers formerly exercised by
elected bodies. However, the prefectoral corps had been highly
politicized and particularly linked to the Radical party. Vichy did
move or dismiss some prefects whose politics attracted its disapproval, but the need for administrative continuity often overcame
the desire for political change: only 18 per cent of Vichy prefectoral
appointments came from outside the corps. The Third Republic also
survived in local government. All municipal councillors in communes of less than 2000 inhabitants had been elected before the
war; even in urban communes where the government appointed new
councils, many of these were simply the old elected representatives.
In some areas of the northern zone, the Germans pressured Vichy
not to purge groups such as Socialists and freemasons from local
government because it did not wish to impede administrative
efficiency.

Some Vichy policies also had republican ancestry: its attempt to
regulate work and its suspension of parliament had been anticipated
under the Daladier government. Even the Popular Front, which was
denounced by Pétain and whose leaders were imprisoned by the
regime, can be seen as having contributed some things to Vichy.
Pétain was granted full powers by the same parliament that had
voted for the Popular Front. He enacted the Popular Front's intention of creating a state pension, remarking with characteristic smug-
ness that 'we keep promises, even those of other people', and Vichy's
interest in the organization of leisure and youth obviously owed
something to the lessons of the Popular Front.

Social and Economic Policy

Vichy can be seen as a response to economic as well as political
developments. The government's propaganda looked back to a way
of life that preceded large-scale industry. The virtues of peasants and
artisans were lauded. The fact that Pétain was 'the son of a family

attached to the land for generations' was stressed in Vichy propaganda, which also declared: 'It is the heroic patience of the peasant that has created France. The peasant ensures our economic and social stability.' The government also made much of the favour with which it regarded artisans and small business; men purporting to represent this group, such as Pierre Nicolle, Aymé Bernard and Léon Gingembre, gathered at Vichy. It is tempting to suggest that Vichy's rhetoric about the virtues of a 'traditional' economy were a product of fears that the French *petite bourgeoisie* and peasantry had felt about 'proletarianization' during the years preceding the war, but this was not the case. The very fact that economic growth in France had been slow meant that small production had been much less marginalized in France than in, say, Germany. This was especially true in the south where Vichy exercised its greatest power. Furthermore, those who proved most vigorous in the defence of a 'traditional economy' often had very little relation to such an economy. Pétain's Saint Etienne speech, in which he attacked the power of big business, was written by François Lehideux, a former director of the enormous Renault company. Even Pierre Nicolle, whose diary is often taken as the classic expression of small business opinion at Vichy,[17] was really a professional business organizer rather than a businessman and, for most of his career, he had drawn his money and power from his relations with large-scale business. In short, the relationship between Vichy's rhetoric and the class that it sought to represent was a complicated one, ridden with deception and self-deception. In one of Pétain's earliest speeches he used the phrase: 'the earth does not lie.' These words seemed to sum up Vichy's respect for the wholesome values of the countryside, but in fact they had been written by Emmanuel Berl, a half-Jewish Parisian intellectual who was soon obliged to flee Vichy's anti-semitic laws.[18] Gordon Wright quotes a French peasant who offered a slightly different interpretation of Pétain's social vision: 'I like the marshal because he is like me ... a good liar.'[19]

Vichy did introduce some concrete measures in its bid to transform the French economy. It gave slightly greater security of tenure to tenant farmers, it provided subsidies for those wishing to return to the land, which were only taken up by about a thousand people, and for those wishing to improve rural housing, which were more successful. Vichy's peasant charter, promulgated on 2 December 1940, sought to create a corporation that would exercise control over French agriculture. The new corporation was dogged by difficulties over whether or not membership was compulsory, and whether or not it was to be controlled by the state. Furthermore, the corporation, like all Vichy's economic bodies, found it difficult to enforce discipline or persuade members to pay their dues. However, it did leave an important legacy. Any degree of organization, however awkward, was a novelty in many parts of the countryside and often laid foundations that were to be built on after the war. Furthermore, around 30,000 leaders across the country were elected to serve in various agencies of the peasant corporation. These men were not a representative cross-section of the peasantry: they tended to be unusually prosperous and old (most of the younger peasants had been taken away from the land by the war), and many of them had already acquired experience in pre-war agricultural organizations. However, they were genuine farmers, unlike the notables who had often spoken for agriculture before the war, and the rural elite formed during the Vichy period was to last after the Liberation.

Vichy policy also sought to reform French industry. In a bid to prevent the creation of large interlocking networks of companies, a law of 1940 banned any individual from holding more than one directorship. Three large employer associations – the *Comité des Forges*, the *Comité des Houillères*, and the *Confédération Générale du Patronat Français* – were dissolved. All of these measures proved relatively easy to evade and caused big business little but passing annoyance. The most important industrial measure, at least as far as the government was concerned, was the labour charter which was enacted in October 1941. The charter was the product of a long and bitter dispute in the government. At the centre of the regime, the marshal's cabinet, the minister of justice, and ministers such as Bouthillier and Baudouin wished to create a truly corporatist regime in which trade unions and employers' associations would be replaced by 'vertical' organizations uniting both workers and employers in each industry, and acting with a high degree of autonomy vis-à-vis the state.

Everyone paid lip service to such corporatist ideas. However, in reality, many supporters of Vichy were reluctant to see such a regime established. The minister of labour, René Belin, and many of his entourage were themselves former trade unionists who did not want to destroy institutions that had provided their own power base. Vichy supporters who had risen up through the employers' associations often had similar reservations. Many of these supporters were members of interprofessional associations that had sprung up since

1936; such bodies were suited to dealing with labour relations in the aftermath of the Popular Front but they could not have had any role in a corporatist system based on organization within single professions. Businessmen, especially large-scale employers, showed little interest in the labour charter. Few bothered to give an opinion on corporatist reform to the committee set up to draft the charter and, of the twenty 'professional families' foreseen by the charter, only three had begun to operate by 1944.

Alongside those seeking to restore some vanished economic order were a group of Vichy ministers and officials who seemed to embrace a certain view of industrial modernity. Members of this group were known as the 'technocrats' or the *jeunes cyclistes*. The most prominent of them were Yves Bouthillier (who became minister of finances from June 1940 to April 1942); Jean Bichelonne (who became secretary general for commerce and industry, secretary of state for industrial production, and eventually, from April 1942, minister of industrial production); Pierre Pucheu (secretary of state for industrial production from February to July 1941 and then minister of the interior from July 1941 until May 1942); and François Lehideux (secretary of state for industrial production from July 1941 until April 1942). These men had all been born in the first four years of the twentieth century, They often came from the elite educational background of the *grandes écoles*; Bichelonne had graduated first from the *École Polytechnique*. Whereas the political elites of republican France were usually lawyers and teachers from *le sud qui gouverne*, these men all came from the *nord qui travaille*. Bouthillier and Bichelonne had both been civil servants; the former described Vichy as 'the triumph of administration over politics'. Lehideux and Pucheu had both worked in large-scale industry.

The 'technocratic' ministers had often been linked before the war by membership of intellectual discussion circles, such as that based around *Nouveaux Cahiers* or the alumni of the *École Polytechnique* who met in 'X crise'. This gave them contacts with men like the industrialist Auguste Detoeuf or the banker Jacques Barnaud. The *jeunes cyclistes* were full of plans for reforming the French economy. Historians have paid particular attention to the two plans for industrial production drawn up by the Vichy government, in 1941 and 1944, which seemed to anticipate the experiments in economic management that would take place in France after 1945. Some at Vichy suggested that the modernizers at Vichy were part of a semi-masonic conspiracy – synarchy – designed to promote the interests of large-scale industry at the expense of Pétain's vision of a traditional French economy and society. The centre of this plot was said to be Jean Coutrot, a graduate of the *École Polytechnique* who had written widely on industrial and social matters during the 1930s and who died under mysterious circumstances in 1941. Those who claimed to be small business representatives, such as Pierre Nicolle, were particularly vigorous in their denunciations of synarchy, but even the *synarque* Jacques Benoist-Mechin recognized that he was a part of a network.

However, on close examination the idea that there was a tightly knit and self-conscious group of industrial modernizers at Vichy begins to seem less plausible. There were many divisions among the modernizers. Some of these men, like Pucheu, came from the fascist *Parti Populaire Français*; others, like Bouthillier, came from the traditional Catholic right or from no party at all. Their political development under Vichy also differed. Bouthillier, Pucheu and Lehideux all left power at the same time (April 1942) that Bichelonne achieved his greatest influence as minister of industrial production. Pucheu was subsequently to try to join de Gaulle in Algeria; the Free French rewarded him with a firing squad. Bichelonne became ever more engaged in economic collaboration and ultimately died in Germany where he had fled with the retreating occupier. It is also far from clear that the 'modernizers' really saw themselves as linked to such a new conception of the French economy. Many of them had worked in large-scale industry, but this did not mean that they represented industrial interests: François Lehideux had come to blows with his former employer, Louis Renault, in 1940. The economic plan of 1941 was designed as much to sop up unemployment, mainly a problem of the non-industrial south, as to transform the economy, and it was full of rhetoric about the virtues of rural life. Bichelonne made great efforts to defend small business in his discussions with the Germans and it was he who established the committee for the defence of small business under Léon Gingembre. Most importantly, both 'technocrats' and 'traditionalists' were united by their lack of realism. Both the 'traditionalists' and 'technocrats' went in for touchingly absurd projects to 'save' France: Jean Coutrot believed that France could solve her energy problems by persuading housewives to position saucepans properly on the stove. The truth was that in an economy of penury, where the Germans wished to extract as much as possible in the shortest possible time, plans for long-term economic restructuring of any kind were impractical.

Industrialists disregarded the projects of both 'technocrats' and 'traditionalists': indeed many of them treated the whole regime with disdain. Most of French industry was located in the northern zone while Vichy's power was based in the non-industrial south. Furthermore, much of France's heavy industry was in the Nord and Pas-de-Calais. The Germans declared this to be a 'forbidden zone' and did not allow Vichy officials to enter it until 1941. Some industrialists feared that they had been abandoned by the regime altogether and that their region might be annexed by the Germans. Vichy's labour legislation and its attacks on the Popular Front offered industrialists little; they had already reversed labour gains of 1936 during the rule of Daladier and Reynaud and most of them regarded Vichy as a reactionary regime with nothing to react against. Such gains as French industry made under Vichy came from the economic strength that it had vis-à-vis Germany rather than the political strength that it had vis-à-vis the Vichy government. It was their role in the German war economy that allowed certain French industries, such as coal mining, to shake off the threat of Vichy regulation and obtain resources, particularly labour, that they needed.

The Vichy organisms that had most impact on the economy were those that carried the least ideological baggage. The organization committees, established by a law of 16 August 1940, were hastily improvised by Belin and a few civil servants to deal with the immediate needs of the economy. One committee was set up to oversee each industrial sector: by 1944 there were 231 such committees, grouping sectors that ranged from steel production to the wholesale potato trade. Committees could be means for the state to impose its will on industry, or a means by which industry expressed its desires to the state. Usually they came closer to the second of these roles than the first – although strong-minded committee presidents (such as Detoeuf, in the electrical industry, Lehideux, in automobiles, and Aimé Lepercq, of the coal industry) might impose policies of their own, which did not entirely fit in with the aims of either industrialists or the government. Alongside the COs stood the *Office Central de Répartition des Produits Industriels* (OCRPI) which was created in September 1940 to allocate supplies of raw materials. The OCRPI was under the direct control of the ministry of industrial production, but in reality it became increasingly clear that neither Vichy nor industrialists were able to guarantee supplies of materials which had been made scarce by the consequences of the war or of German policy.

The reality of economic life under Vichy was far removed from the grand projects drawn up by any of the factions in Vichy or Paris. This reality was dominated by scarcity. Two resources were particularly scarce. The first of these was labour. Initially, the disruption of the economy caused by the defeat meant that there was substantial unemployment in many areas of France. This changed as the German war economy began to make demands on French industry, and the absence of so many young men who were held in prison camps was felt. Light industries often continued to work short hours, but fierce competition developed in heavy industries, which were involved in war production, to obtain and retain workers. Hours of work were pushed up: in steel companies the 56-hour week was introduced in the summer of 1941. However, the productivity of workers tended to drop during the war. In the mines around St Etienne productivity dropped by 15 per cent in just six months during 1941. This fall was produced partly by the fact that inexperienced young men were being drafted into industries which had a particular need of labour. It was exacerbated by a rise in absenteeism as workers succumbed to hunger and exhaustion: absenteeism in some coal mines, where conditions were particularly harsh, reached as high as 50 per cent. The second scarce resource was energy. France had always imported around a third of her coal. These imports were not available after the defeat, and the Germans began to demand part of France's energy supplies. Soon many factories were having to interrupt production when they could not obtain coal or when electricity was cut off.

The Vichy economy was dominated by short-term considerations. The Germans were interested in immediate production that would contribute to their war effort. The replacement of plant, or even the diversion of labour for maintenance, became increasingly difficult. Industrialists themselves were reluctant to make long-term investments. They knew that a peace economy would eventually reduce demand in the very industries that found it easiest to expand during the war, and they knew that German victory might mean the complete elimination of French industries that were seen as competitors for Germany. In short, Vichy presided over a make-do and mend economy in which patched-up equipment, inexperienced labour, and low grade materials were pressed into service with a view to survival rather than reconstruction.

Far from mitigating the disruptive effects of the war economy, the Vichy government exacerbated them. The structure of Vichy economic organization seemed to present a sharp contrast to the chaotic, Malthusian competition of the Third Republic. However, in reality the endless committees and delegations set up by Vichy often exercised little authority. The authority attributed to different bodies often overlapped and there were fierce administrative battles for the control of particular resources. Industrialists sought to play off one body against another, and certain industries were able to ignore Vichy altogether and obtain what they needed directly from the Germans. Furthermore, a black market developed in the coupons that industrialists were allocated to obtain raw materials. Under these circumstances, it is not surprising that the economist and banker Charles Rist wrote that Vichy represented 'integral confusionism'.[20] Roger Martin, a young civil servant and graduate of the *École Polytechnique*, was employed in the Vichy industrial administration. He described his experience thus: 'industrialists, employers and the nation itself were tied up in a bitter struggle for survival and the total absence of information made all preparation for the future impossible. The real function of these organisms was to offer a welcoming structure to uprooted men and to offer them some means of subsistence.'[21]

Life and Death under Vichy

It is hard to sum up the impact that Vichy's policies had on the French population. This impact varied from one region to another. Article three of the armistice had recognized that the French government remained sovereign throughout France, but in practice the degree of power that Vichy was able to exercise depended on the Germans (see Map 3). At one extreme stood Alsace-Lorraine. It was annexed by the Germans in 1940. Thereafter it was ruled from Berlin with the help of local Nazi sympathizers. Here Vichy counted for nothing. From the beginning, local people were given no middle way between collaboration and Resistance. Thousands were expelled from their homes and flooded into the rest of France: the exiled University of Strasbourg in Clermont-Ferrand soon became a centre of Resistance. Young people who stayed were obliged to accept service in the German army – about 100,000 men and 5000 women fell into this category. Some of them were captured while fighting on the Russian front and only returned to France after many years of terrible hardship. Some joined units of the SS that were responsible for atrocities in the rest of France. The trial relating to the massacre at Oradour-sur-Glânes in the 1950s involved several Alsatians. The area around the Belgian frontier underwent experiences that were somewhat similar to those of Alsace-Lorraine. It was not annexed, but it was assimilated with the German administration based in Brussels rather than that based in Paris, and Vichy administrators were prevented from entering the area until 1941.

The northern and western parts of France remained, in theory, under Vichy rule and were always in contact with the southern zone. However, these areas were also occupied by German troops, and subject to German influence. The Germans overruled Vichy on matters that concerned them directly, and they protected some of their associates from Vichy's authority. Paris was a particularly strange place during the occupation. A city of youth, glitter and hysterical energy, it could not have been further removed from the senile provincialism of Vichy. It was here that the youthful technocrats of Vichy spent most of their time. It was also the centre of a large German occupying authority. Otto Abetz, the German ambassador to France, was a cultivated francophile under whose aegis a lively intellectual life flourished. Early plays by Sartre were performed, the classical abstraction of existentialist theatre making it acceptable to political censors. In the occupied zone, Vichy clearly counted for less than it did in the free zone. This difference was exacerbated by the social structure of the two areas. The northern zone contained most of French large-scale industry, although it also contained some rural areas such as Brittany. The economy of the southern zone was based mainly on agriculture and small production This social structure seemed to fit in with Vichy's vision of France – though the south, and especially the *midi rouge*, had often voted for the left before 1940. The southern zone was not occupied by German troops until December 1942. Consequently it was much easier for inhabitants of this area to separate Vichy and the Germans. Pierre Poujade, a small business leader from the Lot, entitled one of the chapters in his memoirs 'Pour le maréchal contre les Nazis'. Matters were made more complicated by the fact that large numbers of people fled from the northern to the southern zone in order to escape German invasion in 1940. It was reckoned that the population of the eight central departments of France doubled at one point during 1940 and the population of Clermont-Ferrand, normally 110,000, was increased by between 30,000 and 60,000 throughout the war.

The area in which Vichy was most successful was Algeria. This area never saw German troops at all during the occupation. Vichy rule proceeded without any sign of German intervention. The area was spared some of the material deprivations that afflicted mainland France; general Weygand, who was sent there as Vichy's delegate, seemed to be rebuilding the army of Africa in a way that some saw as designed to prepare revenge against Germany. Most importantly, this area was liberated directly by the Americans in November 1942. The Americans were aided in this operation by a number of right-wing Frenchmen and they eventually came to terms with admiral Darlan who happened to be in Algeria. Algeria was spared the civil war between Vichy and the Resistance that affected the mainland. The smooth transition from Vichy to American control, which Laval failed to achieve in mainland France, succeeded in Algeria. The purge of Vichy supporters was comparatively restrained in Algeria and control passed only slowly from American nominees to Gaullists and Communists. The fact that Algeria's memories of Vichy were so different from those of mainland France was to have important consequences in the future.

About one million Frenchmen did not see France at all during the Vichy period because they spent the war in German prison camps. A total of 1,800,000 French soldiers were taken prisoner during the battle of France; about 200,000 of these managed to escape before being taken to Germany. Just over half a million were subsequently released for various reasons. The experiences of prisoners of war varied greatly. Some of them were kept in comparatively comfortable conditions alongside civilians with whom they worked. Others spent the war in grim *Stalags* that were unbearably cold in winter, unhygienic and flea-ridden in the summer. Conditions were particularly harsh in the first year of imprisonment, before proper camps had been constructed, and in the last year, when shortage of food and allied bombing began to take a heavy toll. Prisoners of war were not all young single men: their average age was over 30 and around half of them were married. They left behind wives, children and professions. All prisoners other than officers and non-commissioned officers (i.e. about 95 per cent of the total) were obliged to work. Initially, most of these worked in agriculture, later many were switched to work in industry as the Germans sought to increase arms production. A total of around 30,000 prisoners of war died in captivity. Something between 30,000 and 70,000 succeeded in escaping; one writer estimated that only around 5 per cent of escape bids were successful.

The experience of prisoners of war has received comparatively little attention from historians. The enforced passivity and regimentation of prisoners of war presented a stark contrast to the heroic activists of Resistance mythology who dominated post-war discussion of the occupation. Nonetheless, the *Stalags* often exercised a formative influence over those who were imprisoned. Many of the Breton peasants who began to modernize French agriculture during the Fourth Republic had first used tractors while imprisoned in Germany. Fernand Braudel wrote the first draft of *The Mediterranean in the Age of Philip II* while he was imprisoned in Germany. Bourgeois young men like Jean-Paul Sartre and François Mitterrand experienced their first, and last, intimate contact with their ordinary countrymen while they were prisoners of war. Mitterrand went on to play a large role in the *Mouvement National des Prisonniers de Guerre*, initially set up under Vichy aegis, and prisoners of war were to provide him with an important political springboard after the war. Prisoners of war also played a large role in Vichy propaganda. The blind veteran of the First World War, Georges Scapini, set up a 'mission' to French prisoners. They were presented as the suffering heroes whom Vichy would save. Many of Vichy's initiatives were designed to defend the interests of prisoners: it was even made an offence to have sexual relations with the wife of a prisoner. Prisoners of war fitted in with Vichy mythology in several ways: they were all ex-soldiers; many of them came from peasant backgrounds; their life, surrounded by mud and barbed wire, was a curious bloodless echo of that experienced by the First World War soldiers who also played such a role in Vichy's thinking. The enforced passivity, discipline and unity of the prisoners of war also made a welcome contrast to the increasingly rebellious behaviour of young men who remained in France, although curiously the internal organization of prisoner of war camps was more democratic than that of France.

Some French people were also imprisoned in German concentration camps. In addition to the Jews, whose fate is described below, about 63,000 French people (mostly members of Resistance organizations) fell into this category. The treatment of these people, though less horrific than that inflicted on racial deportees, was very harsh and around 40 per cent of them died in captivity. Those imprisoned in German concentration camps included some of the post-war political elite such as the Gaullist politician Edmond Michelet, or the business leader Georges Villiers. Their sufferings were described in their memoirs and the fate of the Resistance heroes occupied much attention in the press when the concentration camps were discovered by allied troops. Indeed, the perception that concentration camps were part of the Resistance experience tended to obscure the fact that the Jews had been the main victims of Nazi persecution. However, in spite of, or perhaps because of, the attention devoted to lauding the heroism of the political deportees, it is hard to recapture the precise effects that this experience had on those who underwent it. The politician Edgar Faure, himself a Resistance leader, wrote of his colleague Charles Laurent-Thouverey: 'his experiences [in Buchenwald] had left a basis of anguish that could occasionally be discerned beneath his gaiety.'[22]

Prisoners were not the only Frenchmen to spend the war in Germany. The Germans sought to fuel their war economy with foreign labour. On 16 June 1942 Vichy instituted the 'relief' scheme. The aim of this, as Laval explained in a broadcast on June 22, was to persuade Frenchmen to volunteer to work in Germany. For every two such volunteers, one French prisoner of war would be released. This attempt to provide volunteer workers failed and in September 1942 *Service du Travail Obligatoire* (STO) was instituted, compelling men whose age would normally have made them subject to military service to make themselves available for work in Germany. About 650,000 men went to Germany. They often endured harsh conditions there: around 35,000 died; almost 60,000 became infected with tuberculosis.

The institution of the STO programme brought about a great change in the perception of the Vichy government. It identified the regime with the German war effort and did so in a manner that had a direct impact on the lives of most French families. Many French people now lost whatever lingering faith they had maintained in Pétain's government. The existence of STO also brought about great changes in the lives of young men who remained in France. Labour service in Germany could sometimes seem attractive to people in poor departments, such as the Ariège, but generally young men were extremely reluctant to go to Germany. Their reluctance was rooted partly in patriotism, partly in prudence – Pierre Nicolle noted that young men refused to sign documents that might make them seem to have volunteered for service in Germany – and partly in distaste for the privations and inconvenience that were involved in STO. In Haute-Savoie only 62 out of the 245 men convoked for the STO had attended preliminary medical examinations by January 1943 and only two had left for Germany. STO could be avoided in two ways.

The first of these was to find work in some industry that was judged to be of use to the German war economy, and hence provided with a right to 'protected labour'. This created a curious situation. It transformed the pattern of labour relations as workers and employers often developed a joint interest in defending their industry. It also showed how difficult it was to divide France neatly into 'collaborators' and 'resisters': employers who 'collaborated' by providing for the German war economy might also be 'resisting' by protecting part of their labour force from deportation. The French coal industry, which benefited from the greatest access to protected labour, even created a special 'mine' near St Etienne to prevent students at the *École Polytechnique* from being sent to Germany, although the students proved useless at all practical tasks. The impressive crowd scenes in Marcel Carné's film, *Les Enfants du Paradis*, were said to have sprung partly from a desire to employ extras who might otherwise have been sent to Germany. Those unable to find protected employment escaped STO by running away from home. Many of these young *réfractaires* took refuge in the hills and forests of the Corrèze or Haute-Savoie in order to escape detection by Vichy or the German authorities, and eventually most of them developed tentative and ambiguous relations with the organized resistance to the German occupation: the resultant force became known as the *maquis.*

The *Service du Travail Obligatoire* programme exposed another important division under Vichy: that between country and city. Most of the prisoners of war liberated under the programme were from rural backgrounds, and fathers of families. The men sent to Germany, by contrast, were mainly young industrial workers from cities. This seemed to fit in with the general sense that Vichy represented rural areas rather than industrial ones. The gulf between the two groups was reinforced by the flight of those called for STO to the countryside and the hills. Young men from industrial areas did not necessarily fit in well with the cultures of the remote rural areas where they could most easily find physical shelter. Much *maquisard* activity was designed to secure access to provisions rather than to counter the Germans. Cigarettes were a particular obsession for the *maquisards;* a whole mythology grew up around the American cigarettes which were intermittently parachuted in by allied aircraft. In Haute-Savoie tobacconists more than any other institution were attacked by *maquisards.*

Relations between *maquisards* and local populations varied considerably. Such relations were best when large numbers of *maquisards*

were themselves from the region. Sometimes such groups were supported by their wives and mothers, and by figures of authority such
as mayors, gendarmes or local schoolteachers, most *maquisards*
having only recently left school. Urban *maquisards* were less likely to
be well received. Politics also had an effect on relations between the
maquis and the population of the areas in which they operated. In
conservative areas, such as Haute-Savoie, groups organized by the
armée secrète of former officers were more favourably received than
those organized by the Communists. Other areas of rural France,
such as the Corrèze, had strong traditions of Communist support
even though they did not contain an industrial working class. In
such areas politics might help to bridge the social gap between
maquisard and peasant. Finally the sheer number and nature of the
maquisard groups had an important effect on the public perception
of their activity. Towards the end of the occupation ever larger
groups of young men took to the *maquis,* and thus placed a larger
burden on the areas in which they took refuge. Organizing and dis-
ciplining such groups became more difficult and, in some areas,
maquisards became increasingly concerned with seeking revenge
against real or alleged supporters of the Vichy government as the
occupation neared its end.

Town–country relations were further worsened by the difficulty of
obtaining food in Vichy France. Vichy extended the rationing system
that had been set up at the beginning of the war. It was estimated
that official rations under Vichy fell short of average requirements by
about 1000 calories per day. The writer Simone Weil, who spent the
war in London, decided to live on official French rations: she died of
malnutrition. Shortage of labour and materials impeded agriculture
during the war: in the area around Clermont-Ferrand pork production, or at least officially declared pork production, dropped to half
of its normal level. Shortage of food was probably the strongest
memory that most ordinary people preserved from the war. Such
shortages were particularly severe in cities. Certain groups involved
in heavy labour, such as coal miners, had access to extra rations, and
some employers sought to maintain their workforce with factory can-
teens or by providing small plots of land to employees, but even
these were inadequate and drops in productivity were attributed to
the deteriorating health of industrial workers. Those who had
money could supplement their diet on the black market. In some
areas, the black market price of butter was over ten times the official
one. Wealthy people flocked into agricultural regions, such as

Haute-Savoie, in search of food. Having friends or relations in the countryside could be highly useful in these circumstances. Sometimes a 'grey' market provided food to acquaintances of the vendor at prices that were between those of the official and black markets. In Clermont-Ferrand it was estimated that over 60 per cent of the average household income was spent on food; in St Etienne consumption of coffee had dropped to 17.1 per cent of its 1938 level by October 1941. It was widely perceived that the peasantry benefited from their direct access to food; in some rural areas mortality rates dropped during the occupation. The peasants were also seen to benefit from their ability to sell at advantageous prices on the black market. Similar accusations were made about small shopkeepers. Such a view of Vichy is reflected in the novel by Jean Dutourd, *A bon Beurre*. Since black market activities were unrecorded, it will probably never be known precisely who gained and who lost from such transactions. Accusations of profiteering often accompany penury and it may be that the peasantry and shop-keepers simply provided the most obvious target for the resentment that was caused by starvation: certainly shopkeepers were more likely than large-scale businessmen to fall victim to post-war purges.

Some groups became particular targets of Vichy hostility. This hos-tility was partly rooted in the traditional Maurrassian disgust for the 'anti-France'. However, not all of the groups who had attracted right-wing hostility in the past suffered at Vichy. The regime made no attempt to put Maurras' attacks on Protestants into practice; indeed Pétain expressed personal admiration for protestantism and a number of Protestants, such as Couve de Murville, served his regime. The freemasons suffered worse. This was partly because the Germans shared the French right's hostility to masonry and partly because masons had been associated with recent political controversy. During the Dreyfus case, masonic lodges had been used to collect information on Catholic army officers who might be hostile to the republic. After 1940, Vichy acted against the lodges. Lists of masons were published and members of the order were forbidden to hold public office. Bernard Fay, the Pétainist director of the French National Library, collected 120 cartons of documents relating to the role of the masons in French history. However, the conflict between masons and the government was blunted by the fact that most masons were property owners who feared Marxism as much as they feared 'reaction'. The Grand Orient Lodge rushed to dissolve itself in August 1940, and special dispensations were passed to allow several masons to serve in the Vichy government. It is significant that the masons who were most closely linked to anti-Vichy activity, such as the Radical politician Pierre Mendès-France, often did not bother to rejoin the order after the war.

Many Communists had already been imprisoned during the last year of the Third Republic. Vichy continued this persecution and from July 1940, French police arrested Communists. In the department of the Seine, 988 Communists had been arrested by the end of 1940; by May 1941 this figure reached 2208. This persecution became particularly severe when the Communists entered into large-scale Resistance after the invasion of Soviet Russia in June 1941. Both Vichy and the Germans were prone to blame the Communists for Resistance attacks. Furthermore, the Vichy minister of the interior, Pierre Pucheu, agreed that his government should provide the Germans with lists of French hostages to be shot by the Germans in the event of Resistance attack. Many of these names were drawn from amongst imprisoned members of the Communist party.

The victims of Vichy who have attracted most attention in recent years are the Jews. Vichy repealed the Crémieux decree of 1875 that had granted French citizenship to Jews in Algeria – a measure that was regarded with considerable satisfaction by many North African Muslims – and, in August 1940, it repealed the Daladier–Marchandeau law of 1938 that had outlawed racial attacks in newspapers. Finally, in October 1940 Vichy introduced a *Statut des Juifs*. Jews, defined as anyone with two Jewish grandparents, were to be excluded from public employment and the media; their numbers were to be sharply limited in many other professions. Robert Paxton and Michael Marrus have shown that these measures were not taken in response to German pressure. The Germans showed little interest in the fate of Jews in France and, initially, sought to deport Jews from the occupied zone, and even from Germany itself, into the unoccupied zone.

Vichy's anti-semitism bore some resemblances to that of Nazi Germany. Vichy's legislation defined Jews in purely racial terms. In general, however, Vichy anti-semitism stressed culture rather than biology. Where the Nazis, and some Paris-based collaborationists, regarded assimilated Jews as being particularly dangerous, Vichy gave assimilated Jews special exemptions from its legislation: particular tolerance was shown to men, such as the historian Marc Bloch, who were seen to have 'proved' their Frenchness through service in the First World War. Furthermore, Vichy did not share the Nazis' obsession with racial purity or with physical characteristics. Indeed Vichy propaganda lauded the black and Muslim inhabitants of the French Empire, who were seen as spontaneous and loyal, and who were valued ·for their contribution to the French army. Henry Lémery, a black senator from Martinique, held office at Vichy as minister for colonial affairs in the summer of 1940.

Vichy's attitudes to the Jews had specifically French origins. In part these derived from the Maurrassian perception that Jews lacked the communal and local associations that made up the real nation. Hostility to Jews was increased by memories of the Dreyfus case and by the prominence of some Jewish politicians – Blum, Zay, Mendès-France – on the left. The Vichy attitude towards Jews was also part of a wider attitude towards foreigners that had grown up during the last years of the Third Republic. Because of her low population, France had always attracted large numbers of immigrant workers and, because of her traditional tolerance, she had always attracted large numbers of refugees. In the late 1930s the number of refugees increased, as people tried to escape from Nazi Germany and Spanish republicans fled across the Pyrenees. The refugees arrived at an unfortunate time: recession meant that competition for jobs was unusually severe and the political climate meant that many viewed potential revolutionaries with suspicion. Even before the defeat, France had begun to subject refugees to draconian controls and special camps had been established for them. Vichy continued this struggle against recent arrivals: many German and Spanish refugees were handed back to the governments of their respective countries. · On 22 July 1940 Alibert, the minister of justice, set up a commission to review the citizenship of all those who had been naturalized since 1927. This commission examined 500,000 cases and stripped 15,154 people of their citizenship.

Many of those who had come into France during the 1930s were Jews, and 6307 of those who were deprived of their citizenship by Alibert's commission were Jewish. There was a sharp contrast between Jews who had been long established in France and those who had arrived recently. Foreign Jéws were poorer than their French co-religionists; they were less likely to speak fluent French; and they were concentrated in certain areas, notably eastern Paris. Only 5 per cent of French Jews, as opposed to 60 per cent of immigrant Jews, worked in industry, whereas 25 per cent of French Jews, compared to 8 per cent of foreign Jews, worked in the liberal professions. Some French Jews resented the arrival of new immigrants,

whom they regarded as likely to bring their community into disre-
pute. In June 1934, a right-wing league of Jews – the *Union Patriotique
des Français Israélites* – had been formed. The Union made much of
the role of Jews in the First World War and espoused an ideology
that bore strong resemblances to that of the *Croix de Feu*: in
December 1934 it decided to exclude immigrants from its ranks.
Vichy's policies need to be seen in the context of this distinction in
the Jewish community. The brunt of Vichy's persecution fell on
foreign Jews. A decree of 4 October 1940 allowed prefects to intern
foreign Jews: by 1942, 20,000 people were in Vichy camps as a result
of this measure. Jews were often forced to work and sometimes were
shunted around the country as local authorities sought to divest
themselves of what they regarded as excessive numbers: in January
1941, 3000 Jews were expelled from Lyon. By contrast measures
against French Jews were relatively restrained at first. Many highly
assimilated Jews were uncertain about whether Vichy's legislation
was intended to be applied to them: an engineer from the Loire who
had converted to catholicism in 1934 wrote to the prefect, asking
whether he was defined as a Jew. Some conservative French Jews
even looked on the new regime with favour: the Jewish deputy
Achille-Fould voted for the granting of full powers to Pétain.

Although Vichy and German anti-Jewish actions were initially separate, they became increasingly connected as time went on. German
efforts to 'aryanize' Jewish property in the occupied zone began in
October 1940. The French were concerned that these measures
risked transmitting large amounts of property to German control
and in March 1941 established a bureau for Jewish affairs which
worked with the Germans. In March 1943 control of this bureau
passed from the Maurrassian Xavier Vallat to Darquier de Pellepoix,
a fascist whose biological racism resembled that of the Nazis. More
importantly, the Germans had begun systematically to exterminate
European Jews in 1941, and Vichy institutions often made it easier
for the Germans to carry out their policies. Organizations set up to
administer and control the Jewish community were used to manage
deportations to concentration camps. French police often helped to
carry out such deportations, the most notorious of which occurred
in July 1941 when 13,000 Parisian Jews were assembled at the
Vélodrome d'hiver.

Once again, the distinction between French and foreign Jews was
crucial in determining the extent to which they suffered. Vichy made
some effort to protect French-born Jews, but it offered to help with

the deportation of foreign Jews. Increasingly Jews lost faith in the ability of any official institution to protect them. They fled into the unoccupied zone. Some Jews also sought sanctuary in the area of France occupied by the Italians, who were less anti-semitic than either Vichy or the Germans and whose zone was conveniently located for crossing the Swiss frontier. However, southern France was occupied by the Germans in December 1942 and the Italian zone suffered the same fate in September 1943. Thereafter Jews had to rely on their capacity to hide or escape abroad for survival. French Jews were more likely to have the money, contacts and capacity for blending into the background that were necessary to survive in this situation. At the end of the war, around 60,000 foreign Jews and 6000 French Jews had been deported to concentration camps in the East. About 5 per cent of them survived.

Conclusion

As allied troops pushed south from the Normandy landing beaches, the German forces occupying France withdrew, taking Pétain and his government with them. A government that had justified itself in terms of the need to remain on French soil now found itself in igno-minious exile. Many of those involved were frightened that the Germans would install the French government at Coblenz where the royalist émigrés of 1793 had been based; in fact the Germans gave Pétain and his entourage a castle at Sigmaringen in the Rhineland. The life of the Vichy government at Sigmaringen was rich in farce, a characteristic that was exploited by Céline in his autobiographical novel, *Un château en allemagne*. Most of the original Pétainists had prudently distanced themselves from the regime and Pétain was now surrounded by a bizarre squabbling group of collaborationists who were either unwilling to accept the possibility of German defeat or so closely identified with collaboration that they could not hope to survive in France. Doriot discussed absurd plans to parachute agents who would incite Resistance in 'American-occupied France'.

The indignity of Vichy's end suited those who replaced it. They were able to present Vichy as a mere parenthesis which had no significance for the proper course of French history. This point of view was expressed by de Gaulle in newly liberated Paris: when asked to 'declare the republic', he remarked tersely that this was unneces-sary since the republic had never ceased to exist. François

Mitterrand made the same point in 1992 when he denied that the republic could be held responsible for the crimes of the *état français*. Historians have reacted against the idea that Vichy can be dismissed as a parenthesis. They point to the extent to which Vichy was built on long-standing elites and they suggest that there were essential continuities running through Vichy and linking the political divisions of the 1930s to the drives for economic modernization of the 1950s. However, the continuities that can be discerned in the politically conscious elite are less obvious when the mass of the French population are examined. Pétain's advisers and ministers drew on ideas that had been developing for years before 1940, but the majority of those who looked to Pétain for reassurance in 1940 were simply motivated by the shock of defeat. Thereafter the majority of French people were more affected by the consequences of war, defeat and occupation than by any specific Vichy policy. The regime that prided itself on realism came to seem abstract and remote to most of those over whom it nominally ruled.

5   Resistance: London, France, Algeria

London

Charles André Joseph Marie de Gaulle was born on 22 November 1890. The name says much about his origins: Charles hinted at royalism (Charles X had been the last Bourbon to rule France); Joseph Marie evoked the devout catholicism which often accompanied royalism; *de* Gaulle was a sign of noble descent. The French upper classes did not choose names at random: de Gaulle's own first son was to be named Philippe after his godfather Philippe Pétain. De Gaulle's family belonged to a section of French society that had never accepted the Revolution of 1789. They regarded the Third Republic constitution of 1875 with particular distaste and they encouraged their children to seek careers in institutions such as the church and the army that were seen as untainted by France's recent political history.

De Gaulle broke with his family traditions by becoming a republican. However, in many ways his upbringing among traditional conservatives continued to mark him: as late as 1934 de Gaulle dedicated one of his books to the royalist thinker Charles Maurras. Renouncing belief in a hereditary king did not necessarily mean acquiring faith in the unstable governments and squabbling parliaments of the Third Republic. Throughout his political life, de Gaulle wanted a single strong leader to exercise power and he emphasized the direct relations that such a leader might have with his subjects though plebiscitary democracy. It might be argued that de Gaulle had abandoned the political traditions that were believed to have been incarnated by the Bourbon kings for the traditions of Bonaparte. De Gaulle's ideas on France's place in the world were also rooted in the traditions of the French right: he was obsessed by the belief that 'France cannot be France without greatness'. He believed that the primary duty of government was the conduct of foreign policy and war. He regarded the nation state as the only important focus of political loyalty and he was to have no enthusiasm for international bodies, such as NATO or the United Nations, or for international ideologies, like communism or anti-communism.

In the context of the early twentieth century, the most humiliating sign that France could not regain the greatness that she had once known under Louis XIV was the greatness that Germany had acquired under Bismarck. France had been defeated by Prussia in 1870 and the army in which de Gaulle spent the early years of his adult life was haunted by the idea of revenge. De Gaulle learnt to speak almost fluent German as part of his preparation for the coming war. His personal and patriotic ambitions came together when he contemplated the prospect of war against Germany: at the age of 15 he had written a school essay about the day when 'general de Gaulle' would save France from a foreign invader. But the mud and trenches of the First World War provided little scope for the military glory of which the young de Gaulle had dreamed and in 1916 the war came to an end for de Gaulle when he went missing in action and was presumed dead. In fact he had been wounded and captured by the Germans. The two years that he spent in a prisoner of war camp were intensely frustrating: he made numerous unsuccessful escape attempts. But this was also an important period of reflection for de Gaulle. He prepared an interesting book, published in 1924, entitled *Discord among the Enemy*. A central argument of this work was that the Germans' failure during the war had sprung from the inability of civilian politicians to keep the generals in check. It was unusual for a professional soldier to argue for the elevation of civil over military power and de Gaulle's endorsement of such arguments may be seen as a turning point in his career. Thwarted in military ambition, he turned his attentions to the political sphere. He was to remain a professional soldier until 1940 and he was to wear uniform, when it suited him, until the end of his life. However, from the end of the First World War de Gaulle turned his back on the values that were most highly regarded in the army: obedience to superiors and loyalty to subordinates. He was increasingly associated with civilian politicians, and all the violent conflicts of his life were to set him against soldiers.

The new direction of de Gaulle's career was visible in the postings that he took. Unlike most of his brother officers he never served in the French Empire; he spent much of the interwar period in Paris studying, teaching and annoying his superiors at military college. He also worked as a ghostwriter, producing speeches and articles for marshal Pétain, his first and most powerful patron. Eventually de Gaulle and Pétain fell out when de Gaulle insisted on publishing *France and her Army*, a work originally prepared for Pétain, under his own name. This argument also reflected broader disagreements between de Gaulle and Pétain. Pétain came from a humbler and less conservative background than de Gaulle. When Pétain married a divorcée, de Gaulle's devout Catholic wife refused to call on the couple. There were also growing differences between the strategic conceptions of the two men. Pétain was associated with defensive warfare; de Gaulle began to advocate mobile warfare in which tanks would be used in large and concentrated groups. De Gaulle exacerbated the conflict with Pétain, and the army hierarchy in general, by seeking to gain political allies who could impose the strategic ideas of a lieutenant colonel on the senior ranks of the army. De Gaulle's first article on mechanized warfare was published, not in the *Revue de Défense Nationale*, but in the *Revue Politique et Parlementaire*. A wide range of politicians – including the neo-Socialist Marcel Déat, the Socialist Léon Blum and the conservative le Cour Grandmaison – took an interest in de Gaulle's ideas. The man who was most convinced by them, and most willing to try to convince others, was Paul Reynaud. However, as has been argued above, the politicization of mechanized warfare, and its association with what was seen as an undemocratic professional army, reduced its chances of being accepted.

If de Gaulle's political manoeuvres had little impact on French policy, they had a substantial impact on his own career. When Reynaud became prime minister, in March 1940, he plucked de Gaulle from his comparative obscurity as a tank commander and made him undersecretary of state for war. Since Reynaud himself held the ministry of war, this was an important position for de Gaulle to occupy, and it gave him the opportunity to draw himself to the attention of the British, especially Winston Churchill, as a determined advocate of continued French resistance during the debacle of May–June 1940. These links were to lead to the most astonishing event of de Gaulle's astonishing career. De Gaulle, who had joined the government in Bordeaux, was contacted by Churchill's emissary, general Spears, who suggested that de Gaulle should fly to London and advocate continued resistance to Germany from there. De Gaulle accepted this offer and the two men left Bordeaux on June 17.

Churchill welcomed de Gaulle warmly to London, but it was unclear what the new arrival was to do. All early attempts to present him with an acceptable public image fell flat. Cecil Beaton took photographs of the general standing stiffly to attention while his wife fed the ducks in Regent's Park. De Gaulle himself issued a public statement in which he declared his belief in God and France. He also, somewhat disingenuously, stressed his lack of links with party politics. The statement probably baffled most Englishmen, though a Frenchman would have recognized religion, nationalism and 'apoliticism' as hallmarks of the right. Finally, on the evening of 18 June 1940, the anniversary of the battle of Waterloo, de Gaulle broadcast what was later to be described as his 'call to honour'. He argued that France need not accept defeat and that she should fight on from her overseas possessions with the help of her allies. De Gaulle was effectively setting himself up as the incarnation of the true France and calling on his compatriots to rally around him. It is almost impossible to overstate his isolation and weakness when he made this audacious move. He was still a comparatively junior officer, having been promoted from the rank of colonel to that of 'acting general' the previous month. He had been a minister for only a couple of weeks. In France he was known only as a man on the fringes of political life with eccentric right-wing views, an offensive personal manner and a high opinion of his own importance. 'The call to honour' was to assume great importance in Gaullist mythology, but very few people in France heard it in 1940.

De Gaulle fought a political war. From June 1940 until the Liberation of France in July 1944, he took little interest in the military details of campaigns and battles against the German enemy. What concerned him was the assertion of French rights and prestige against the English and, especially, American allies. At first de Gaulle's claim to represent the 'real France' was based on the support of a very small number of heroes, fanatics and far-sighted opportunists who came to join him in London. Unlike the Poles or the Czechs in London, the French were not a 'government in exile'. The Vichy government, which sentenced de Gaulle to death in July 1940, was recognized as legitimate by most powers. Even the British accepted only that de Gaulle represented 'the Free French', and French troops evacuated at Dunkirk who wished to return to France were allowed to do so. The first event that changed de Gaulle's position occurred in July 1940 when the British, fearing that French ships might come under German control, sank the French Mediterranean Fleet at Mers-el-Kebir with the loss of 1500 lives. The attack probably damaged de Gaulle's reputation, such as it was, in France. However, it also made a rapprochement between England and Vichy France, which might have deprived de Gaulle of a role, less likely.

De Gaulle's hopes of finding a genuine home for Free France during this period were fixed on France's overseas possessions. In August 1940 Chad, Cameroun and the French Congo rallied to Free France. In September, de Gaulle sought to extend this territory by leading an expedition to take the African port of Dakar. The mission failed. It was so badly organized that even the novelist Evelyn Waugh, who accompanied the French forces during his improbable incarnation as a marine commando, came to regard the Free French as unreliable and indiscreet. In spite of this setback, de Gaulle established a council for the defence of the French Empire in Brazzaville in October 1940. In 1941, he tried to extend his influence further when Vichy France allowed German forces to use their possessions in the Levant. De Gaulle hoped that this would provide him with a chance to take over the area, and he named general Catroux as 'plenipotentiary for the Levant'. The British, to de Gaulle's fury, signed the Saint-Jean d'Acre agreement with Vichy officials. In December of the same year, de Gaulle enraged the Americans by sending admiral Muselier to rally the French island of St Pierre et Miquelon off the Canadian coast to his cause. Finally in May 1942, the British seized the French island of Madagascar without allowing the Free French to become involved.

De Gaulle's relations with the British deteriorated during this period. The British supported admiral Muselier's attempts to wrest control of the Free French from de Gaulle in 1941 and 1942, and at one point the Free French were obliged to defend themselves from the accusation that they were torturing prisoners in the basements of their headquarters. The personal affection that Churchill had felt for his protégé soon dissipated. Churchill is said to have remarked that 'de Gaulle thinks he is Joan of Arc but I can't get my bloody bishops to burn him'. Roosevelt was even more hostile. However, de Gaulle had several advantages during this period that prevented him from being entirely eclipsed. Firstly, British and American public opinion, or at least the group of articulate intellectuals who were assumed to represent public opinion, was often more favourable to the Free French than the governments of these two countries. A.J.P. Taylor and his friends wept while watching the film *Casablanca*; Charles Bagley, professor of French at Dartmouth College, bombarded newspapers with letters in favour of de Gaulle. Secondly, the British Foreign Office, initially hostile to de Gaulle, came to see his potential uses and sought to restrain Churchill's hostility. Thirdly, the USSR entered the war in June 1941, and in September of that year, made contact with the Free French. There was no natural affinity between de Gaulle (who had fought with Polish troops against the Red Army in 1920) and Stalin's Russia, but the two sides were pragmatic enough to recognize that they had a mutual interest in checking Anglo-Saxon power. Fourthly, and most importantly, de Gaulle was increasingly seen as the representative of Resistance fighters within metropolitan France.

France

Many French people were hostile to the German occupation and to the Vichy government from an early stage. However, very few of them translated this hostility into action. Furthermore, those who did seek to establish Resistance networks in the months after the defeat came from very different political traditions. On the one hand were nationalist right-wingers, often influenced by the writings of Charles Maurras. These men shared Vichy's hostility to what they saw as the decadence of the Third Republic, but their hostility to Germany made them reluctant to accept the defeat. Jacques Lecompte-Boinet, who founded *Ceux de la Résistance* in the northern zone, Henri Frenay and Philippe Viannay, who founded *Combat* in the southern zone, all fitted into this category.

On the other hand was the *Parti Communiste Français*. The PCF condemned Vichy, Germany and de Gaulle (seen as the tool of the city of London) with equal vehemence. Some individual Communists did take action against the Germans and Vichy. In the Nord Charles Debarge and others sabotaged German equipment; in Brittany and the Limousin guerrilla bands were established. In Bordeaux Charles Tillon called for resistance to Germany. However, all these men were acting without the authority of the party leadership. In the immediate aftermath of the defeat some Communists had approached the German authorities in Paris and, unsuccessfully, requested permission to resume publication of the Communist paper *Humanité*. Some of the PCF's actions during this period were open to more than one interpretation. The strike of coal miners in the Nord and Pas-de-Calais, which party leaders helped to organize in May and June 1941, can be seen as an act of Resistance, because strikers demanded the return of their comrades who were prisoners of war. However, it might equally well be seen as a purely economic strike or even, since the strikers exploited their role in the German war economy, as an act of collaboration. Similar doubts surround the clandestine *Organisation Secrète* (OS), which Communist leaders founded in the autumn of 1940. The OS is sometimes presented as an early Resistance organization, but there is evidence that its main purpose was to assassinate enemies of the PCF including some of those dissident Communists who wished to fight Germany.

Communist activity between the defeat of France and the German invasion of Russia in June 1941, at which point the PCF came down unambiguously in favour of anti-German struggle, aroused resentment from other elements of the Resistance. Lecompte-Boinet, Frenay and Avinin all believed that the Communist party had been 'allies of Hitler' during this period. In fact, things were more complicated. The Communists argued that their history was marked not by a period of treachery between September 1939 and June 1941, but by a continuous period of clandestine resistance to the forces of reaction that began with their being banned under the Third Republic in 1939 and continued until the Liberation. The Communists were anti-Vichy without taking much action against the Germans, while the right-wing Resistance was often anti-German without being against the Vichy government, or at least marshal Pétain. It was alleged that an early issue of the Resistance publication *Défense de la France*, produced by Viannay, excused Pétain's actions at Montoire. Furthermore, in the early days, right-wing resistance leaders ran comparatively few risks. Many of them had no known political associations. Some had protectors at Vichy. Even in the northern zone, the Germans were so convinced that opposition would come from the working class and the left that they often overlooked conservative Resistance groups. By contrast, Communists were frequently arrested and sometimes executed even before the party began to resist the German occupation. It was not until August 1942 that René Bousquet, Vichy's chief of police, ordered that non-Communist Resistance should be repressed as hard as that of the Communist party.

As time went on, the Resistance movements in France expanded. The growing unpopularity of the Vichy government provided networks with new members and, perhaps more importantly, with the sympathizers who provided the varieties of discreet support – food, information, documents – on which Resistance depended. The STO programme ensured that there were growing numbers of young men on the run from whom Resistance leaders might gain recruits. The invasion of the Soviet Union in June 1941 ensured that the Communist party leaders threw their full weight behind the struggle against the German occupation. The Communists formed a group of *Franc-Tireurs et Partisans* (FTP) and a wider umbrella organization: the Front National. These movements gave the struggle a violent dimension that it had previously lacked. Communist organizations carried out 107 acts of sabotage between June and December 1941, and on 21 August 1941 the Communist 'Colonel Fabien' shot a German naval officer in a metro station. Militants were dedicated to their cause and already experienced in clandestine organization. In spite of, or perhaps because of, the fact that so many Communists had been arrested before the party's whole-hearted entry into the Resistance, its capacity to keep secrets and conceal its leaders was exceptionally good: the leader of the Communist-dominated FTP in Clermont-Ferrand was able to live in his own house as late as spring 1943.

The Resistance was never united. Deep hostility between Communists and non-Communists persisted, and the effectiveness of the former only exacerbated this hostility: non-Communist Resistance leaders often felt that 'their' movements were being colonized. The Communist party was suspected, with some justification, of using Resistance activity as a cover to eliminate its own enemies and dissidents. Marcel Gitton, a former Communist who had denounced the Hitler–Stalin pact, was executed by members of the OS in September 1941. Other Communists who had shown themselves too independent of the party line, such as Gabriel Peri, were denounced to the German authorities. Sometimes former Communist Resistance leaders, such as Guingouin in the Limousin, took up arms against their former colleagues from the Communist party. Numerous arguments arose within the Resistance. Some argued that violence against Vichy supporters was wrong or even that attacks by fighters in civilian clothes against unprepared Germans were dishonourable. Some disliked the growing intrusion of politics into the Resistance. Many disliked those whom they regarded as 'latecomers' to the movement. The personality of the most prominent leaders did not help matters. Such men were often natural rebels who had been noted for their bloody-mindedness even before 1940. In the Resistance such men became 'unelected emperors of clandestine empires', and their jealousy of potential rivals was increased. Conflicts flared between networks in different regions and, especially, between those in the northern and southern zones:

the former regarded the latter as mere politicians who had not endured the real test of conflict with the Germans. Suspicion was a feature of all Resistance activity, and since only the suspicious survived, this characteristic increased as time went on. Years after the Liberation, books on the betrayals and conspiracies of the Resistance were still appearing.

In spite of all the problems described above, the Resistance did gradually begin to unify. In January 1942 the *Mouvements Unis de la Résistance* brought together the three main networks in the southern zone, and in March a similar agreement was reached in the northern zone. Networks from all over France met in the *Conseil National de la Résistance* (CNR) in 1943. Unity was speeded by three things. Firstly, the dissolution of the Comintern in 1943 changed Communist tactics. Emphasis was now placed on alliances within each nation rather than on revolution. The PCF now emphasized trade union action more and violence less. It also eventually agreed to join the CNR. Secondly, Third Republic politicians began to enter the Resistance. These men were often deeply despised by their colleagues: Henri Frenay wrote that no one had died for the *Alliance Démocratique* or the Radical party. Furthermore, some of the new enthusiasts for Resistance, such as Joseph Laniel, had voted in favour of granting full powers to marshal Pétain in 1940. Others, such as Louis Marin, were subject to such intense surveillance by Vichy that it was almost impossible for them to make contact with the Resistance. In spite of these obstacles, politicians did become involved in Resistance activity. Henri Queuille, a Radical from the Corrèze in his late fifties, clambered aboard a Lysander aircraft bound for England, and Pierre Brossolette, a Socialist, joined a Resistance network before committing suicide after capture by the Germans in 1944. The Third Republic politicians brought particular advantages to the Resistance. They lent it legitimacy in the eyes of the Americans, and the worldly tact of men like Pierre Cot helped to smooth relations between gruff young activists.

The third thing that helped to unify Resistance networks was the intervention of Gaullist agents. Christian Pineau of the *Libération Nord* network persuaded de Gaulle to issue a message to the Resistance on 23 June 1942 in which he emphasized that the struggle against Vichy was a political one in favour of democracy as well as a military one against defeat. De Gaulle's emissary Jean Moulin was the driving force behind the CNR and all Resistance networks began to recognize de Gaulle as a symbol of their activity.

Algeria

The most important moment in the development of the Free French and the Resistance came on 8 November 1942 when the Americans invaded French Algeria. This operation took place without de Gaulle's knowledge. The Americans were helped by a group of right-wing Frenchmen. Initially French forces in Algeria, commanded by admiral Darlan, who happened to be in the area, resisted the Americans. After this Darlan came to terms with the Americans, implying, incorrectly, that he had Pétain's authority to do so. The Americans ruled Algeria in collaboration with Darlan until his assassination on Christmas Eve. After this date the Americans placed their faith in general Giraud, a conservative French officer who had escaped from German custody. De Gaulle badly needed to gain access to Algeria which was seen as being part of France and which contained a substantial portion of the French army, but the Americans were determined to avoid a Gaullist take-over. The American representative in Algeria, Robert Murphy, had good relations with a number of Pétainists and a former Vichy minister of the interior, Marcel Peyrouton, was appointed as governor-general in Algeria. In January 1943, the Anglo-Saxon allies sought to stage a reconciliation between de Gaulle and Giraud at the Casablanca conference. The occasion was so tense that when de Gaulle met Roosevelt the latter's aides positioned guards with machine guns behind a curtain, but it did produce photographs of de Gaulle and Giraud shaking hands.

The next six months saw a struggle between Giraud and de Gaulle. The former was a purely military man who claimed that his only goal was victory; de Gaulle had a more sophisticated view of the role of Free France, which revolved around the maintenance of French prestige and suspicious vigilance over her allies. Rapprochement between the two men was facilitated by Jean Monnet who became Giraud's political adviser. Under Monnet's influence, Giraud made an unenthusiastic speech in favour of republican institutions in March 1943. De Gaulle responded by sending out general Catroux as his representative in Algeria. De Gaulle insisted that Giraud should denounce the Vichy regime and that a joint committee should be formed by the representatives of the two men: significantly, he also insisted that Giraud should accept the subordination of military to civil authorities. On 30 May 1943, de Gaulle himself finally arrived in Algiers and formed a *Comité Français de*

Libération Nationale (CFLN) with Giraud. In theory, de Gaulle and Giraud exercised equal powers within the committee. In practice de Gaulle enjoyed the support of Third Republic politicians and of the internal Resistance; Jean Moulin sent a telegram affirming this support on 15 May 1943. De Gaulle was also helped by the relations that he nurtured with Harold Macmillan, the British plenipotentiary in the Mediterranean. The two men even went on a picnic to Tipassa together though de Gaulle sweated in his full uniform while Macmillan swam naked. By October 1943, de Gaulle was recognized as president of the CFLN (the civil power) and Giraud as commander-in-chief (the subordinate military power).

De Gaulle's establishment of a base in Algeria was a turning point. He now had a reservoir of support, and he came to be seen in mainland France as a rival to the Vichy government. The new authorities in Algeria began to carry out purges of those who had supported Pétain: governor Peyrouton was forced to resign on 1 June 1943 and a number of individuals were imprisoned. These purges sent a clear message to those on the mainland, which was reinforced on 3 September 1943 when it was announced that ministers and officials of the Vichy government would stand trial. In 1943 prudent French civil servants and ministers such as Maurice Couve de Murville, a future Gaullist prime minister, and Jacques Le Roy-Ladurie left Vichy and fled to join the *maquis* or de Gaulle's forces. Algeria gave de Gaulle control of 120,000 French soldiers who had been trained by Weygand and access to the young Frenchmen who now made their way to North Africa via Spain. Finally, Algeria provided de Gaulle with a suitable location to begin acting as a head of a provisional government. In the autumn of 1943 a pseudo-parliament or 'consultative assembly' of politicians and Resistance leaders was summoned to Algeria.

De Gaulle's battle with his Anglo-Saxon allies was not over. They still hoped to prevent him from taking over the government of France at the Liberation. They flirted with the idea of running France as an occupied country, as they had run Italy. They were keen to prevent de Gaulle from finding out about the D-day landings in Normandy that were planned for June 1944. For some time de Gaulle was kept in Algeria and communications between London and Algiers were impeded. De Gaulle himself did not arrive in England until 4 June 1944. Negotiations between Churchill and de Gaulle over the precise status of French officials who would accompany the allies were so savage that one of the unfortunate diplomats who shuttled between the two men died of a heart attack before agreement was reached. De Gaulle was even more awkward than usual because he was nervous. He had no idea what kind of reception he would receive in mainland France. His national reputation had been built while he was abroad: he was the first politician whose public persona was entirely created by radio broadcasts. Furthermore, de Gaulle had seen film of the enthusiastic reception given to Pétain when he visited Paris in 1944. No one knew how de Gaulle would be received when he stepped on to French soil. In fact de Gaulle's visit to Bayeux in Normandy in June 1944 was a huge success; it was now clear that the French people recognized the general as their leader and that the allies had no choice but to do likewise. De Gaulle's relief was reflected in an uncharacteristically gracious letter to Churchill. He had fought hard to preserve his independence at a time when he laboured under terrible disadvantages: now he could afford to be generous.

6   Rebuilding Bourgeois France: 1944–1951

In an uncharacteristically tactless moment, general Eisenhower remarked that all the sacrifices of the French Resistance had only damaged the German occupiers as much as 15 divisions of regular troops would have done. The French took an equally sceptical view about the contribution that the Anglo-Saxons had made to the Liberation of France: polls showed that 50 per cent of the population (almost twice the Communist electorate) believed that the Soviet Union was the power that had played the largest role in defeating Germany. The reasons for tension between the western allies and the French were rooted partly in the struggles of de Gaulle during the Occupation; they were also linked to the difficult circumstances of the period after the Liberation. The allies were blamed for the impact of bombing on France, for the disruption of French life caused by requisitions and controls and for their apparently contemptuous attitude towards the French. National stereotypes abounded. Vichy propaganda films had shown Popeye and Donald Duck at the controls of a Flying Fortress attacking France; later the Communist party was to launch a campaign against the influence of Mickey Mouse.

The misunderstandings between French and Americans were also due to a more important gulf between their views of the war. The Americans saw France as a battleground to be fought over whereas the French Resistance saw it as a nation to be liberated. The French were interested not just in the military battle against Germany, but also in a political battle that pitted them against their allies and compatriots. De Gaulle was particularly concerned to maintain French grandeur that had been so badly compromised during the previous four years and it was for this reason that he enthusiastically supported French participation in the war. Several incidents illustrated the political dimension that the Liberation assumed in France. The first of these was the Liberation of Paris. American troops were persuaded to hold back and allow French troops under general Leclerc to enter the city with the help of Resistance fighters. This allowed the creation of the myth that 'Paris had liberated herself'. It also allowed certain groups, such as the Paris police, whose role in the Occupation had been notably unheroic, to redeem their reputations. Similar considerations governed de Gaulle's response when general Eisenhower, faced with German counter-attack, decided to abandon Strasbourg at the beginning of 1945. On military grounds the decision made sense, but on political grounds the sacrifice of a town so embedded in national mythology would have been a disaster. De Gaulle ordered de Lattre to defend Strasbourg at all costs. De Lattre succeeded and Strasbourg was to be a Gaullist stronghold from then on. Further dispute with the Americans arose when de Gaulle was forced to withdraw the troops that he had sent to occupy the Val d'Aosta, a part of Italy claimed by France.

Purges of those who had supported the Vichy government accompanied the Liberation of France. At first unfortunate individuals who fell into the hands of vengeful crowds or *maquisard* units were lynched or executed after brief trials in kangaroo courts. Later commissioners of the republic, the local officials appointed by the Free French, managed to bring events under control, and purges were increasingly conducted in the law courts as suspects accumulated at Fresnes prison on the outskirts of Paris. Pétainist representatives, such as the abbé Desgranges, compared the purges to the repression that had been imposed by the Germans, and even Tixier, the Socialist minister of the interior, believed that 105,000 had died in 1944 and 1945. Recent research has tended to demythologize these events and to suggest that the number of people who fell victim to reprisals was actually comparatively small – probably less than 10,000. Furthermore, the purges were not systematic in their selection of targets. The directors of Paribas, a merchant bank that had had extensive dealings with the Germans, escaped almost unscathed while the singer Sacha Guitry was punished. Obscure teenage *miliciens* were shot while fanatical and unrepentant collaborationists, such as Lucien Rebatet, François Brigneau and Charbonneau, were freed after a few years. Most significantly, a large number of the reprisals taken after the Liberation affected women; 40 per cent of those tried for collaboration in Orleans were female and the shaved heads of women accused of sleeping with German soldiers provided an enduring symbol of the purges, although few women had held positions of real power under Vichy.

Variations in the intensity of the purges were partly due to geography: casualties were much higher in regions where the Resistance had been most active and where reprisals immediately after the

Liberation were least restrained. Time was also important. Courts
began by imposing severe penalties and subsequently moderated
their behaviour. Most importantly, social class influenced the purges.
In Valenciennes, the court acquitted one third of all employers, and
one quarter of all middle-class suspects, but only one tenth of
working-class or peasant suspects. This was explicable in several
terms. Firstly, wealthy men could afford to hire effective defence
lawyers and to absent themselves from France during the first few
crucial months when the purge was at its most intense. Secondly, the
'Franco-French civil war' that had occurred under Vichy had really
been a civil war within the working class. It was from this group that
the most violent members of the Resistance had been drawn. It was
also among the working class, or at least amongst some of its more
marginal elements, that the collaborationist groups and the *milice*
had gained much of their support. By contrast, many members of
the elite had remained prudently distant from the conflict. Most
upper-class Pétainists had resigned from their offices before the
Liberation. Furthermore, at the highest levels of society, contacts
between the Resistance and Vichy had always remained open.
Businessmen who had supported the Resistance, such as Georges
Villiers, Aimé Lepercq or Raoul Dautry, had often been protected by
Pétainist officials such as André Boutemy. After the war, the
Resistance elite returned the favours that had been done to them.

Those connected with economic activity, particularly at a high
level, were also less likely to fall victim to the purges than those connected with the enforcement of order: 86 prefects and 267 subpre-
fects were replaced but almost no senior official in the finance
ministry was punished. This was partly because economic activity was
often intrinsically ambiguous; industrialists and civil servants were
able to claim that they had protected French labour and resources
by dealing with the Germans. It was also because industrialists and
civil servants continued to be necessary to the French war effort and
to the subsequent 'battle for production'. Indeed, it was often those
heavy industrialists who had been most useful to Germany who also
proved most necessary to the provisional government. By contrast
writers and artists were hit hard at the Liberation. Writers could
hardly deny views that they had expressed during the Occupation,
and the polemical tradition of French literature meant that many of
them had expressed such views with great vigour. Furthermore, they
provided important symbolic victims and their removal was not likely
to damage the French war effort.

The fact that the purge was comparatively restricted in its scope, and that it disappointed many Resistance leaders, should not be taken to mean that it had no effect on French society. There were several reasons for this. Many right-wingers believed that the purges were much more widespread than they really were. Charbonneau, a prominent writer of the extreme right, claimed that 1 million people were arrested and that 200,000 had been put on trial. This psychological impact was exacerbated by the fact that some of those imprisoned or put on trial belonged to the privileged classes who were unused to such treatment: one neo-fascist entitled a chapter in his memoirs, 'le tout Paris à Fresnes'.[1] Secondly, the purges were felt far more widely than judicial statistics would suggest. Many individuals suffered informal or covert punishment for what they had done: some tainted company directors were encouraged to resign by their colleagues, many army officers were discreetly retired and large numbers of people were placed in 'preventive detention'. Thirdly, purges did not merely affect individuals: they were also felt because of their effects on that great French bourgeois institution, the family. The father of the Sidos brothers, who played an active role in the French extreme right until the 1960s, had been shot in 1946. Philippe Ariès never forgot the humiliation inflicted on his brother, a Pétainist army officer. Maurice Bardèche, who became the editor of the neo-fascist *Défense de l'Occident*, was deeply affected by the execution of his brother-in-law, the poet Robert Brasillach. Those hurt by the purges provided an important part of the conservative electorate: one political analyst estimated that about a million families had been touched in some way by anti-Pétainist purges. Those who had been punished more directly provided the leadership of a new hard-core extreme right. A survey carried out by *Rivarol*, the leading paper of the extreme right, in 1957, discovered that 36 per cent of its readers had been imprisoned at the Liberation and that 3 per cent of them had been reprieved after death sentences.

Curiously, the purges made it more easy for parts of the French right to reintegrate themselves into political life. This was partly because the common experience of imprisonment often created new alliances within a group that had been divided by fierce ideological conflicts. Royalist reactionaries began to work with fascist revolutionaries and republican conservatives. The extent to which such alliances could transcend previous hostilities was shown by the fate of Georges Albertini. Albertini had been an aide of Marcel Déat, the anti-semitic and anti-capitalist politician who devoted particular energy to denouncing the 'synarchic conspiracy' that was seen to centre on the Worms Bank. In 1945 Albertini was put in the same cell as Hippolyte Worms, a Jewish capitalist and head of the Worms Bank. The two men became friends and, on their release; Worms funded Albertini's anti-Communist propaganda. Right-wing leaders, who had traditionally despised the *pays légal*, also acquired a new respect for legality now that a precise interpretation of law was the only thing between them and a firing squad. It was no accident that the two leading figures of extreme right post-war politics, Jean-Louis Tixier-Vignancour and Jacques Isorni, both made their reputations as defence lawyers. The fact that those who had voted full powers to Pétain were declared ineligible caused particular offence: abbé Desgranges' Association of Representatives of the People, which brought together 900 ineligibles for a banquet in 1948, spoke on behalf of this group. This new emphasis on republican legality created a common issue that united some Pétainists with the old parties of the Third Republic

Almost every group that emerged from the Resistance had high hopes for reform in 1945: they were all disappointed, and most historical accounts echo the sense of disillusion that is found in the memoirs of the Resistance leaders. Some argue that the fate of the Fourth Republic was determined by the nature of the constitution that was accepted by a referendum of October 1946. This new constitution gave great power to the national assembly, which was the only body to be elected directly by universal suffrage. The president of the republic was elected by parliament. He was to possess fewer powers than his Third Republic predecessors and, in particular, he lost much of his say over military appointments. The old senate was replaced by a 'council of the republic' which was little more than a forum for discussion. Governments had no power to govern without parliament and dissolution of the national assembly was made difficult while it was easy for the assembly to overthrow governments. The constitution did not make strong government easy, but is not in itself a sufficient explanation of the fate of the Fourth Republic. The way in which the constitution operated was itself dependent on the parties that exercised power in the national assembly and on the personalities of the prime minister and president of the republic.

Explanations for the broader political nature of the Fourth Republic vary. Some believe that the crucial moment came in January 1945 when the congress of the *Mouvement de Libération Nationale* failed to agree on unity around the 'charter' of the *Conseil*

National de la Résistance. After this congress the Resistance divided
between the mainly Communist *Mouvement Unifiée de la Renaissance
Française* and a variety of non-Communist groups, some of whom
eventually formed the *Union Démocratique et Socialiste de la Résistance*
(UDSR). Gaullists believe that the turning point came in January
1946 when the general, apparently disillusioned with party politics,
resigned from the provisional government. Philippe Viannay, by contrast, blames de Gaulle himself for the decline of the Fourth
Republic and dates that decline from the moment in 1945 when de
Gaulle, by insulting a Resistance hero, made it clear that the
Resistance would not play a large role in post-war politics.[2] Henri
Frenay dates the decline of the Fourth Republic from January 1946
when the UDSR, of which he was a member, joined with parties from
the Third Republic and Vichy to form the *Rassemblement des Gauches
Républicaines.*[3] Finally, many believe that the Fourth Republic fell
victim to the Cold War. They believe that American pressure forced
the Communist party out of government in May 1947 and thus
ended the 'tripartite' period during which France had been governed by an alliance of the Socialists, Communists and Christian
Democrats.

   In reality, the very diversity of explanations offered to explain the
'failure' of the Resistance shows how inevitable that failure was.
Resistance leaders did not share any coherent vision. Many of these
men talked of *travaillisme* and suggested that it might be possible to
create a large party of the united left. But *travaillisme* was a mirage.
Those, such as Frenay, Bourdet and Viannay, who described themselves as *travailliste* were seeking to distinguish themselves from the
Communist party and from their own conservative backgrounds, but
they did not advocate any specific set of policies that would have
been recognized as socialist. There had always been hostility between
Communists, Gaullists and those who were neither. During the war
the need for anti-German unity had helped to suppress such
antagonisms; after the war disputes about the division of the spoils of
government helped to expose them. Resistance veterans tended to
be young, impatient, and contemptuous of convention. None of this
fitted them for the compromises and petty disappointments of ordinary politics. They failed to appreciate that the Third Republic,
which seemed utterly discredited at national level, continued to exist
in the networks of contacts and mutual back-scratching of local politics. Only those few Resistance leaders (like Edgar Faure, Jacques
Chaban-Delmas and François Mitterrand), who were canny enough

to come to terms with the notables of the Third Republic and dig themselves into local fiefdoms, succeeded in post-war politics. Most Resistance leaders abandoned party politics altogether and sought more satisfying, prestigious and lucrative careers in the civil service, business or journalism: Jacques Lecompte-Boinet became an ambassador, Pierre Lefaucheux became managing director of Renault.

There was not much hope of a new left emerging from the Resistance, but there was a chance that the Resistance might produce a new right. This was precisely because a comparatively small proportion of right-wingers had been active in the Resistance. Traditionally, the right had been composed of small, poorly disciplined parties: real power was held, not by official party leaders, but by 'notables'. The notables drew their power from their own wealth, reputation and contacts and national politicians were obliged to compete for their support. After the Liberation, the balance of power between notables and national politicians changed. On the one hand the notables badly needed representation in order to alleviate the impact of the purges and to gain access to the greater resources that the state now distributed. On the other hand, in order to obtain that representation, notables had to rely on a very small number of conservative leaders who had the legitimacy, and the legal right, to hold office. It seemed possible that the Resistance elites might use their new monopoly of right-wing leadership to sweep away the old fragmented, notable-based parties of the right and create a large-scale and disciplined group that would be similar to the English Conservative party. Three attempts were made to create such a party: the first, the *Parti Républicain de la Liberté*, involved economic liberals who were closely linked to big business. The second, the *Mouvement Républicain Populaire*, was Christian Democratic. The third, the *Rassemblement du Peuple Français*, was Gaullist. The real political drama of the early Fourth Republic was not the struggle between right and left, but that between these three competing parties of the right and the older version of conservatism which they all sought, without success, to displace.

The *Parti Républicain de la Liberté* insisted that its members yield to strong party discipline; it also sought to subordinate old conflicts about religion, and new conflicts about Vichy, to the need for unity to defend the interests of the bourgeoisie and especially large-scale industry. Initially certain sections of big business seemed willing to back the party, apparently because they felt that capitalism needed a strong protector in the *dirigiste* climate of the Liberation. The party's leaders hoped that they would obtain around 100 seats. In fact they only obtained 40 and their representation in parliament declined so much that the party had ceased to exist by 1951. The PRL's leaders originated in the Resistance and its failure was, in some respects, part of the general political failure of the Resistance. The party's insistence on central discipline annoyed established leaders of the right such as Louis Marin, and perhaps more importantly, conservative notables such as André Baud in the Jura. The PRL was also disappointed by the scale of subsidy provided by big business. It became increasingly obvious that businessmen themselves were too divided – by economic differences, commercial rivalry, political disagreement and personal dislike – to unite behind any single party. Furthermore, as the general political climate for capitalism improved, businessmen could often get what they wanted through direct approaches to government or civil service departments: they needed party representation less and less. Some capitalists believed that a single strong party of the right, which might acquire considerable autonomy vis-à-vis its financial backers, was undesirable. They preferred to scatter their largesse over a large number of competing conservative parties.

The PRL was also undermined by competition from another new party, the *Mouvement Républicain Populaire* (MRP). The MRP was France's first large-scale Christian Democrat party. At first it achieved great success: in the elections of 10 November 1946 it gained 26.3 per cent of the vote and 167 seats in parliament, making it the second largest party in the national assembly after the Communists. The MRP's opponents dubbed it the '*Machine à Ramasser les Pétainistes*'. The MRP drew most of its support from areas such as Haute-Savoie, Brittany and Alsace-Lorraine, that normally voted for the right. A number of the MRP leaders had past associations that might have been expected to make them attractive to conservative voters: Pierre Pflimlin had been a member of the *Jeunesses Patriotes*, Francisque Gay had denounced republican atrocities during the Spanish Civil War, Robert Schuman had voted in favour of granting full powers to marshal Pétain in 1940.

The MRP represented a particular kind of conservatism. In one sense this was an old conservatism which rejected the modernizing 'orleanism' of parties like the PRL. Intimate associations with the church recommended it to rural and traditionally devout regions. Its opposition to large-scale capitalism, which many historians have identified as a 'left-wing' characteristic, also appealed to a conservative electorate in economically backward regions and to those who

had been influenced by the denunciations of the 'trusts' made by
Dorgères, Maurras and Pétain. On the other hand, the MRP represented a new kind of conservatism. The very fact that the party was
new meant that it appealed to those who had despised the parliament of the Third Republic, or those, such as women, who had been
excluded from politics before 1940. The MRP was also well placed to
gain the support of those people who felt that they, or their families,
were threatened by the post-war purges. The MRP emphasized legality and order. Furthermore, as a member of the tripartite coalition
that ruled France between January 1946 and May 1947, the MRP was
able to act from within the government to protect those whose interests seemed threatened where a more explicitly right-wing party
would have been reduced to crying in the wilderness.

The success of the MRP in synthesizing new and old conservatism
raises an important question. Why was the party unable to sustain its
success? The MRP lost support in the five years after 1946 and eventually saw its representation in parliament drop to 86. The extent of
the MRP's failure is thrown into sharp relief by the success of similar
movements elsewhere in Europe: Christian Democrats became the
dominant political force in Italy, West Germany and Austria. The
MRP might have sought to emulate its German or Italian counterparts by becoming the major conservative party, but it failed to do
so. There were two reasons for this. Firstly, although many MRP supporters and voters came from right-wing backgrounds and many of
the party's policies fitted in with traditions of the right, the party's
style was that of the left. The MRP was a party of 'militants' rather
than one of 'notables'. Its most active supporters were dedicated, disciplined and priggish individuals who eventually repelled many conservative voters. The MRP was also influenced by the French
church's obsession with rechristianizing the working class. This
meant that the party devoted excessive energy to mobilizing its
limited support in industrial cities and neglected its natural constituency in the countryside. Most importantly, while other Christian
Democratic parties in Europe, and other conservative parties in
France, devoted much energy to the provision of jobs and favours
for their supporters, the MRP remained preoccupied with high principles. When armament workers in Bordeaux came to talk about
their salaries with an MRP deputy, they were treated to a long speech
on the duty of public service. The MRP's naïvety in matters such as
this was rooted in inexperience: it is significant that in Alsace-
Lorraine, the only region where Christian Democracy had been

strong before 1940, the MRP leaders were both less high-minded and more successful than their counterparts in the rest of France.

The MRP's failure to become a party of large-scale Christian conservatism was also linked to the behaviour of particular individuals. Several potential leaders of Christian conservatism, such as Jean-Louis Terrenoire and Jacques Vendroux, were also Gaullists and defected from the MRP to join de Gaulle's RPF in 1947. Of those who remained in the MRP, the man who saw most clearly the potential of Christian conservatism was Georges Bidault. Bidault believed that the threat of communism was the dominant issue of French politics and he believed that the MRP should subordinate other considerations to this fact. Eventually Bidault did try to create a large-scale Christian conservative party when he established *Démocratie Chrétienne* in 1958. However, the man who saw the possible right-wing future of the MRP most clearly was also one of the few MRP leaders with an authentically left-wing past. Bidault's role in the Resistance and his opposition to Franco made conservatives reluctant to accept his leadership.

The voters who deserted from the MRP often turned to the RPF, founded in April 1947. De Gaulle did not regard the RPF as a political party: he hoped that it would group people from a wide range of political groups who were united by a desire to defend the national interest and to impose a new constitution which would lead to stronger government. The creation of the RPF coincided with the moment when the Cold War was felt most intensely in France. De Gaulle made much of the fact that the advance guards of the Red Army were only separated from the French frontier by a distance equivalent to that of two stages in the Tour de France, and that 25 per cent of the French population voted for the 'separatist' Communist party. The RPF achieved great success: it won 40 per cent of the vote in the municipal elections of 1948. However, it did not sustain this level of support and although, with 106 seats, it was the largest party in parliament after the 1951 election, it was not able to enforce its policies on the nation. Gaullists attributed the failure of the RPF to a variety of particular causes: the fact that the MRP refused to allow its members to belong to the RPF; the fact that senatorial elections were delayed for a year at the moment when the RPF seemed most successful; and, most importantly, the *apparentement* law enacted to cover the 1951 elections, which gave enormous benefits to alliances of centre parties at the expense of the Communist and Gaullist extremes.

There were also more deep-rooted reasons for the failure of the RPF. The party's supporters were only really united by opposition to the existing regime: on almost every issue of policy the movement was divided. It contained Resistance heroes, but at the same time, its anti-communism attracted many who had supported the Vichy government. Pétainists like Louis Rougier and even fascists like Maurice Bardèche praised the RPF, though not its founder. It contained working-class leaders, like Manuel Bridier, who had come from the Communist party and remained hostile to capitalism, alongside wealthy businessmen who hoped that the RPF could be used to break strikes. Divisions in the RPF were exacerbated by two things. The first of these was de Gaulle's insistence on rigid central discipline which left little scope for amicable agreements to accept diversity. The second was the personal awkwardness of many RPF militants. The RPF's confrontational style attracted aggressive men and some who joined it had already broken with other parties. A prime example of such a person was Jean Nocher, a former Resistance leader from the Loire, who frequently settled political arguments with his fists and who published a book with the title *Messieurs les grands, un petit vous dit merde* (1947).

With friends like Nocher, the RPF did not need enemies but, as it happened, it did have some very effective ones. These men were to be found in the parties of the so-called 'Third Force' which were neither Communist nor Gaullist. Particularly important in this context were Jules Moch, Socialist minister of the interior, Henri Queuille, Radical prime minister, and Vincent Auriol, Socialist president of the republic. Third Force politicians also damaged the RPF in more subtle ways. Some joined the RPF or allied with it. Such men could ensure that their own parties benefited from the wave of Gaullist enthusiasm while arranging matters so that the representatives elected on an RPF ticket were really not committed Gaullists. Radicals proved particularly good at such manoeuvres. Their experience of local politics meant that they almost invariably gained more than they conceded in electoral arrangements with the RPF. Sometimes politicians maintained a studied ambiguity about their real views of the RPF. Pleven, leader of the UDSR, pretended to be a secret Gaullist working to undermine his own party, when he was really a secret anti-Gaullist working to undermine the RPF.

The parties of the Third Force also damaged the RPF by proving that it was unnecessary. De Gaulle had blamed Fourth Republic politicians for being weak, but now he was faced, in Queuille, Moch and Auriol, with three very strong leaders. De Gaulle had blamed the Fourth Republic parties for being divided, but they proved capable of uniting in coalitions, alliances and *apparentements* designed to exclude the RPF. De Gaulle had blamed the Fourth Republic for being soft on communism, but the government expelled Communist ministers the month after the RPF was formed. The RPF leaders had hoped that the state would be obliged to turn to them to maintain order against Communist agitation. However, Jules Moch's riot police, the CRS, after having been purged of Communist sympathizers, proved very effective and, unlike the RPF *service d'ordre*, the CRS could be relied on to return to their barracks when told to do so. In short there was what the Gaullist Olivier Guichard described as a 'parallelism' between the RPF and the Third Force. Both developed in similar ways, and where de Gaulle had hoped to create an anti-Communist 'rassemblement' of parties under the aegis of Gaullism, he actually helped to create an anti-Communist rassemblement of parties held together by a common desire to exclude de Gaulle from power.

The Cold War in France?

In some respects, the early history of the Fourth Republic can be interpreted as part of the broader international conflict. Of all the west European Communist parties, the *Parti Communiste Français* was the most obedient to the orders issued by Moscow. Front organizations, such as the *Banque Commercial e pour l'Europe du Nord*, transmitted money from the Soviet Union to support strikes or Communist activity in France. Equally, the United States intervened heavily to support the non-Communist elements in France and funded institutions such as *Paix et Liberté* and publications such as *Est/Ouest*. The division between the two blocs became particularly intense in 1947. This was the year that the Americans offered Marshall Aid to rebuild the economies of Europe. In theory the offer was open to both East and West; in practice it was widely assumed that the Americans did not expect their offer to be taken up by the Communist bloc. At a meeting of Communist parties in Warsaw, it was made clear that no Communist country would accept Marshall Aid and that Communist parties in the West would be expected to resist the 'Marshallization' of their countries. An association of Communist parties, the Cominform, was now set up to replace the Comintern, which had been dissolved in 1943, and to mark the fact that Communist parties were now expected to look to their international counterparts rather than to their former allies in national anti-fascist coalitions. The split between East and West was accompanied by the departure of Communist ministers from the governments of both France and Italy in May 1947, which marked the end of tripartite government by Christian Democrats, Socialists and Communists.

The conflict between Communists and non-Communists could be seen in many areas, and it often started before the break up of tripartism. Communists attempted to build up a basis of support in the administration. They were so successful in the ministry of veterans that the minister, Henri Frenay, was kept out of his own office by Communist civil servants who were on strike. The social and economic reforms of the Liberation offered scope for new kinds of political empire building. Nationalized companies had workers' representatives on the board and all large firms had 'enterprise committees'. The social security system was also administered by elected committees. The Communist party exercised considerable power in all these institutions: in April 1947, 101 of the 111 representatives elected to family allowance committees were members of the party. Labour relations were also affected. There were strikes in France in 1947 and 1948, and these strikes had a particular impact in the Renault car factory and in the northern coal mines, which were both important symbols for the Communist-dominated *Confédération Génerale du Travail* (CGT). In 1948, a group of non-Communists in the CGT, supported by Irving Brown from the American Federation of Labour, broke away to form a new union: *Force Ouvrière.*

Anti-communism produced a degree of pragmatic unity among all the non-Communist parties of the Fourth Republic, including the Socialists. The most effective anti-Communist slogan of the Fourth Republic was launched by the Socialist Léon Blum, who described the PCF as 'a nationalist party dedicated to a foreign cause', and the most effective practical measures against the Communist party during the Fourth Republic were taken by the Socialist minister of the interior, Jules Moch. Moch and Blum both attracted plaudits from sections of the right-wing press. Certain institutions facilitated anti-Communist cooperation. Agencies like the CNIP or the RGR grouped two or more parties for electoral purposes. The *apparentement* system that was established for the 1951 election allowed parties to conclude bizarre alliances that would ensure that their votes were counted together even when they had campaigned against each other. The *Paix et Liberté* organization, led by the Radical Jean-Paul David, provided propaganda and advice for all the anti-Communist parties, and André Boutemy, dispenser of funds for large-scale industry, handed discreet unmarked envelopes to all the non-Communist leaders who came to his headquarters at the Rue de Penthièvre.

However, it would be simplistic to suggest that French politics can be seen as just one front in the Cold War. International conflicts were always refracted through a particularly French prism. The departure of the Communist party from the French government in May 1947 was not produced by either Moscow or Washington. Members of the central committee of the PCF were divided about whether or not to remain in government, and some Americans seem to have assumed that the PCF was less dangerous in government than it would have been out of it. It was Ramadier, the Socialist prime minister, who manoeuvred the Communist leaders into a position where they were forced to resign. Ramadier and his associates presented the Communists as being behind the strikes in 1947: Jules Moch talked about a 'secret conductor' who coordinated these strikes. The truth was more complicated. Strikes occurred in industries where the PCF was traditionally seen as powerful, but in fact such strikes exposed the weakness of the party. The CGT had never managed to subject large parts of the workforce to effective discipline. The events of 1936 had exposed its inability to control spontaneous outbreaks of labour protest. In addition to this, Trotskyist agitators sometimes sought to promote strikes which they could use to gain advantage over the PCF. In the immediate aftermath of the war, the Communist party and the CGT had sought to prevent strikes and check working-class demands in order to contribute to the 'battle for production', a battle that was particularly important to the party while the USSR was an ally of France. However, in 1947 strikes broke out in protest at wage controls that were imposed by the government of which the PCF was a member. The PCF could not afford to condemn them or to stand aside for fear that it would be discredited in the eyes of its supporters and lose ground to its more audacious rivals on the left. The disciplined nature of the PCF put it in a particularly awkward position. In other parties, militants could distance themselves from measures taken by ministers from their own parties; the strikes of 1947 were vigorously supported by some elements of the SFIO. No such stance was possible for the Communists: the party's ministers were unable to accept Ramadier's demands that they condemn the strikes and they were therefore forced to leave the government.

The Communist party itself was not simply an obedient tool of Stalin's Russia. This was particularly true in the immediate aftermath of the Liberation when certain prominent Communists had discovered the possibility for independent action through their experiences of Resistance, and especially Resistance before June 1941. It was often the Resistance activists who had caused most disruption at the Liberation and who were the most enthusiastic supporters of a Communist insurrection within France; many of them admired Tito's Yugoslavia which was the only Communist state to have been born directly out of an anti-fascist guerrilla war. The Soviet Union, and the PCF leadership, by contrast did not believe that insurrection was appropriate in France and their hostility to the Resistance activists tied in with their hostility to Yugoslavia as Tito broke with the Soviet Union. Curiously, it was the democratically minded Resistance activists who presented most threat to the social order within France, while the elements in the PCF who were most loyal often acted as functional conservatives and restrained attacks on bourgeois institutions.

Most Resistance activists yielded to party discipline; one of them, Charles Tillon, was given the deliberately humiliating task of responding to the attacks of the Yugoslav delegation at the Warsaw conference of 1947, but fissures remained in the party, as was to be shown by the purges of the early 1950s. Even the most apparently Stalinist leaders of the PCF were not puppets of Moscow. The creation of a personality cult around Maurice Thorez and the imposition of strict party discipline could serve specifically French purposes. Such measures allowed the PCF to claim to be the true representative of the Leninist tradition. Furthermore the French Communist party's propaganda often irritated Moscow by the emphasis that it laid on a French revolutionary tradition. Relations between Stalin and the French 'Stalinists' could be odd. In 1945 Stalin is said to have shocked de Gaulle by asking whether he proposed to have Maurice Thorez shot, and in the early 1950s the Communist leader was to become a virtual prisoner in the Soviet Union.

The divisions within the anti-Communist/pro-American front were even more extreme than those in the Communist party. These splits began in America itself. Often particular individuals had particular attachments within France: Robert Murphy, for example, was a conservative Catholic who sympathized with the French right-wingers whom he had got to know when a diplomat at Vichy. Some individuals shuttled between the Americans and the French while pursuing aims of their own: Michel Debré remarked that it was hard to know whether Jean Monnet was 'the skilful representative of France to America or America to France'.[4] To make matters even more complicated, a variety of private or semi-private American bodies sought to intervene in French politics in ways that often bore only a tangential relation to the initiatives of the American government. The American Federation of Labour supported anti-Communist trade unionists while American companies like Standard Oil subsidized anti-strike activity. Further complexities and contradictions were produced by the nature of Franco-American relations. America was linked to Britain by common language and wartime alliance, to Italy by the presence of a large immigrant community, and to West Germany by her role as an occupying power. Ties between America and France were much less intimate. When Léon Blum visited America in 1946, his English was rarely understood by those whom he met, and American officials frequently failed to note the difference between Robert Schuman and Maurice Schumann.

French anti-communism was not made in America. Even ferocious French anti-Communists often distanced themselves from the policy of the United States. During the war Henri Frenay had complained about the unwillingness of the Americans to recognize the role of the Communist party in the Resistance and, in 1945, Georges Bidault tried to persuade the US ambassador that it might be possible to integrate the Communist party into French national life. Many of the most effective French anti-Communists originated on the left and some of them remained members of the SFIO. As has been suggested above, Léon Blum was particularly important in this context and the French expected that this would make the Americans sympathetic to Blum. In reality, many Americans failed to make much distinction between Blum's politics and those of Thorez: when Blum visited the United States to appeal for fresh loans, the *Wall Street News* greeted him with the headline 'Karl Marx is coming to see Father Christmas'. If the Americans were more likely to be anti-Socialist than their friends in France, they were less likely to be opposed to trade unions. American policymakers were used to union leaders who accepted the existence of capitalism and they tried to encourage French capitalists to draw trade unionists into a productivist consensus. When the French government cut off subsidies to an increasingly militant *Force Ouvrière* in 1949, the CIA increased its subsidies to the movement to make up the shortfall.

Franco-American relations were further complicated by the fact that, in France, atlanticism was seen to be connected to anti-Gaullism as well as to anti-communism. America had recognized the Vichy government until the end of 1942 and many Frenchmen expected her to be hostile to measures taken against those who had supported or served that government. Furthermore, the Americans had backed general Giraud, who became a conservative deputy in 1946, and they were known to have had bad relations with de Gaulle during the war: a fact revealed by the American diplomat Kenneth Pendar in a book that was gleefully reviewed in the French right-wing press.[5] Many Pétainists and some right-wing Resistance leaders expected that the Americans would intervene in French politics not merely to combat the Communist party but also to prevent purges and to weaken general de Gaulle. Indeed, in January 1946, some attributed de Gaulle's departure to American pressure. In fact, right-wing expectations about the pro-Pétainist and anti-Gaullist thrust of American policy were almost entirely wrong, but such beliefs did have an influence. They made it easier for the Pétainist and Third Republic parties to reform and restore some of their former influence.

Even French anti-communism itself was not a homogeneous bloc. Apart from the religious, factional and personal quarrels that cut across anti-Communist alliances, there were three different varieties of anti-communism. Capitalist anti-communism was mainly concerned with the defence of property. Nationalist anti-communism was concerned with the military threat of the Soviet Union and with the treason of those within France who gave allegiance to a foreign nation: this vision of the world bore many resemblances to the Maurrassian one though the USSR had now replaced Germany as France's traditional enemy. Libertarian anti-communism was concerned with the defence of human rights and individual freedom. These divisions bore some relation to party divisions within the anti-Communist bloc. The PRL was the natural home of capitalists, the RPF was that of nationalists and the SFIO contained many libertarian anti-Communists. However, divisions were never clear-cut: the RPF contained many who were bitterly hostile to the Communist social vision as well as those who were hostile to the power of the Soviet Union; the PRL defended capitalism, but those of its leaders who had gone to German concentration camps were clearly motivsated by something other than naked class interest; the SFIO contained deputies who were sponsored by the pro-business *Front Economique.*

The most curious feature of all of the 'Cold War in France' is the fact that it was a static conflict. Generally speaking, Frenchmen were either Communist or not, and the Communist vote remained almost entirely stable at around 25 per cent of the population. A few artisans, whose political lives were dominated by fiscal grievances, seem to have hovered between the two political blocs; the SFIO and the PCF might compete for working-class votes in some areas, and prominent intellectuals flounced in and out of the PCF. However, all these were exceptional. Generally, it was difficult for anyone to switch from a party that believed Joseph Stalin to be a living saint and the Soviet Union to be an earthly paradise into one that regarded communism as the most pernicious doctrine of modern times. In this context, the millions of francs that were lavished by big business and the Americans on anti-Communist propaganda were so much wasted money. In fact anti-communism often served unexpected purposes. It provided a means by which Pétainists could work their way back into the political mainstream. Less obviously anti-communism provided those, such as Georges Albertini or Jean Jardin, who were too compromised by their wartime behaviour to re-enter politics, with a new role in the shadowy directing organizations of the anti-Communist struggle.

Most importantly, anti-Communist rhetoric was designed not to convert Communists but to rally the existing anti-Communist electorate. In the 1951 election, the manifesto of each conservative party tried to present it as the real leader of anti-communism in France. RPF propaganda pointed to the role that the MRP had played in alliance with Communists between 1944 and 1947, and claimed that it was the formation of the RPF that had driven Communist ministers from government. MRP manifestos pointed to the role of the RPF in 'dividing anti-communism' by refusing to ally with other bourgeois parties. Independent manifestos drew attention to de Gaulle's wartime cooperation with the Communists; a poster showing de Gaulle shaking hands with Thorez was circulated. In short, anti-communism became a means by which the struggle between non-Communist parties was fought out.

7   The Fall of the Fourth Republic: 1951–1958

In 1959, Nathaniel Leites published a book on French politics between 1951 and 1958. *The Game of Politics in France* argued that the activities of the French parliament were connected with small-scale struggles over local issues or personal prestige and that they bore little relation to grand ideological debates. The last seven years of the Fourth Republic were marked by a series of scandals, quarrels, and party schisms that often made it seem impossible to provide any rational account of political motives. The large-scale disciplined parties, in which so many had placed their hopes after the Liberation, lost influence. Politics came to be dominated by small formations with modest ambitions. There were five separate 'Independent' groups in France between 1949 and 1953: Chanoine Kir of Dijon even contested the 1951 election as an 'independent Independent'. In addition to this, lists to represent professional groups, taxpayers, motorists and *mécontents* were all presented at elections. The parties that did well in the 1951 election were gathered into loose alliances which did not seek to exercise much discipline over their members. Two of these groups were particularly important. The *Rassemblement des Gauches Républicaines* was founded in 1946 by the Radical party, the *Union Démocratique et Socialiste de la Résistance* and several Third Republic parties that had been discredited by their support for Pétain. The *Centre National des Indépendants et Paysans* was founded in 1949 to bring together the small Peasant party with the various conservative notables.

The general pattern of politics in France changed after the 1951 elections. Governments became even more short-lived than before. The kaleidoscope of parties in parliament seemed to be divided on a variety of highly complicated issues. Furthermore, many of these divisions ran within, as well as between, parties. The Independents were divided between the faction loyal to Antoine Pinay and that loyal to Joseph Laniel; the Peasant party was divided between those who supported Paul Antier and those who supported Camille Laurens; the UDSR was riven by a conflict between Pleven and Mitterrand; Edgar

100

Faure and Pierre Mendès-France fought for control of the Radical party, which eventually split into several different elements.

Extreme fragmentation and instability were not new in France, but immediately after the war, most political parties had been encouraged to subordinate old hatreds by the threat that communism seemed to pose to their most essential interests. As has been stressed above, the anti-Communist alliance was never completely homogeneous or free from strife. However, until the 1951 election, the immediate threat of communism was so great that it created a certain working unity among parties ranging from the Socialists to the extreme right. After 1951 the threat of communism diminished. The international balance of power stabilized: America and the Soviet Union confronted each other in the remote proxy war in Indo-China, but no one expected them to fight in mainland Europe. Stalin's death, in 1953, made Russia seem less threatening. Purges within the French Communist party during the early 1950s neutralized many of the Resistance leaders who had been the most enthusiastic exponents of revolution in France. The changed climate in France was reflected in reactions to the large-scale public sector strike of 1953. This caused less concern than the strikes of 1947 and 1948, which had been seen as potentially revolutionary. It was also reflected in the growing current of 'neutralism' as people began to feel that France need not choose between the eastern and western camps.

The diminished Communist threat left other parties free to pursue their squabbles. These squabbles were rendered all the more confusing by the fact that French political parties did not merely have different aims: they had entirely different views of what political activity was about. The RPF, or at least its leader, wished to overthrow the existing constitution. In order to achieve this, the Gaullists needed to gain a sufficiently large representation in parliament to make it unworkable. They did not do this, and having failed to overthrow the political system, their refusal to accept ministerial office ensured that they would not exercise any influence within that system. Other political parties were willing to work within the system, but even here their views of success varied considerably. The MRP wished to implement particular policies, especially ones relating to foreign affairs. For this reason, the party was willing to remain in government even when this meant incurring electoral unpopularity. The Radicals and the SFIO, by contrast, both aimed to preserve their own support. However, the means by which they sought to accomplish this differed. The SFIO frequently left government to take a *cure d'opposition* which would please their austere militants; the Radicals remained in government at all costs in order to ensure that their clients had access to the benefits that the state controlled.

The Fourth Republic was made even more unstable by the fact that very small parties were often able to exercise influence that was disproportionate to their electoral support. Such parties might provide 'hinges' between right and left that were crucial for determining which side would be able to form a government. They could then use the influence that they acquired from this position to conclude beneficial electoral alliances or to gain government office. It was through such machinations that the Radical party was able to increase the number of seats that it held in parliament between 1945 and 1956 in spite of the fact that its vote was in continuous decline. Even more strikingly, the UDSR was able to increase its representation in government and, on one occasion, to provide the prime minister, in spite of the fact that its representation in parliament had dropped to only nine deputies in 1951.

The diminished threat of communism meant that older divisions became important again. The first such division was that between clericals and anti-clericals: a division that was fought out in the Fourth Republic by means of a debate over the desirability of state subsidies to church schools. In the long term, divisions over the church would be rendered less important by the secularization of French society. This secularization was reflected in the fact that the number of clericals (who regularly attended church) and, more significantly, anti-clericals (who never set foot in church) was declining. However, in the short term, secularization created more rather than fewer divisions in French politics. In the past the clerical parties, which were principally those of the right, had confronted the anti-clerical parties, the Radicals, Communists and Socialists. Now new divisions arose within many parties between those who cared about the clerical issue, one way or the other, and those who wished to end the clerical issue altogether. By the early 1950s even the Radical party, traditionally the party most associated with anti-clericalism, contained 11 deputies who supported state subsidies to church schools. Indeed in 1951, it was a Radical minister of education, André Marie, who introduced legislation to restore subsidies to church schools.

The second issue to divide French politics in the 1950s was that caused by the Vichy–Resistance conflict. In the immediate aftermath of the Liberation, Resistance veterans had enjoyed great advantages, particularly in the right-wing parties, and many Pétainists had been excluded from politics altogether. However, Resistance conservatives became victims of their own success: their efforts to reduce the impact of measures taken against those who had supported the Vichy government ensured that increasing numbers of Pétainists returned to public life and became their rivals. In 1951 Jacques Isorni, Pétain's defence counsel, created the *Union des Nationaux et Indépendants Républicains* which was explicitly dedicated to defending Pétain's reputation and which gained several seats in parliament. Other Pétainists were elected on behalf of other parties. Two amnesty laws, in 1951 and 1953, released many Pétainists from prison. Most importantly, in 1952 Antoine Pinay was elected as prime minister. Pinay had been a member of Pétain's National Council. He was also the owner of a small family business, a tannery, in a small provincial town, St Chammond. He had made his reputation as a finance minister who emphasized the need for balanced budgets, though his financial practices were less orthodox than his public pronouncements. Pinay seemed to incarnate a return to the values of traditional conservatism and an end to the ambitions that had characterized sections of both the right and left at the Liberation. Tension between Pétainists and opponents of Vichy underlay the Pinay–Laniel conflict in the Independents, as it underlay the Laurens–Antier dispute in the Peasant party.

The return of Pétainists to power in the bourgeois parties was accompanied by similar changes in the Communist party. Of 29 members who were removed from the party's central committee at the congress of the Aubervilliers in 1950, 23 were Resistance veterans. This purge sprang partly from the suspicion that elements of the party leadership always felt towards those whom they believed to be dangerously independent. It also sprang from a conflict within the Communist party between Maurice Thorez, who had surrounded himself with Resistance veterans after the war, and Jacques Duclos. In 1951 this conflict reached farcical proportions when Thorez fell ill and was removed to Russia for treatment. To the delight of the right-wing press, Thorez was then held as a virtual prisoner in the Soviet Union and was not able to return to France until after the death of Stalin.

French politics was further fragmented by several new issues that became important during the 1950s. The first of these was the debate over the European Defence Community (EDC). The EDC was designed to bring troops from the major powers of continental western Europe together in order to shift some of the burden of containing the Soviet Union away from the United States. The proposal was first discussed in December 1951, and a treaty laying down the framework in which it would operate was signed in Paris in May 1952. However, in 1953 argument over the ratification of the treaty began to affect French politics. De Gaulle called for the rejection of the treaty on 25 February 1953; on 30 May 1954 the SFIO, after a vigorous internal debate, agreed to support ratification; on 13 August 1954 Gaullist ministers who opposed the EDC resigned from the government of Pierre Mendès-France; finally Mendès-France himself abandoned his efforts to get the treaty ratified. Conflict over the EDC reflected several elements in French politics. It showed that the Communist threat was seen to have diminished: bourgeois politicians would not have squabbled over defence measures so much five years previously. The EDC was also controversial because it involved some measure of German rearmament. Such moves revived the split between the Resistance and Vichy. The atrocities that the German army had carried out in France had been recalled in 1953 by the trial of those responsible for the Oradour massacre, and many argued that such a nation could not be trusted to rearm. Traditional anti-German nationalists, many of whom were to be found among the Gaullists and among right-wing deputies for the eastern provinces, were also hostile to the EDC. Debate over the EDC even tied in with the clerical issue: Christian Democrat parties were always the most vigorous supporters of European integration and many opponents of such measures talked of a 'clerical international'.

The next issue to trouble French politics was that produced by struggles over decolonization. After the Second World War, nationalist forces began to contest French power in a variety of imperial possessions. Eventually the French ceded full independence to Morocco and Tunisia and, after military defeat at the hands of Ho Chi Minh's guerrillas, they left Indo-China in 1954. Apart from Algeria, which will be discussed in a later chapter, few of these imperial conflicts had any great interest for the majority of Frenchmen. The population of European settlers in Indo-China, Morocco and Tunisia was small, as was the scale of French investment in these areas. It is true that the French fought a war in Indo-China, but this war was fought with professional soldiers and funded, in large measure, by American money. Ho Chi Minh and his associates were Communists, and the struggle against them was presented as part of a global struggle between the two blocs. But the very fact that the struggle was global reduced its significance for France: no one seriously believed that Communist victory in Saigon would threaten Strasbourg or Mulhouse.

The disputes over decolonization were important mainly because they touched on other issues in the politics of mainland France. Indo-China became tied up with clericalism: the country contained a large Catholic population and the MRP proved the most intransigent opponents of concessions there. Debate over alleged atrocities by the French army blended into the Vichy–Resistance dispute, especially because of the widespread belief that the most brutal soldiers in Indo-China were German members of the foreign legion. Most importantly, debate over decolonization helped to launch a new kind of left in France. In the immediate aftermath of the Liberation, attempts to build a new kind of left-wing party on the foundation of the Resistance had been thwarted by the fact that the men who supported such initiatives remained attached to bourgeois class interests and virulently hostile to communism. However, by the 1950s, the Communist threat was no longer sufficiently intense to be frightening and the struggle in the colonies provided would-be left-wingers with a cause that could be separated from the interests of their class in France. Opposition to French policy in Indo-China crystallized around a number of newspapers and periodicals such as *L'Express*, and mobilized Resistance leaders like Claude Bourdet. It also affected party politics. François Mitterrand began his long march from the Fourth Republic right to the Fifth Republic left under the influence of his parliamentary allies in the *Rassemblement Démocratique Africain*.

For a time it seemed that the fragmentation of French politics might be brought to an end by one man: Pierre Mendès-France. Mendès-France was invested with an unusually large majority of 419 on 18 June 1954. The date was the anniversary of de Gaulle's call to honour of 1940, and the symbolism of the date was appropriate for a man who, after beginning his career in Léon Blum's Popular Front government of 1936, had escaped from a Vichy prison in order to join de Gaulle's Free French forces. He is one of the most admired French politicians of the twentieth century, an admiration that is particularly acute among intellectuals and Anglo-Saxons. He was the only major public figure to feature prominently in *The Sorrow and the Pity*, Michel Ophuls' film on Vichy. He became the hero of *L'Express* newspaper and was even quoted in the resignation speech of a

British cabinet minister in 1989. Mendès-France's admirers believed that he stood apart from the petty squabbles and archaic preoccupations of most French politicians. He was the first French minister with an academic background in economics, and he seemed to have broken free of many traditional divisions in French politics: in particular he appealed to a certain section of progressively minded Catholics in spite of his own origins in the Radical party.

Mendès favoured decisive government, a preference illustrated by his often quoted phrase 'to govern is to choose'. Parliament granted him special financial powers on August 10, and he brought in a small constitutional reform on 30 November 1954. Mendès did tackle some of the problems that had been haunting France. He ended France's war in Indo-China by signing an armistice with the Communist forces on July 21. Ten days later he visited Tunisia and promised to recognize the right of self-determination.

However, it is possible to overemphasize Mendès' originality. He was a protégé of Edouard Herriot, doyen of radicalism and an archetypal figure of Third Republic politics. He was also a supporter of the *scrutin d'arrondissement*: the electoral system of single member constituencies that had underlain the localism of Third Republic politics. In economic terms, Mendès was a liberal who believed in balanced budgets and ruthless restraints on inflation; indeed Antoine Pinay remarked that Mendès' economic views were not very different from his own. Mendès' colonial policy was also less original than it seemed at first. He was less enthusiastic about the independence of Morocco, which he regarded as a backward and feudal nation, than he was about the independence of Tunisia, and even Tunisian independence was granted by Mendès' successor and rival, Edgar Faure. Most importantly of all, there is no evidence that Mendès envisaged the possibility that France might withdraw from Algeria. Indeed he wrote the introduction to François Mitterrand's book of 1953 which proposed withdrawal from Indo-China so that *more* resources might be diverted to North Africa.[1]

In some respects Mendès' accession to the premiership actually introduced new divisions into French political life. The admiration that was felt for Mendès in some circles was matched by the distaste felt in others. He appeared, misleadingly, a cold, emotionless man. He was said to have picked his parliamentary constituency at random by looking at a map of France. As a Jew, a resistant, and a supporter of decolonization, Mendès was loathed by a large part of the right; as a technocrat and a proponent of modernization he was disliked by many representatives of small business and peasant farmers. His campaign against alcoholism only increased his unpopularity in a nation where millions of people made money from home distilling and wine-making.

Mendès became a particular target for one movement that was to have an important role in the last years of the Fourth Republic: Poujadism. Poujadism started as a protest of small shopkeepers against value added tax. It was led by Pierre Poujade, a stationer from the town of St Céré in south-west France, who founded the *Union de Défense des Commerçants et Artisans*. In 1954 the UDCA organized tax protests in many parts of France and began to gain seats in elections to chambers of commerce. Initially the UDCA sought to apply pressure to existing deputies from the established political parties, but at the end of 1955 Poujade formed a new political party, the *Union de Fraternité Française*, which astonished everyone by gaining 56 seats, and more than 10 per cent of the popular vote in the 1956 general election. After this success Poujadism faded almost as quickly as it had risen. The grocers and bakers who represented the UFF in parliament seemed like bumpkins alongside the lawyers and journalists in the Palais Bourbon. Poujade himself was defeated in a by-election of 1957. Most importantly, Poujade began to lose control of the UFF deputies. Few of them obeyed his instructions not to vote in favour of de Gaulle's return to power in 1958 and in the elections shortly after this, only four UFF deputies were returned to parliament.

The Poujadists attracted much derision At best Poujadism was seen as a movement of petit-bougeois vulgarity and philistinism, and the literary critic Roland Barthes devoted some of his most scathing essays to mocking Pierre Poujade's pronouncements. At worst it was seen as fascist, the English cartoonist Vicky dubbing Poujade 'Poujadolf'. Many suggested that the Poujadists represented an outdated France of slow economic growth, provincialism, nostalgia and crude prejudice. Those groups – intellectuals, Anglo-Saxons, progressive Catholics – who were favourable to Mendès-France were often particularly hostile to Poujade; the two men were often explicitly contrasted. However, even the extreme right had trouble taking Poujade seriously: the neo-fascist François Brigneau said that he could no more pledge loyalty to Poujade than he could to Johnny Hallyday.

The reality of Poujadism was more complicated than its detractors allowed. It was not just an outpouring of rage against economic change, but a focused, and largely successful, attempt to deal with one particular grievance, the high burden of value added tax that shopkeepers were obliged to collect. Furthermore, Poujadism was quite different to the other lower-middle-class movements of the twentieth century. In England and Germany, the lower middle class defined itself by contrast with, and in opposition to, the working class. When large-scale industry had arisen in these countries during the nineteenth century, the lower middle class had made increasing efforts to distance itself from the proletariat. In social terms this meant an emphasis on respectability, correct dress, elocution lessons and the avoidance of manual labour. In the southern and western provinces of France where Poujadism originated, however, there was no large-scale industrial working class. These areas were almost exclusively populated by small property owners – peasants, shopkeepers, artisans. Consequently, artisans and shopkeepers still maintained the style that was often associated with the working class in other European countries. They were not afraid of manual work or vulgar appearances. Poujade himself had worked as a docker before establishing his small shop; he talked with an Auvergnat accent and ostentatiously removed his jacket in public. The Poujadists were rumbustious, hard-drinking, loud-mouthed men, and their tactics – strikes, boycotts, mass demonstrations – were those that are normally associated with the working class.

Most importantly, Poujadism was distinguished from other European lower-middle-class movements, and from most other political parties in France, by the fact that it was not systematically anti-Communist. Indeed Poujade himself made much of the role that the Communist ironmonger of St Céré, Frégéac, had played in the movement, and the Poujadists continued to work in alliance with the Communist party, when it suited them, until 1955. The absence of anti-communism was associated with other peculiarities of Poujadism. The Poujadists resented many aspects of the Fourth Republic political system that had been constructed at the height of the Cold War, and which were rooted in anti-communism. In particular, they were violently hostile to the United States and to France's alleged dependence on that nation.

The crisis caused by Poujadism blended in with that caused by the insurrection in Algeria that began in 1954 (see chapter 12), and it was Algeria that delivered the *coup de grâce* to the Fourth Republic. Army officers and European settlers became increasingly sceptical of the regime's ability or willingness to defend French Algeria. This discontent was played on by agents working for the return to power of general de Gaulle, though de Gaulle refrained from public pronouncements on politics after 1954. On 13 May 1958, a demonstration by settlers in Algiers led to the storming of the government headquarters. A number of army officers joined the 'committee of public safety' that was formed by the demonstrators. The Gaullist colonel Massu became head of this committee and he appealed to general de Gaulle to form a government. This call was echoed, unenthusiastically, by the French commander in Algeria, general Salan, on May 15. Some in Algeria planned to secure de Gaulle's return by military action on the French mainland; troops from Algeria did seize Corsica. De Gaulle himself did not entirely rule out military action, but he also began negotiations with the political establishment and notably with the Christian Democrat prime minister, Pierre Pflimlin. De Gaulle's aim was to play off the army and the politicians against each other so that he would avoid being either an ordinary Fourth Republic prime minister, controlled by parliament, or the leader of a putsch, controlled by the generals. Eventually, he was successful. Pflimlin resigned, René Coty, the president of the republic, threatened to resign if parliament did not accept de Gaulle, and on 1 June 1958 de Gaulle was granted full powers for six months.

In part the collapse of the Fourth Republic reflected the particular problems presented by French Algeria, which will be described in chapter 12. In part it reflected the weaknesses of the regime that have been described above. Anti-communism had imposed a degree of discipline on the French political system and had given power to strong leaders like Vincent Auriol. When the Communist threat diminished, politics became more chaotic and weak compromise candidates, such as René Coty, who succeeded Auriol in 1954, rose to prominence. However, the fall of the Fourth Republic was also linked to the social and economic changes that had occurred during the 1950s. Economic change had political consequences. It exacerbated the political fragmentation of the 1950s. It split the 'neo-Radicals', like René Mayer, who were linked to large-scale business, from the traditional radical base among the shopkeepers, artisans and peasants of the south-west. Similar splits occurred among the Independents and even in the Peasant party which included such odd figures as André Boutemy, who distributed political funds on behalf of big business, and Maurice Petsche, son of an electricity magnate. Economic change also helped to fuel discontent by

Poujadists and peasant organizations who felt that they were not benefiting sufficiently. There was also a broader sense in which economic change undermined political stability. The Fourth Republic political system had developed to suit a particular kind of society. It hinged around the large electoral power of those who owned small enterprises (shops and peasant farms), and around the power that notables exercised in small towns. Economic change began to undermine this system, and developments as varied as urbanization, the spread of television, and the growth of a 'technocratic' managerial class in both private and public sectors all made new forms of political organization possible. The 1950s may have seen the destruction of one form of politics, but they also saw the foundations laid on which a new political system would later be built.

8   Trente Glorieuses

Between 1948 and and 1963, the French gross national product grew at an average of 4.6 per cent per year. During the 1960s, this growth reached 5.8 per cent per year. These figures were all the more spectacular when compared with the bleak years through which the French economy had passed between 1932 and the end of the war; many French people look back on this period as the 'thirty glorious years' which they associate with the end of French backwardness and the transformation of everyday living standards. Economic historians have been less sure. Some argue that post-war economic growth did not mark a turning point in French history, but rather a return to the healthy industrial growth that had been seen before the exceptional period of depression and war. Others argue that the growth of the post-war period was not unique to any one country and that France merely participated in the general prosperity of western Europe. Some contemporary perceptions of the French economy also suggest that economic growth was less straightforward than it appeared at first glance. Many of those involved with economic planning in the 1940s, such as Jean Monnet, Mendès-France or Etienne Hirsch, had spent the war in England or America. They thought of their early works as imitations of Anglo-Saxon models more than attempts to create specifically French institutions; most of them would have been satisfied if French growth had merely kept pace with British growth. In the 1950s, French leaders were worried by persistent problems of inflation and labour shortage. Even in the booming 1960s, some remained unhappy. Michel Crozier's book on the 'stalled society' of French industrial management was published in 1966 and quoted approvingly by Jacques Chaban-Delmas in 1969.[1] Jean-Jacques Servan-Schreiber expressed concern about an American takeover of the French economy in 1967.[2] It was only in the early 1970s that Frenchmen began to believe that they were enjoying really spectacular economic success and to talk of overtaking Germany. In fact French growth peaked at 6.3 per cent per year in 1973 and was then badly hit by the oil crisis which produced a small drop in GNP in 1975.

111

Questions arise from any attempt to isolate the causes of post-war growth. Can the causes of growth be ascertained simply by studying the period in which growth occurred? To what extent was prosperity after 1945 rooted in long-term changes or in restructuring that occurred between 1932 and 1945? Should the failings of the French economy after 1975 make us revise our views of its success before this date? Most importantly, is it possible to separate causes and effects of growth? Did consumerism, new managerial techniques and technological change come about because of changes in the level of gross domestic production or did they bring such changes about?

Economic growth is usually taken to be almost synonymous with industrial growth, but in some respects the most spectacular changes in post-war France concerned agriculture. These changes were important because agricultural stagnation had slowed down the rest of the economy during the interwar period. After 1945, agricultural production grew at an average of 2.5 per cent per year. Productivity per man hour grew by an average of 7 per cent per year. The Monnet Plan encouraged investment in tractors and agricultural machinery. Before the war France had contained 35,000 tractors and 260 combine harvesters; by 1967 these figures had risen to 1.1 million and 110,000 respectively. The modernization of agriculture was linked to a reduction in the numbers of small family peasant farms. In the early 1960s, government experts reckoned that the peasant population was twice as large as it should have been. Legislation was introduced to make the consolidation of peasant land-holdings easier. As technology replaced labour in the countryside, and as economic growth drew farmers' children into the cities, the proportion of the population employed by agriculture dropped from 2 million in 1954 to 1 million in 1968. However, such developments did not mark the total extinction of the peasantry. Peasants remained an important electoral constituency and were able to secure tax concessions and subsidies from the French government. Indeed the Common Agricultural Policy, established in 1962, was to ensure that French farmers eventually received such subsidies from the European taxpayer: the French consumed 36 per cent of European agricultural subsidies while contributing only 26 per cent of the funds that supported these subsidies. Peasants became better organized, especially under the influence of militants who had risen up in Catholic youth movements during the 1930s. Farming cooperatives were able to give small producers access to machinery and to marketing networks: eventually 70 per cent of French wine was produced in cooperatives.

France also benefited from new resources after 1945. Shortage of energy had been a bane of the economy. Government planning sought to overcome this problem. Heavy investment was made in the French coal mines and attempts were made to gain access to German coal fields; French coal production peaked at 60 million tonnes in 1952. However, the real key to the expansion of energy reserves lay in finding new sources of power. Natural gas was discovered in 1951 in south-western France. Hydroelectricity had provided 25 per cent of French electricity in 1938, but production quadrupled after 1945 and came to provide one third of all French electricity. The shift to these new sources of power was symptomatic of shifts that had a wider significance in two respects. Firstly, it changed French economic geography. Industry had formerly been clustered around the coal fields in northern, eastern and central France, but hydroelectricity and natural gas were available in remote and mountainous regions that had formerly seen little industry. Hydroelectricity also became the centre of sharp debate over the management of the French economy. The construction of dams required enormous investments, largely provided by means of American aid. However, in the early 1950s some liberals, such as Taix of the French electricity company, began to argue that the state should not support such large and long-term investments and that it should return to thermal generators.

Ultimately French electricity generation did shift back to thermal production, but it relied less on coal and more on oil. Petrol accounted for 67 per cent of French energy use in 1973, compared to only 18 per cent in 1950. Oil was cheap in the 1960s and also had the advantage, unlike coal, of being easy to transport. Once again this contributed to changes in French industrial geography and also made the spread of motor cars in France possible (see below). However, French dependence on oil carried dangers as well as benefits. France was particularly vulnerable to rises in the price of oil and it was such rises that accounted for the sharp slowdown of the French economy during the early 1970s.

The most scarce resource in France for much of the post-war period was labour. The low birthrates of the Third Republic and the casualties of both world wars meant that the adult male population was low. Unemployment never rose above 1.8 per cent, and labour shortage accounted for the severe inflation that France suffered throughout the period, though the inflation of the 1960s was also part of a larger worldwide tendency. Labour shortage was exacerbated by the fact that decreasing numbers of women worked, by the drafting of men for military service in Algeria, and by the increasing numbers of young people who were involved in education. The net result of these changes was that, though the total population increased from 40.5 million to 52.6 million between 1946 and 1975, the total working population increased by only 1.3 million (from 20.5 million to 21.8 million). Two things made it possible for the French economy to survive the labour shortage. The first of these was the substitution of machinery for labour; the second was movement of labour. The mechanization of agriculture meant that decreasing numbers of people were required for farm work. Between 1945 and 1972 the agricultural labour force dropped from 7 million to around 2 million. Those who had been formed in the harsh world of rural France proved particularly good workers because they were willing to endure long hours in often uncomfortable conditions. A study of French bakers in the 1960s found that it was mainly the sons of peasants who were willing to take on the crippling workload involved in running such enterprises. By 1976, 7.1 per cent of French people lived in a department other than the one in which they had been born. France had always depended heavily on immigrant labour. By 1978 she had 882,000 immigrants from Portugal, 529,000 from Spain and over a million from various parts of North Africa. A crucial turning point in the French labour market occurred in 1962 when France left Algeria. This freed young Frenchmen who had previously been in the army; it encouraged large numbers of Algerian Muslims to come to France in order to escape from the chaos and poverty that gripped their native land after independence; and, most importantly, it meant that almost one million *pieds noirs*, the European settlers, returned from Algeria. The *pieds noirs* had a particularly stimulating impact on the French economy. They were French in terms of culture, language and education so they did not experience the usual problems of assimilation faced by immigrants. Furthermore, many of them lacked formal qualifications and were therefore obliged to take the semi-skilled jobs that were available in France during the early 1960s. However, the desire to rebuild their fortunes and regain their former status encouraged the *pieds noirs* to display exceptional enterprise and diligence. In many ways they resembled the German-speaking immigrants from East Europe who had done so much to rebuild the economy of West Germany after 1945.

The area of the post-war French economy that has attracted most attention from historians is that relating to state intervention. Before 1940, French economic orthodoxy had been liberal. Doyens like Charles Rist and Jacques Rueff had educated generations of civil servants to be suspicious of state intervention in the economy and to aim for balanced budgets, though in practice the Third Republic had often intervened to protect certain politically powerful groups. After 1945, the state's role in the economy increased greatly. The period after the war saw the most important wave of nationalizations in French history. A few of the companies affected, notably the Renault automobile firm, were taken over to punish them for collaboration during the war. More frequently, companies were nationalized for economic reasons and compensation was paid to former shareholders. Particularly important were the nationalizations of the coal mines, the electrical and gas distribution networks (which created *Electricité de France* and *Gaz de France*), and the nationalization of the major deposit banks. These moves placed the state in control of two key resources, energy and credit. By the mid 1950s, around 25 per cent of capital formation occurred within the nationalized sector. The French state used nationalized industries in various ways. It encouraged them to invest in great projects on a scale that private enterprise would not have countenanced; it used them to pressure private firms into cooperating with government; finally, nationalized industries, especially EDF, became showcases for certain kinds of technical and managerial innovation. The state also exercised control through a variety of other mechanisms. Control of prices allowed it to force rationalization on industries that it believed to be inefficient; this strategy was applied to the steel industry during the 1960s. Control of securities issues, given by a law of 1947, allowed the government to prevent certain industries from obtaining funds to invest, and to ensure that those selected industries that were allowed to raise money in this way gained from artificially low interest rates. Even safety rules could be manipulated by civil servants who allowed companies that accepted state direction to be exempted from unworkable regulations: a practice that came to be known as *exceptionalisme*.

Changes in the role of the state were also reflected in the existence of a new ministry (founded by Vichy) of industrial production, and in the attempts of Pierre Mendès-France, finance minister in de Gaulle's provisional government, to create a new ministry of national economics that would concern itself with a whole range of industrial concerns and not simply with financial ones. Finally, planning came to assume a new role in French economic life after 1945. This began with Mendès-France's aborted plan of 1945. In 1946, a new *Plan de Modernisation et Equipment* was launched by Jean Monnet. Monnet had several advantages. Firstly, he was able to strike chords which were not purely economic. He was conscious of the psychological role of economics and the need to create a 'mystique du plan'. He also appealed to many influential figures, particularly de Gaulle, by presenting planning as a means of restoring national power and prestige. Secondly, Monnet benefited from his own background. As a cognac merchant he was more trusted by business than Socialist planners such as Jules Moch could ever have been. Thirdly, Monnet benefited from the fact that he was perceived to be closely linked to the Americans and this increased his influence within France.

The initial Monnet Plan was drawn up in 1946 and designed to operate between 1947 and 1950. It concentrated on certain key sectors: coal, steel, transport, tractors, cement and electricity. The plan initially ran into financial difficulty, but was saved by an influx of American funds under the Marshall Aid programme, which paid for most of the investment foreseen under the first plan. The first plan was extended to last until 1952 and after a brief gap a second plan was launched by Etienne Hirsch in 1954. Thereafter plans were always part of government economic policy.

However, it would be wrong to present France as a particularly *étatist* economy in the period after 1945. The first plan was deliberately supple and indicative rather than coercive. Monnet worked with a small staff and with few formal powers in a deliberately relaxed atmosphere. He sought to obtain the cooperation of industry through regular meetings of commissions that were set up under the aegis of the plan. As has been suggested above, Monnet's reputation for being sympathetic to capitalism made it easier for him to obtain cooperation from business. His attention to the psychological side of planning also proved important: the American economic historian, Charles Kindleberger, described meetings of planning commissions as being 'like revivalist prayer meetings', in which enthusiasm was whipped up for the achievement of particular economic goals.[3] Later plans changed direction again. The second plan laid greater emphasis on profitability rather than production, a shift that reflected a more general tendency for financial considerations to reassert themselves. Finally, in the 1960s plans came to lay a heavier emphasis on social considerations. Planning also moved away from Jean Monnet's original intentions and became increasingly prescriptive and precise: the fifth plan revolved around no less than 1600 equations.

Liberalism co-existed with economic planning. Sometimes such liberalism came into conflict with planning. The high taxation involved in supporting investment and state enterprises was a subject of particular complaint – the *Front Economique*, established in 1949 to combat *étatisme*, sponsored over 300 successful candidates in the 1951 elections. Liberalism became increasingly influential during the 1950s and reached a peak of influence during the first few years of the Fifth Republic when Antoine Pinay was finance minister, Jacques Rueff was head of planning, and even Claude Gignoux, leader of the *patronat* in the Third Republic, was consulted about economic policy. However, the relations between liberalism and economic planning were complicated. Sometimes the two currents could complement each other. Jean Monnet recognized that his own efforts to subsidize key sectors had to be matched by equal efforts to withdraw subsidies from traditionally protected groups such as small peasant farmers. For this reason, Monnet applauded the liberal project of René Mayer, finance minister in 1948, which aimed to cut agricultural incomes relative to those of industry.

It should also be stressed that state intervention in the French economy was not always well coordinated and clearly thought out. In St Etienne, the nationalized armaments manufacturers, having been granted exemption from many economic regulations on account of military necessity, made hunting rifles, much to the annoyance of their private sector competitors. In May 1950, the government allowed *Electricité de France* to issue 15 billion francs worth of bonds but then discreetly diverted half of the funds raised into its own coffers. Different factions struggled for control of the state's economic apparatus. The various *corps d'état* (roads and bridges, mines, finances, etc.) preserved an intense sense of group identity. Members of these *corps* remained loyal to each other even when they had left their original civil service departments. In the nationalized electricity industry there was a struggle between members of two *corps d'état* (mines versus roads and bridges) as well as between former employees of two private sector firms (Messine and Durand). Sometimes the state intervention in the economy acquired an impetus of its own: the number of people involved in the process ensured that it became increasingly difficult to return to a liberal order. Indeed, as state planners began to talk an increasingly liberal language during the 1950s and the early 1960s, institutional interest often ensured that planning was actually acquiring increasingly complicated and heavy structures. The first plan had set up only six commissions; the sixth plan, running from 1971 to 1975, established 100 commissions, which contained 4000 participants and employed 2900 people.

The increased state intervention in the post-war economy was facilitated by two things. The first of these was American money. America lent France money with arrangements such as the Blum–Byrnes agreement of 1946, and then gave substantial aid in the form of the Marshall Plan that was instituted in 1948. The Marshall Plan was crucial for purely financial reasons. The Monnet Plan would not have been feasible without the injection of cash that the Americans provided in 1948. It was also crucial for political reasons. Monnet had spent much of the war in America and was perceived to have good relations with the USA. He was able to persuade other Frenchmen to support his projects by convincing them that the Americans would be more well disposed towards France if she planned her economy. Finally, American aid was important because it helped to ensure that the Monnet Plan would be accepted by French business. Business leaders would have regarded a plan funded by the French government as a dangerous beginning of *étatisme*. However, they were more favourable to measures that were funded, and perhaps controlled, by a government that was seen as favourable to capitalism, hostile to communism and tolerant of those who had supported the Vichy government.

The creation of what Jean Monnet called a 'concerted economy' took place in the private sector as well as in the public sector. Employers' organizations acquired a new importance after 1945. Industrialists had acquired habits of organization from their experience under Vichy. After 1945, the powers and resources of Vichy's industrial committees were sometimes devolved to private industrial syndicates. Employers' organizations also benefited from the general tendency to cohesion that the French bourgeoisie showed when under threat between 1944 and 1947. A particularly important beneficiary of this tendency was the main employers' organization, the *Conseil National du Patronat Français* (CNPF), formed in 1945. By the mid 1970s, 900,000 companies, with 6 million employees, were affiliated to the CNPF. The CNPF's first president, Georges Villiers, was one of the few businessmen to have been active in the Resistance and this gave him a unique authority over his peers. The last leader of the main business association in the Third Republic had survived in office for only three years; Villiers remained president of the CNPF for over twenty years, which was longer than the entire life of the Fourth Republic. The activities of business organizations and the state often became interlinked. The former provided the latter with information and attempted to persuade their members to participate in economic planning, but business organizations also benefited from their own increasing role in the distribution of state resources. Many business leaders were themselves former civil servants: Pierre Ricard, vice-president of the CNPF, had worked for fifteen years in the *corps des mines*; Jean Fabre, another CNPF official, had run the French coal industry under Vichy. Such men often seemed to have more in common with their former colleagues in the administration than with their present colleagues in the private sector.

Some sympathy for the aims of state planners could also be found in the larger French companies. Large companies had the resources to integrate the information provided by government into their own strategy: by 1967 over half of firms employing more than 5000 people said that their own projects were influenced by state planning. The state was also often the major customer of large firms. Traditionally iron, steel and armaments manufacturers had sold much of their production to the state. After 1945 these industries were joined by many firms producing high technology goods: in 1976, 57.3 per cent of aircraft fuselages made in France were bought by the government. Such companies tended to be run by professional managers rather than owners, and these managers were often former members of the *corps d'état* or graduates of the *grandes écoles* which prepared students for the civil service. Industrial concentration after 1945 increased the proportion of French production that took place in such firms. At the same time a new class of manager appeared who gravitated between the civil service, the nationalized firms, the private sector and a variety of parapublic institutions. These managers displayed immense self-confidence: Roger Martin, a graduate of the *École Polytechnique* who moved from the *corps des mines* to the Pont-à-Mousson works, entitled his memoirs *Boss by Divine Right*.[4] Commentators have often contrasted the technocrats of French large-scale business after 1945 with the 'Malthusian' risk-averse family businesses that were seen to have dominated the French economy before 1945. However, the legacy left by this new breed of industrial managers was not an entirely positive one. The managers were not necessarily any more 'rational' than the industrial dynasties that they replaced. Indeed large, and especially nationalized companies, often pursued highly expensive projects of construction or technical innovation that were designed to earn prestige rather than to make money. Furthermore, the managers of French industry often seemed like an independent caste who pursued the interests of their own colleagues and associates rather than those of either the state or any private company.

The modernizing politicians and civil servants of post-war France regarded small business with hostility: the economist Jeanneney complained that France had an excessive number of small retailers. Similarly small business leaders, such as Léon Gingembre, often railed against planning, technocracy and the trusts. In fact, 'modernization' and the survival of small business were not mutually exclusive. The reasons for this were partly political. Small businessmen remained an enormous electoral power and they were sometimes able to survive by pressuring governments into giving them special concessions. The political power of small business was particularly strong after 1947 because the high proportion of working-class voters who supported the Communist party reduced the potential constituency on which governments depended and therefore made petit-bourgeois voters more important. During the early Fifth Republic, the political power of small producers was weakened by de Gaulle's appeal to a section of the working-class electorate and by the eclipse of some of the parties that had traditionally represented them but, by the late 1960s, de Gaulle had lost much of his appeal to the working class and concessions to the small businessmen regained their importance. In some ways the rapid growth of the French economy meant that small business acquired more political concessions because the resources available to politicians to buy off discontent increased.

There were also economic reasons for the survival of small business. Sometimes large factories needed small subcontractors who could maintain equipment, provide a degree of flexibility and, frequently, evade labour regulations. There was a lag between the concentration of production and the concentration of distribution so that small shops often benefited from the falling wholesale prices that came from the growth of factory production. New technology could provide new opportunities for small business. The technologies of the nineteenth century – steam engines, railways, telegraphs – had been agents of centralization and concentration. They were expensive and they gave benefits to those who operated at the centre of communications networks. The technologies that came into widespread use after 1945 were ones that small isolated producers found easy to use. Electrification of the French countryside meant that small workshops had access to power. Most importantly, the motor car created a cheap form of transport that was within the reach of every baker or carpenter. The spread of motor cars also created a new form of small business as garages spread through provincial France.

The spread of motor cars and electricity was linked to the creation of a consumer society in France. Such a society had existed in parts of the country for many years: the boulevards of Paris had been part of a consumer society by 1900. However, much of provincial and especially rural France had remained dominated by a culture of self-sufficiency, utilitarianism and meanness. The peasantry had often preferred the purchase of land or the saving of money to spending on comfort. After 1945, several forces spread consumerism through France. The first of these was the influence of America, the homeland of consumerism. American films exercised a particular influence during the 1940s and 1950s. The American government consciously fostered the growth of certain consumer items produced in the USA: the Blum–Byrnes agreement of 1946 required the French to accept Coca-Cola and Hollywood films in return for American loans. French companies also became aware of the need to nurture a consumer culture and some firms did succeed in building a strong sense of brand awareness around their products. The greatest success in this field was the maker of kitchen appliances, Moulinex, which increased its turnover from 1 billion to 2 billion francs between 1958 and 1968.

The spread of consumerism was connected to other social changes. The decline of religious practice meant that the stern ascetic catholicism, which had prevented even the very wealthy northern textile industrialists from spending most of their money, exerted less influence. Changes in banking also encouraged consumption. The number of French banks dropped from 411 to 308 between 1945 and 1958, but the number of branches increased from 3616 to 3838. Banks and the government were successful in encouraging individuals to settle large transactions with cheques rather than cash. Total bank reserves multiplied by twelve between 1945 and 1958, while cash in circulation increased by a factor of only 3.5. Banks encouraged their clients to spend more freely. The *Union de Crédit pour le Bâtiment* (founded in 1951) and the *Compagnie Bancaire* (founded in 1959) lent against the anticipated income of those who were expected to have successful careers; they also lent to support certain specific purchases, such as motor cars, houses and electrical goods.

The rise in the birthrate that had begun in 1940 also affected consumption. Children born in this period did not enter the economy as producers until the early Fifth Republic, but they became consumers straightaway. The rising birthrates helped to bring about a change in family structure. Before 1945, much of the French bourgeoisie and peasantry had been strongly influenced by a sense of dynastic duty: they were concerned to maintain the reputation and prosperity of their families over many generations, and in order to bring this about they were willing to forgo or defer gratification. After 1945, the French lived increasingly in nuclear families made up of two adults and their children: a unit that encouraged a more short-term view of consumption.

It was widely recognized that women played a key role in the creation of the consumer society. Domestic appliances were specifically targeted at women. Women's magazines, which advertised such products and conveyed the image of leisured and comfortable life, began to be widely read during the 1940s and 1950s. *Elle* had been founded in 1937. By 1951 there were 90 separate magazines concerned with fashion or homemaking and aimed at women; these sold a total of 15 million copies per month. The head of *Electricité de France* told the surprised technocrats in his company that they should read *Marie-Claire* and *Elle* if they wanted to learn how to make electrification attractive in the countryside and a sociological study of a Breton village, published in 1967, contained a chapter entitled '*La femme: agent secret de la modernisation*'.[5] Women's new role may have been linked to a certain increase in their power – they had been granted the vote for the first time in 1945 – but it was also linked to a diminution of their power in certain spheres. Historically women had made up a large proportion of the French workforce. This proportion had begun to diminish in the aftermath of the First World War, when it began to increase in most other countries, and it continued to diminish during most of France's rapid post-war economic growth. Furthermore, women in the countryside who had exercised a certain power in the household economy of the peasant farm did not transfer that power into the market relations or the agricultural organizations that came to play an increasing role in the lives of peasants. Women were becoming consumers at the same time as they were ceasing to be producers.

Changes in the nature of employment stimulated consumption. Self-employed peasants and artisans were reluctant to spend money on consumption for two reasons. Firstly, such people had to choose between immediate consumption and future production; under the circumstances they often chose to buy new equipment rather than consumer goods. Secondly, the self-employed tended to be assessed for taxation on the basis of visible signs of wealth, and they were therefore reluctant to advertise prosperity: in 1948 Jules Moch ordered his tax inspectors to investigate the owners of all American cars in Paris. However, in the post-war period the number of self-employed people diminished and the number of employees increased. Employees had no means of avoiding tax and no interest in investing for future production. The growth of the *cadre* or professional manager was particularly important for the increase of consumption. Previously management had been dominated by engineers: such men might be very wealthy but they belonged to a production culture and spent much of their time on the factory floor; the new *cadres* were more likely to work in marketing. They spent their time meeting clients and were immersed in the consumption culture of expense account lunches, designer suits and company cars. The insecurity of the *cadres'* social position also pushed them to purchase. Unlike the more established sections of the bourgeoisie, the *cadres* rarely had distinguished ancestors, inherited property or even qualifications from the most prestigious institutions. This was a group that defined itself by consumption.

The development of consumerism in France was reflected by the increase in spending, particularly spending by the lower classes, on non-food items. The bourgeoisie turned increasingly to devices such as vacuum cleaners and washing machines as alternatives to domestic servants. The electrification of the countryside meant that electrical appliances acquired a much wider potential market. Most importantly, motor cars spread throughout France; after 1955 half a million motor cars per year were sold. However, it is important not to overestimate the extent to which consumerism spread in France. Fashion and status played a smaller role in French consumption than in America or Great Britain, and advertising took up a relatively small proportion of French GNP (only 0.8 per cent in 1972). The consumer society also spread through France in a very uneven way. In 1952 there were an average of more than two bathrooms for every household in the Alpes-Maritimes, but in Lozère only 9 per cent of households had bathrooms. Often it seemed that two quite different economies existed within the same country. *Maison et Jardin*, an upmarket women's magazine, defined a fridge as 'essential' in 1951 although only 9 per cent of rural households possessed such a device. Alongside the Parisian *cadre* who lived in the post-cash economy of bank accounts, cheques and mortgages, was the Breton peasant who lived in the pre-cash economy of auto-consumption and barter, an economy that had often been strengthened by black market practices during the war. As late as 1967, Edgar Morin described the attitude of Breton peasants to money in words that could have come from Eugen Weber's description of peasants in the late nineteenth century:

> For the old peasants money is still not the universal unit and agent of economic relations. The values of exchange, service and gift persist outside of, or inside of, monetary values. The real measure of value for small prices is the pound of butter, the litre or the glass of wine, or the packet of tobacco; the measure of large prices is the horse, the pig or the tractor.[6]

Furthermore, the French could display a surprising resistance to the consumer society: a study of Vienne in 1950 discovered that a couple, who had recently moved to a new flat with a modern bathroom, continued to heat water in the kitchen rather than using the central heating system.

In many respects post-war France underwent two sorts of associated and overlapping forms of economic change: one associated with consumption and one associated with production. Generally speaking, the changes in production were concentrated in the 1950s while the changes in consumption were concentrated in the 1960s, but the relations between the two processes could be complicated. The countryside was still modernizing production while the city had turned to consumption, and recent immigrants from the countryside often worked in factories while the urban working class moved to jobs in the tertiary sector concerned with consumption. Women often pressed for spending on consumption while their menfolk were preoccupied by production. When Lawrence Wylie visited the Vaucluse in 1957, he discovered that farmers spent much on agricultural machinery but that 'there are none of the external signs of modernity, no chrome, no enamel, no electrical items, no deep freezes, no television, no white kitchens, no glamorous bathrooms'.[7] Ten years later, sociologists visiting the Breton village of Plodémet talked of internal modernization (i.e. that concerned with the house and often promoted by women) and external modernization (i.e. that concerned with the farm and often promoted by men). They recorded the following conversation between a 43-year-old farmer and his 40-year-old wife:

SHE   'When one has something one always wants something more. To start with, television.'
HIM   'Bah.'
SHE   (*Laughs*)
HIM   'I would prefer to see two horses in my stable.'[8]

Certain changes might be associated with both consumption and production. Electrification was one such change. Generally speaking, electricity facilitated the modernization of production during the early 1950s and then shifted to consumption. In 1962 only 29 per cent of electricity was used by residential and tertiary customers; by 1972 this figure had risen to 37 per cent. The spread of motor cars was another such change. Roland Barthes identified the motor car, especially the Citroën DS, as the ultimate bourgeois consumerist icon. However, small businessmen and peasants saw motor cars as economic necessities rather than as luxuries and chose utilitarian models. The France that was interested in cars for consumptionist reasons bought new cars while those who saw them as economic necessities bought battered second-hand models. In Seine et Oise 68 per cent of cars bought in 1954 were new; in the Vaucluse the statistic was only 41.6 per cent.

The institutions most associated with consumerism often sought to deny that they were associated with the grimy world of production, or indeed with capitalism at all. The most striking example of such denial was provided by the Club Méditerrané holiday company, which was founded in 1950. Club Med publicity presented its camps as a means of escape from work and ordinary life: clients even purchased their drinks with beads instead of money. In reality, of course, Club Med was a successful capitalist enterprise: it had 400,000 clients by 1967, and in 1959 it established a mail order catalogue to sell products that would remind clients of their annual month in the sun. Furthermore, Club Med's success was built on the productive capacity of the company's 2000 employees as well as on the French industrial production from which the *cadres* and office workers who used its service drew their prosperity. There was a tension between the hedonistic individualistic images that were generated by consumer capitalism and the reality that underlay those images. It is this contradiction that explains the fact that the most vigorous assaults on consumerism during the 1960s would come from the very groups, the prosperous young, on which it had been founded.

Many historians have been attracted to the study of the French post-war growth by the belief that they will be able to learn lessons that can be applied to their economies. This chapter has suggested that such enquiries are futile. The reasons for French growth are rooted in a whole variety of political and social circumstances: it would be impossible, and undesirable, to reproduce these circumstances. The success of new economic strategies cannot be separated from the legacy of perceived economic decline, defeat and Communist threat that made influential people willing to accept them. Furthermore, it is difficult to isolate any single cause of economic growth after 1945. It might be argued that post-war France was characterized not by a successful economy, but by several kinds of economic success that had little to do with each other. It might, for example, be argued that the planned economy with a heavy emphasis on large-scale heavy industrial production of the late 1940s and 1950s had little to do with the consumer-led boom in electrical goods and household appliances during the 1960s. Such an interpretation would be simplistic. Often even the most apparently disparate elements of economic growth turned out to be connected in complicated ways. For example, the influx of skilled labour that France acquired during the early 1960s seems at first glance to be due to an entirely non-economic cause, France's departure from Algeria. However, this departure was itself linked to changes in the economy, as business began to look to European rather than imperial markets. Most importantly of all, the various forms of growth that France underwent after 1945 were linked by the infuriatingly intangible quality of confidence. The civil servant who laid down objectives for government plans, the industrialist who decided to build a new factory, the peasant who decided to buy a new tractor and the housewife who decided to buy a new washing machine may have had little in common, but they did all share a belief that the French economy was growing and that growth would make their ambitious projects feasible. If the *trente glorieuses* was a myth then it was one that came to influence reality.

9   The Second Sex

In 1949 Simone de Beauvoir, a former *lycée* teacher who was then mainly known as the lover of Jean-Paul Sartre, published *The Second Sex*. In this book de Beauvoir examined the various disadvantages under which women laboured. In 1971 de Beauvoir's name appeared at the top of a petition in favour of the legalization of abortion: all the 343 signatories claimed that they themselves had undergone abortions. It would be possible to present the period between these two events as one in which de Beauvoir's ideas spread to influence almost all Frenchwomen. In his study of a Breton village, Edgar Morin even talked of the spread of 'Beauvoirism' among peasants. In reality changes in the lives of women in post-war France cannot be attributed simply to the spread of feminist ideas, or to any other single process. De Beauvoir's own, highly mythologized, life raises interesting questions about the changing role of women in France. Her relationship with Sartre – the two lived apart and enjoyed the freedom to pursue 'contingent' relationships – can be seen as a liberating alternative to the constraints of bourgeois marriage. But it can also be argued that de Beauvoir lived in his shadow from the moment when, in 1929, she came second to him in the philosophy agrégation, to the time when, at the end of his life, she nursed him through illness. Furthermore, Sartre's world was one in which a certain idea of masculinity, characterized by boxing, hard drinking and violent revolution, was carried to the point of caricature. It could be argued that de Beauvoir became prominent only by adopting male values and that she defined herself largely through a relationship with a man.

De Beauvoir's career also poses the question of whether feminists could really claim to represent Frenchwomen. Some activists were certainly confident that they could do so; in the 1970s one *groupuscule, Psychanalyse et Politique,* even bought the copyright to the words *'Mouvement de Libération des Femmes'*. However, most feminists were urban, bourgeois and educated. Their lives were far removed from those of peasant and working-class France. De Beauvoir spent almost her entire life in Montparnasse in Paris, she lived in hotels, never did housework and was childless. She had no direct experience of many of the problems of which she wrote in *The Second Sex*. According to her sister, de Beauvoir had not even undergone an abortion: she had merely signed the petition of 1971 out of 'solidarity'. The third question raised by de Beauvoir's life is whether feminist struggles between the Second World War and 1970 really had any unity at all. Huguette Bouchardeau pointed out that during the interwar period feminists had rallied around the issue of female suffrage;[1] she might have added that from the late 1960s onwards feminists increasingly rallied around demands for the legalization and facilitation of birth control. However, between these two dates French feminism was fragmented and different activists were preoccupied with a variety of different issues.

A crucial chapter of *The Second Sex* was entitled 'The Job and the Vote'. This encapsulated the widespread assumption that women would undergo parallel, and mutually reinforcing, processes of liberation. Equipped with the vote they would be able to gain social and economic concessions which would ease their entry into the workforce on equal terms with men. Entry into the workforce would, in turn, eradicate the differences between male and female political behaviour. In fact, economic and political emancipation did not go together. The number of women who worked dropped as they gained political rights and continued to drop for two decades after women were granted the vote. Traditionally women had worked in light industries, especially in textiles; in 1950 the textile industry employed 237,000 women and 105,000 men. But these industries were in decline. Those women who remained in work gravitated towards the tertiary sector, which accounted for 42.3 per cent of women workers in 1946 and 63.5 per cent of them in 1972. Office and secretarial employment expanded rapidly in France after 1945. Women who worked tended to remain subordinate to men. They rarely took senior positions and they earned less than their male counterparts: in 1972 wages for married women were 32 per cent lower than for their male counterparts while wages for single women were 16 per cent lower than those earned by men. Women rarely worked in the heavy industrial enterprises that were most associated with working-class organization – only 4 per cent of employees in heavy industry in 1950 were women – and they displayed less class consciousness than men: a survey of Vienne in 1950 showed that the proportion of women who identified themselves as working class was only 45 per cent while the proportion of men who identified themselves thus was 53 per cent.

Few women showed much enthusiasm for their work. A survey among female workers at Renault in the late 1940s showed that the majority would have preferred to remain at home. It would be unwise to make too much of this statistic: work at Renault was famously tedious and humiliating, and the enthusiasm with which the French took to the culture of retirement showed that many men as well as women dreamed of escaping from the constraints of employment. Work outside the home was also made unattractive to women by the fact that so many of them had to undertake unpaid work in the household. In 1954, 75 per cent of managers continued to eat their lunch at home and a survey of bourgeois Parisians in the late 1940s showed that housework took an average of 56 hours and that looking after children could take anything up to a further 30 hours.

Politicians and journalists had always implied that the ideal woman was the *femme au foyer* who stayed at home. Initially the *femme au foyer* was mainly presented as a mother, but in the 1950s she also began to be seen as a housewife who was concerned with the creation of a comfortable and attractive home for her husband. This shift was partly a reflection of growing prosperity, which made it possible for growing numbers of families to live without the women's salary. It was also a result of the consumerist economy described in chapter 8. Firms that made domestic appliances and the women's magazines that advertised them began to produce plans of the housewife's 'ideal' day in which all the appropriate tasks would be efficiently completed. The upkeep of the house was no longer seen as an hereditary skill that was passed from mother to daughter; rather it was a science, defined by time and motion experts, and taught in domestic science classes or through educational broadcasts on the radio.

The construction of the housewife tied in with other social changes. Traditionally French couples had had little privacy. Many had shared houses with parents; bourgeois families often employed live-in servants; immediately after the war, bombing damage forced many families to share a single flat and most people shared bathrooms or toilets with their neighbours. During the 1950s, all this began to change. Domestic servants became less common and the nuclear family became more widespread. Houses, at least for those who were reasonably prosperous, became private places. As the number of self-employed shopkeepers and artisans dropped, men were less likely to spend their working day close to their home, but they were also encouraged to spend more of their leisure time at home. The emphasis on the private space of the home was increased by the diminishing availability of public space. The government campaigned against cafés, which were seen as likely to encourage alcoholism. Television meant that entertainment was likely to be found at home, and the washing machine removed the need for women to gather together at public washing places. Changes in housing patterns also separated women from public space. In the 1960s the government sought to lessen the housing shortage by building *grandes ensembles* on the outskirts of big towns, especially Paris. The large-scale suburbs were isolated. Women who lived there were unable to get work; at Melaunes outside Paris it was estimated that there were only 35 jobs for 800 women. They also found it hard to get to shops, markets or anywhere else where they might meet people outside their immediate family. Women's magazines celebrated these changes and presented the ideal home as a place of tranquillity that was cut off from the world of work and public affairs, and women were presented as the creators of this private haven.

However, the model of the household as a private space and women as belonging to that space never took hold in France to the extent that it did in, say, suburban America. Sometimes new technologies contributed to communal life rather than creating private space. In the south, where there was a tradition of sociability, television was often watched in bars rather than at home. Similarly, the first washing machines to arrive in Roubaix were communally owned and operated. Most importantly, to the exasperation of domestic science experts, women were often unenthusiastic about losing touch with the outside world. Urban housewives were reluctant to use fridges to shop 'efficiently' once a week, and continued to make daily visits to markets.

All commentators agreed that women played a crucial part in the exodus of people from the country to the city. They became less prone to accept the life that accompanied marriage to a farmer. In 1965 almost none of the girls graduating from the Lycée Jeanne d'Arc in Plodémet remained in the country. A survey of girls attending courses in agricultural domestic science in 1954 showed that only 5.5 per cent of them wished to be farmers; 50 per cent of them wished to work in offices. Some writers, such as Eugen Weber, have argued that rural life was always harsh for women, and that peasants treated their wives as chattels.[2] De Beauvoir did not deny that peasant women were obliged to wait on men, though she stressed that their position varied from one part of the country to another. However, she also pointed out that women enjoyed a certain power that sprang from their economic role in a household that was also a unit of production. This argument has been developed by Martine Segalen, who suggests that the 'modernization' of the countryside diminished women's power: forces external to the household became increasingly important to peasant life and it was men who had exclusive access to such forces.[3] Morin wrote of Plodémet: 'the old women only speak Breton and have never left the locality while the men all know French and have travelled in the army.'[4]

These two interpretations present alternative explanations for women's enthusiasm to leave the countryside after 1945. One inter-pretation would argue that women responded to the opportunity presented by economic modernization which offered them the chance to move to cities and to enjoy a more comfortable life. The other interpretation would suggest that women were forced out of the countryside by economic modernization which deprived them of the role that they had previously played in the household economy. The real explanation probably lies in a combination of these two interpretations. Women's lives were becoming more comfortable after 1945. Peasant girls spoke French, sat at the dinner table and wore slacks, while their mothers spoke *patois*, stood up to wait on men and wore traditional clothes. However, the modernization which young women in the countryside underwent was one that affected their lives as consumers. Their relations with agricultural production were weakened by the perception that an increasingly organized and mechanized agriculture was the exclusive province of men. Women were not allowed to be members of the main farmers' associations if a male member of their family already belonged. Only 80 women graduated from the *Institut National d'Agronomie* in the 30 years that preceded 1968. Of 832 delegates to the farmers' mutual association in the Allier only 8 were women. As women lost their role in production and as their lives centred more and more around con-sumption, it was not surprising that they began to find the comforts of the non-agricultural world more and more attractive.

This illustrates a wider point about women's role in social change. Women's transformation from active producers into housewife con-sumers was neither entirely the product of a male construction nor was it a sign of female power. Women did make choices, but they made them from a limited and unattractive list of options which were largely determined by men. Perhaps it was a sign of how limited and unattractive women's options were, that those of them who had achieved their supposed goals were often unhappy. Morin's study of Plodémet found that the proportion of bourgeois housewives who used drugs to sleep at night, 35 per cent, was higher than that of any other group. Colette Audry, who translated Betty Friedan's *Feminine Mystique* into French in 1964, remarked that the picture of bored and frustrated housewives seemed familiar in France.

The lives of men and women were not only differentiated by their experience of work. As has been suggested above, most men had a wider experience of the world than women because they had undergone compulsory military service. As France became an increasingly urban and sophisticated society, military service ceased to be such a vital means of education. It did, however, remain a rite of passage. Men were better educated than women; in 1962, 60 per cent of women had no educational qualification. By the 1950s the gap between the numbers of boys and girls educated was beginning to diminish, but differences in the kind of education given continued to be important. Men were more likely to study law and sciences, women were more likely to study arts subjects. Women remained entirely excluded from the most prestigious technical *grandes écoles* until the early years of the Fifth Republic. Places at *écoles nationales professionnelles*, which trained people for trades, were four times as numerous for men as for women. Women were also more likely than men to have undergone a religious education.

Rates of marriage reached their historical peak with 9.6 marriages per thousand people in 1950. Most women in post-war France married comparatively young (around the age of 25 in 1946), and the age of marriage dropped until 1970. Marriage among the bourgeoisie had had a large economic dimension. Simone de Beauvoir's own parents had undergone an arranged marriage and Simone was obliged to learn a profession because her father's ruin in the inflation of the First World War made it impossible for him to provide her with a dowry. Formally arranged marriages were rarer after 1945, and a series of laws culminating in 1965 gave women greater rights to dispose of their own property and careers without reference to their husbands. But money continued to play a role in marriage. Only 6 per cent of the sons of industrialists married the daughters of workers, and only 1 per cent of workers married the daughters of employers. It was only the *petite bourgeoisie*, and particularly small shopkeepers, who showed much propensity to marry below their own class. Shopkeepers too were motivated by economic needs, but their main concern was to find a suitable business partner rather than to acquire a presentable or wealthy wife. Thousands of working-class or peasant girls found out too late about the drudgery of long hours minding the till and keeping books: a survey of bakers' wives showed that almost all told their daughters, 'never marry a baker'.[5]

Numerous proposals to give women the vote had been advanced in the French parliament between the wars. By 1936 a majority of members of the Chamber of Deputies had been won over to the cause of female suffrage, but their views were continuously rejected by the French Senate. Division over the political rights of women did not operate on a simple left–right spectrum. Léon Blum, always sympathetic to feminist causes, appointed three women as secretaries of state in the Popular Front government, but other supporters of female suffrage came from the right. Pierre-Etienne Flandin, of the *Alliance Démocratique*, and Justin Godard, of the *Fédération Républicaine*, had both put forward motions in favour of female suffrage during the 1920s, and the *Parti Social Français* also supported the cause. Conservatives wished to give women the vote partly because, like their counterparts all over Europe, they expected women to limit the power of working-class men which seemed so threatening in the aftermath of the Russian Revolution. Women were associated with the home and the family whereas men were associated with the factory and the strike. The right also saw female suffrage as a means to honour and empower the dead of the Great War. Barrès had written of the '*suffrage des morts*' to be exercised by war widows, and the Patureau-Miraud bill of March 1922 proposed to give the vote to war widows who had not remarried. The most vigorous opposition to female suffrage came from the Radical group in the senate who believed that the political behaviour of women would be unduly influenced by the church.

Political parties made little attempt to adjust to the enfranchisement of women. There were few women deputies in parliament in 1945 and those that did get into parliament were often widows of Resistance heroes who were chosen to represent their husbands. Political parties did establish special women's sections, but these concentrated on what were seen as women's issues such as childcare, housing, suppression of alcoholism and prostitution. The parties that contained the most women activists and leaders, particularly the Communist party, tended to be unattractive to women voters, while parties that attracted women voters, particularly the Gaullists, had few women in prominent positions. Political parties could be stunningly insensitive in their attempts to obtain female support. A speaker at a congress of the *Union Démocratique et Socialiste de la Résistance* (UDSR) said that the party should encourage women members by insisting that men brought their wives to meetings: a member of the audience shouted out '*et la liberté*', but it was unclear whether he was defending the right of women to disobey their husbands or the right of men to leave their wives at home. In 1951, a UDSR candidate in the Lozère put his wife second on his electoral list. The list received one vote and it was widely assumed that the wife had voted against herself.

There is a great deal of information about how women used their voting rights after 1945. This is partly because the advent of women's suffrage coincided with the use of large-scale opinion polls. It is also because, on one or more occasions, three constituencies – Belfort, Grenoble and Vienne – operated separate polling stations for men and women and counted the votes of the sexes separately. Women seem to have voted exactly as the opponents of female suffrage had feared they would. The three parties with the highest proportion of female voters in the 1951 election were the Christian Democrat MRP (61%), the Gaullist RPF (52%) and the conservative CNIP (53%). Those with the lowest proportion of female voters in 1951 were the Socialists (40%), the Communists (39%) and the Radicals (49%). Writers on female voters, who were sympathetic both to the political left and to women's suffrage, found this fact embarrassing. Most of them argued that the 'peculiarity' of women's electoral behaviour was merely a vestige of the period when women had been excluded from economic and political life and that this vestige would disappear as women 'entered the modern world'. In fact the differences between the political behaviour of the sexes can be explained as much in terms of the peculiarity of male traditions as in terms of the particular forces affecting women.

Age played a role in the sexual division of politics. Women lived longer than men and so they were more likely to be found among the relatively aged electorate of the RPF and the CNIP, but age cannot explain the support of women for the MRP, which had a smaller proportion of voters over 50 (34% in 1951) than any other party except the Communists. Women's role in the workforce also goes some way to explaining their electoral behaviour. The fact that women were less likely than men to work outside the home, and particularly unlikely to work in large-scale heavy industry, meant that the Communist and Socialist parties, which directed much of their appeal at the industrial proletariat, were unlikely to attract many female supporters. However, this can hardly explain the fact that the Radical party, which drew much of its support from non-industrial areas, appealed to so few women.

Attitudes to the church played a role in the sexual divisions of politics. The CNIP, the RPF, and the MRP all presented themselves as defenders of church interests while the Radicals, Socialists and Communists were all seen as anti-clerical. Since women were more likely to attend church than men it was widely assumed that female 'clericalism' underlay their support for conservative parties, although in public opinion polls only 20 per cent of women admitted that the advice of the church played a role in their vote. Conversely male anti-clericalism played a role in persuading men to support the left. Male anti-clericalism was as irrational as female 'clericalism'. Communist working men often supported Radical candidates on the grounds of anti-clericalism even when they had nothing in common with the social programme advanced by such candidates. It should also be stressed that anti-clericalism was more condemned by modernity than was clericalism. The proportion of people who never attended church, and who voted Radical, was dropping faster than the proportion of people who attended regularly.

After 1945 men continued to be loyal to the parties with which they had been involved in the Third Republic: this gave an advantage to the Radicals, founded in 1898, the Socialist party, founded in 1905, and the Communist party, founded in 1920. Conversely parties founded after 1945 – the MRP, CNIP and RPF – tended to attract disproportionate numbers of female votes. Men also tended to define their political stance in terms of universal ideologies, women expressed less certainty on political matters and were often attracted by political parties associated with strong political leaders, especially de Gaulle. This meant that political parties of the right, which tended to present themselves as 'apolitical' and pragmatic and which focused loyalty on leaders rather than ideologies or organizations, proved more attractive to women.

During the 1960s, French feminism turned its attention away from the broad economic and political issues and towards those of personal freedom for individual women and particularly towards the question of birth control. Indeed by 1971 the campaign for the legalization of abortion had become the main issue on which feminists united. The fact that birth control came to be seen as a specifically women's issue marked an important change. The French parliament, which had outlawed birth control in 1920, had been motivated mainly by military considerations – the need to rebuild the population after the First World War. Thereafter the debate over birth control had been conducted mainly by men and in terms of male interests. 'Natalists' sought to increase the birthrate, either to increase military strength or because they believed that large families were sanctioned by the Catholic church. On the other side 'neo-Malthusians' believed that restraining population growth would lower international tension and maintain wages by keeping labour scarce. Often the focus on men in conflicts over birth control reached ludicrous proportions. The society designed to promote large families gave prizes to fathers rather than mothers; when a couple were arrested for distributing information on birth control, the husband was given a sentence of five years while his wife escaped with two.

The decisions that individuals made over birth control were also often controlled by men. The population of France did not increase at all in the 20 years after 1920 any more than it had done in the 50 years before 1920: birth control was not a 'women's issue' but the social basis of the Third Republic. Given the 'Malthusian' nature of French economic thinking and the effects of inheritance laws on family farms, birth control was often seen as a matter of economic necessity for the family rather than personal freedom for the woman. Furthermore, the most widely practised techniques of contraception – premature withdrawal, and to a lesser extent condoms – were ones that required male cooperation. Abortion was frequent; Simone de Beauvoir claimed that there were between 800,000 and 1 million abortions per year and that their number equalled that of live births. Poor women were often reduced to practising abortion on their own or with the help of friends: 5 per cent of abortions were said to have been carried out with knitting needles. But the rich had access to professional abortionists, and such operations often involved male participation, either because doctors carried out the operation or because men organized and subsidized the operation: Sartre's novel, *The Age of Reason,* describes the efforts of a man to arrange an abortion for his unwilling mistress.

After 1945, debates over birth control continued to be dominated by men. An organization, *Maternité Heureuse,* was founded in 1956 to campaign for access to birth control; in 1958 this changed its name to *Planning Familial* and in 1960 it established France's first birth control clinic at Grenoble. The *Planning Familial* organization contained a large number of men and became increasingly influenced by male doctors and politicians. One feminist writer complained that women were becoming the 'production line workers of sexuality' – acting as receptionists, nurses and secretaries in clinics run by men.[6] Debates over the birthrate contained many paradoxes. Family planning publications were often conservative in tone. They stressed that their aim was to allow women to limit and control childbirth within marriage; sexual freedom or the desire not to have children at all were rarely discussed. Equally, the pro-natalist movement sometimes brought about developments that were later to be applauded by feminists. In particular it ensured that Frenchwomen had the best maternity benefits in Europe; a law of 1946 guaranteed 14 weeks maternity leave.

In the 1960s attitudes to birth control changed for several reasons. Urbanization meant that village constraints were less likely to force men to marry women whom they had impregnated. Secondly, the decline of peasant France and the granting of family allowances meant that men no longer had the kind of economic interest in limiting family size that they had possessed in the Third Republic: indeed an agricultural labourer with four children might expect to gain more from the family allowances given to his wife than from his own wage. Thirdly, the invention of the contraceptive pill meant that a form of birth control that could be managed by a woman, without the participation of her lover or husband, was available. In 1965, François Mitterrand suggested that contraception should be legalized: a poll of women of child-bearing age taken in the same year suggested that 80 per cent of them would use contraception if it was legal. Lucien Neuwirth managed to persuade de Gaulle to support the legalization of contraception. De Gaulle believed that decisions in this matter should be 'lucid' – his own wife had had no further children after the birth of Anne, a child with Down's syndrome, in 1928. The Neuwirth bill was passed in 1967, one year before the Catholic church condemned birth control in unambiguous terms. Contraception remained under an element of male control because a doctor's prescription was still required. Abortion, within 10 weeks of conception, was finally legalized by the Veil law of 1975.

The debate over birth control changed the politics of women's rights in two respects. On the electoral level, birth control was the first issue that mobilized large numbers of women in favour of the left. This was reflected in the votes from women that Mitterrand obtained in the 1965 presidential election. In spite of the efforts that Giscard d'Estaing made to court women's votes during the early 1970s, Mitterrand seems to have preserved the loyalty of an important part of the female electorate for the rest of his career. Mitterrand was probably made more attractive to women voters by the fact that, as a politician who had begun his career as a Fourth Republic conservative, he was not associated with any of the established and male-dominated traditions of the French left. Mitterrand also courted the female vote with some skill and insisted that the *Fédération de la Gauche Démocratique et Socialiste* should put forward at least seven female candidates in the 1967 election. In the 1988 presidential election Mitterrand was to become the first major left-wing figure to attract a predominantly female electorate.

Among committed feminists, birth control also had a dramatic effect in creating the first organizations that were exclusively controlled by women and which did not simply see themselves as part of a broader progressive movement. The development of the feminist movement was stimulated by the student protests of 1968. The protests encouraged radical critiques of society, but also showed how marginalized women were in 'progressive' movements: the *enragés* of Nanterre who 'liberated' the dormitories of female students did not ask the inmates whether they wished to be liberated. Sometimes the rhetoric of the new feminist groups, as was so often the case with the post-1968 left, resembled that of the traditional right. This was shown most strikingly in August 1970 when a group of women laid a wreath at the Tomb of the Unknown Soldier and dedicated it to 'the Unknown Wife'. The feminists of 1970 would probably have been surprised to learn how prominently war widows had featured in right-wing propaganda of the 1920s. The Paris police were equally ignorant and promptly arrested all the women involved.

10   Generation Gaps

In 1945 France was a gerontocracy. She had only just ceased to be ruled by a marshal born in the middle part of the nineteenth century. The split between Resistance and Vichy was, among other things, a fight between youth and age. But the dominant figures of the Fourth Republic were closer to Pétain's generation than to that of the *maquisards* who had fought against Vichy. Edouard Herriot was born in 1872, Henri Queuille first held political office in 1912. The memories that dominated the minds of this generation were of the First World War or even the Dreyfus case. The Radical party, which had the oldest electorate (in 1951, 65 per cent of its supporters were over 50), continued to exercise an influence that was disproportionate to its electoral success. The Communist party had the youngest electorate (42 per cent of its supporters in 1951 were under 34), but it exercised no direct influence at all after 1947. The Mouvement Républicain Populaire was the only bourgeois party to attract significant support from the young, but its fate after 1945 seemed to show that youthful naïvety would always be defeated by experience.

The power of the old was even more entrenched outside the world of party politics. It took years to claw up the hierarchy of French industrial management. The average age of managers in large industrial companies at the beginning of 1954 was just over 46. Léon Daum left the civil service to become a manager at Marine et Homécourt, where he was given to understand that he would succeed Theodore Laurent as managing director. Daum finally gave up waiting and returned to the civil service in 1952 after Laurent had been renewed in his post for a further six years at the age of 90. Those who voted in elections to chambers of commerce were almost all over 50, and those who held office in such bodies had generally retired from active business life. The average age of leaders of the main business association in Bordeaux was just over 62. Every local agency from the departmental *conseil général* to the village *comité des fêtes* was dominated by aged notables.

The extent of the gulf between generations was closely linked to variations between social classes. The peasantry, the *petite bourgeoisie* and the workers were shaken by economic changes which meant that few children could expect to pursue the same careers as their parents. Small shopkeepers set up in business and went bankrupt: many entered self-employment from the working class and many encouraged their children to seek more secure and less demanding lives as salaried workers. Peasant children often left the land to seek work in the cities and even those who stayed often entered a world based on mechanization and organization which seemed unrecognizable to their parents. Peasant patriarchs who had grown up accustomed to being head of the family felt marginalized during the 1960s (see below). The families of workers were also divided between generations. Gérard Noiriel has talked of the heavy industrial working class of the post-war decade as a 'unique generation', which was formed by economic and political circumstances that did not last. Economic change moved jobs out of the old heavy industries during the 1960s and many workers from these industries encouraged their children to better themselves through education. Disappointment with the reality of the few opportunities that were to be found in education accounted for the disillusion of many young workers during the 1960s and explains the participation of some of them in the strikes of 1968.

The group among whom relations between the generations were closest, and in which the power of the old remained strongest, was the elite of big business managers and top civil servants. The size of this group remained remarkably stable. This stability was reflected in the fact that the number of students passing through the elite *grandes écoles*, as opposed to those going to university, remained almost unchanged between the late nineteenth century and 1970. The *haute bourgeoisie* displayed an impressive capacity to pass privilege down across the generations. Indeed, sociologists like Bourdieu argued that social privilege in post-war France was guaranteed by transmission of 'cultural capital' through education more effectively than it had once been maintained through the transmission of property. This process of transmission revolved around the *grandes écoles* and the entrance exams to the *grands corps* (the most prestigious parts of the civil service). Success in this academic struggle was associated with social background. Few stood any change of entering the system unless they had begun life with a good *lycée* and couple of years of *classes préparatoires*. However, background alone was never enough. The French bourgeoisie traded the maintenance of their collective privileges for the acceptance that those privileges could not be passed on to academically unsuccessful children. Similarly, individual bourgeois young men traded their eventual place in the ruling class for the absorption of their youth in a rigorous process of study and testing.

A couple of examples reflect the role of families in transmitting privilege. Jean-Noël Jeanneney, who became a minister in Mitterrand's government during the 1990s, was the grandson of Jules Jeanneney, president of the Senate at the end of the Third Republic and the son of Jean-Marcel Jeanneney, a distinguished economist. Jean-Noël's own career was based on an elite education, at the *École Normale Supérieure*, and on a successful career as a research historian, in which he benefited considerably from privileged access to the private documents of several members of the French elite. An even more dramatic example of bourgeois family success was provided by Valéry Giscard d'Estaing (president of France from 1974 to 1981). Valéry was another educational star, who had graduated from the *École Nationale d'Administration* before entering the inspectorate of finances. He was also the son of Edmond, a banker and business leader and the grandson of a conservative deputy, who bequeathed Valéry his seat in parliament. It is not surprising that commentators, from both the left and the extreme right, sought to explain the French power structure in terms of 'great bourgeois dynasties'.

During the Fourth Republic, the dominance of the old began to be challenged by a variety of groups. Pierre Poujade was only 35 when the *Union de Fraternité Française* achieved such success in the 1956 general elections, and the average age of deputies elected under his aegis was around 40. Among other things, Poujadism was a rebellion by young shopkeepers who had sought to establish themselves after the Second World War, against the domination of small business by the generation represented by the *Confédération Générale de la Petite et Moyenne Entreprise* of Léon Gingembre (who had been born in 1900). The Catholic church had begun to organize the young, or at least young men, during the 1930s. The *Jeunesse Agricole Chrétienne* (JAC) was particularly important in this context. The JAC had trained a leadership who began to take over the main agricultural syndicates during the 1950s: Michel Debatisse, who had been formed by the JAC, became deputy secretary general of the *Fédération Nationale des Syndicats d'Exploitants Agricoles*. These new men were more open to ideas about mechanization and organization than their fathers. The *Centre des Jeunes Patrons*, founded in 1938, sought to promote similar ideas in the world of industrial management: by the 1940s it mobilized 2500 employers. The CJP was less effective than its agricultural counterpart and its greatest support lay in small-scale family companies whose traditional structure contrasted oddly with the movement's modernistic rhetoric. However, CJP veterans also began to exercise some influence in the main industrial organizations during the 1960s: Yves Glotin, a veteran of the Christian business organizations, became head of the Bordeaux Chamber of Commerce.

'Youth' as promoted by the various Catholic-inspired organizations was a relative concept. The upper age limit for membership of the CJP was 45. Furthermore, the generations who had been mobilized under the banner of youth often acquired real power a decade or two later when they had ceased to be youthful in any respect except in their own imaginations. One businessman dismissed the CJP with the words: 'Quand on est jeune, on n'est pas patron, et quand on est patron on n'est pas jeune' (a sentence that might be applied to many areas of French life). This was particularly notable in the 1960s. Jean-Louis Servan-Schreiber, brother of Jean-Jacques, wrote in 1967: 'It was natural to identify with John Kennedy, who embodied the leading ideas of my generation: America, youth, success, beauty, the future.'[1] However, members of the generation for whom, and about whom, Schrieber wrote were already 40 years old. The leaders who claimed to represent youth during the 1960s were often comparatively old: Mitterrand was born in 1916, Mendès-France in 1907. Even student leaders were usually a few years older than their followers. The two leaders of the students in Algeria – Lagaillarde and Susini – were already in their late 20s. The youngest of the student leaders in 1968, Cohn-Bendit, had been born in 1945; the oldest (Alain Giesmar) had been born in 1939.

The continued power of relatively old men during the 1960s was underwritten by the mythology of the French Resistance. In 1959 Claude Nicolet tried to explain the admiration that he and his contemporaries felt for Pierre Mendès-France in the following terms: 'I have always envied those among my elders who were awakened by the political exaltation of the Resistance ... we are, in short, a generation abandoned by history.'[2] The Resistance mythology had had a limited impact in the immediate aftermath of the war, when most people remembered the complexity and ambiguity of the choices that had been under Vichy. However, in the 1960s two parallel processes made Resistance important once again. On the one hand, the men who had been young Resistance fighters between 1940 and 1944 began to reach positions of influence. On the other hand the generation that had been born in around 1940 began to be influenced by the worldwide current of rebellion that was to lead to the students' protests of 1968. This rebellion was expressed in terms of an admiration for the guerrilla fighters of the Third World and opposition to 'fascism'. However, such rhetoric was difficult to sustain in France when the head of state himself had rallied the country against fascism and when so many of the older generation had been guerrilla fighters in their youth. When the journalist Françoise Giroud interviewed young people for her book on the 'New wave' of youth she was struck by the fact that no event had mobilized this generation in the way that the Spanish Civil War and the Occupation had mobilized hers.[3] Even the Algerian war was greeted with sullen resignation rather than rebellion; only a few hundred young men deserted to join the FLN. The leaders of the opposition to the French presence in Algeria were often Resistance veterans and most French people, on the mainland, saw the Algerian war through the prism of events between 1940 and 1944. The slogans of demonstrating students in 1968 – 'nous sommes tous les juifs allemands' and 'CRS/SS' – reflect the extent to which the young were constrained by images passed down from the Second World War. One student leader, Régis Debray, later explained that he had felt obliged to join South American guerrillas in order to rival the monopoly of anti-fascist Resistance that seemed to belong to an older generation.

A youth culture, involving people of under 21, did begin to emerge in post-war France. At the beginning of this period, young people still expected to leave school at 14 with, at most, a *certificat d'aptitudes primaires*, and to begin work straightaway. Many effectively began work before they officially left school and it was still possible for children of 12 to obtain leave from school to perform agricultural work during the late 1950s. However, the numbers of students who remained in school rose steadily and a law of 1959, effective from 1967, raised the school leaving age to 16. In other western countries the 1950s and 1960s saw the rise of the teenager – a group with fashions, habits and, most of all, music of its own. Teenage culture did make some impact on France. International radio stations, notably Europe 1, brought English and American pop music to France during the early 1960s. In the summer of 1963 a meeting organized by a Europe 1 disc-jockey brought around 150,000 teenagers to the Place de la Nation. A number of French pop stars emerged during this period. The most notable of these was Johnny Hallyday, an exponent of 1950s American rock and roll, whose impact in France is incomprehensible to Anglo-Saxon listeners. A Breton teenager interviewed in 1967 remarked that the two most memorable events of his life were the assassination of Kennedy and the marriage of Johnny Hallyday; in 1991 Johnny Hallyday was the main attraction at the *Fête de l'Humanité* organized by the PCF, where he proved more popular than the Communist leader George Marchais.

However, youth culture made far less of an impact in France than in England or America. Rock music never took hold in France as much as black jazz music had done. When the trumpeter Miles Davis visited Paris in 1949 he became intimately involved with the city, he drank with Jean-Paul Sartre, and had a brief affair with the singer Juliette Greco; his music was used as the score for Louis Malle's film *Ascensceur pour l'Echafaud*. By contrast, when Jim Morrisson, singer with The Doors, visited Paris, he did so as a tourist. He had almost no contact with French people and, when he took a fatal overdose in his hotel bedroom, he was buried at the respectable bourgeois cemetery of Père Lachaise rather than in fashionable Montparnasse.

In England and America, the spread of rock music in the 1960s was linked to a sense that the public discussion of sexual behaviour was becoming freer. In France, by contrast, public discussion of sex became more restrictive during the 1950s and 1960s: the 1960 law on homosexuality, for example, was more draconian than that of Vichy and the Fourth Republic. This shift was reflected in popular culture: the boy meets girl world of Johnny Hallyday and Mirelle Mathieu must have seemed naïve to those brought up on the casual bohemianism of Edith Piaf and Arletty. There were also social restraints on the French young people: most of them were not sufficiently prosperous to live the lives described in the songs of the Beach Boys and they were not sufficiently rebellious to live the lives described in the songs of the Rolling Stones. France remained a nation of small towns and villages. Most young people had no more exciting distraction than the prospect of playing 'baby-foot' at the Café de la Paix or racing their *vélomoteurs* up and down the Boulevard Jean-Jaurès. The 'wildness' of young men described in Lawrence Wylie's *Village in the Vaucluse* in the late 1950s took forms that would have been recognizable to their grandfathers. They danced, drank, and went to a brothel (where they played cards).

Most importantly, French youth remained under the influence of those three great pillars of authority: the family, the school and the army. Most young people lived at home throughout their years of study at school or university, and many did not leave the parental home until they married. Furthermore, French parents, and grand-parents, never relinquished authority over the younger members of their family to the same extent that their Anglo-Saxon counterparts did: one young blood from the *Camelots du Roi* had missed the events of 6 February 1934 because his mother had ordered him home to have dinner with the family. Schools were also disciplined institutions where teachers enforced an order that was laid down in the ministry of education: an ordinance of 1921 even regulated the games that could be played in school playgrounds. Most importantly, military service continued to overshadow the lives of every young man in France. Every Frenchman was obliged to join the armed forces at the age of 21. Until the end of the Algerian war, many spent up to two years in uniform. Military service was still the forma-tive experience of many men's lives. It brought them into contact with people from other areas of France and it gave them experience of travel – if only to the grim tedium of Metz or the danger and dis-comfort of Algeria. The knowledge that military service was on the horizon meant that the teenage years had always been seen as an interlude for high jinks. Parents could rest secure in the knowledge that wild *blousons noirs* would be knocked into shape by the drill sergeants. Men returning from military service generally accepted the disciplines of marriage and regular work.

The most striking development in post-war France was not the cre-ation of a youth culture but that of the culture of what the French came to call the 'Third Age'. Life expectancy increased during this period. In 1946 there were 4,355,000 people in France aged over 65, by 1975 this figure had risen to 7,499,000. More importantly, the manner in which old people lived changed. In 1946, 66 per cent of men and 31 per cent of women aged between 65 and 69 still worked; by 1975 these figures had dropped to 19 and 10 per cent. In the past, old age had meant dependence on others: the old had lived with their children. Sometimes this had been a grim experience. Many old people had to suffer the thinly disguised resentment of their children or the utterly undisguised hostility of their in-laws. However, the sharing of houses among three generations had also helped to contribute to the unique flavour of French society, espe-cially rural society. It had provided a means by which folklore and tradition could be transmitted and Braudel suggests that French peasant conservatism was partly due to the fact that grandparents looked after children while parents worked in the fields. In cities the bourgeoisie often kept their parents, especially mothers, in the family house. In the countryside cohabitation among all classes remained common: nine out sixteen of those over 65 in one Breton village in 1967 lived with their children. However, urbanization, which for most people meant living in relatively small flats, and increasing desire for private space contributed to the rise of the nuclear family. By 1969 the proportion of old people living with relatives had dropped to about 24 per cent; Simone de Beauvoir estimated that two thirds of those over 65 received no help at all from their children.

Standards of living among the old were sharply divided after 1945. The Vichy government had introduced old age pensions, and the full pension was 40 per cent of the final salary for those who had paid social security contributions for 30 years. In practice many people, or their employers, had not paid adequate contributions. It was estimated that 1 million old people in 1969 lived on an income that was just sufficient for subsistence. The oldest resident of the Vaucluse village studied by Lawrence Wylie had not paid for his bread or his round of drinks for two years. Alongside this poverty-stricken group stood another group who enjoyed good pensions. This was partly because of the expansion during the Third Republic of public services – such as the Post Office and the railways – that provided pensions. Soldiers and policemen who had seen active service were allowed to retire early: a non-commissioned officer who had been imprisoned in Germany and then served in Indo-China and Algeria might expect to draw his pension at the age of 42. Retirement arrangements for workers, the self-employed and farmers were far less generous (though the government introduced a scheme for early retirement of farmers in order to help consolidate land). In some respects the existence of large numbers of relatively young and prosperous pensioners counteracted other changes. Often the retired moved from the city to the countryside while the young moved from country to city. Sometimes the old took to agricultural and artisanal activities as a hobby and a means of earning a little extra income, a trait that was encouraged by the fact that French pensions did not penalize people for having supplementary incomes. However, the flood of pensioners from city to countryside was not accompanied by a transformation from Frenchmen to peasants. The new arrivals retained many of the habits of the city. Their behaviour may have helped to transform the culture of the countryside. In 1956 Jean Pataut remarked that parts of the Nièvre countryside had been transformed into 'virtual suburbs' by the influx of retired people. In Brittany there was a stark contrast between retired people from the town and the peasants aged between 50 and 65. Those from the towns were relatively prosperous and led relaxed lives; the peasantry were still obliged to work but felt increasingly displaced by new methods and new leadership of the agricultural associations.

Even the comparatively prosperous pensioners were not rich; in 1964 77 per cent of retired managers claimed that their pensions were 'just adequate', and they were reluctant to indulge in the kind of ostentatious consumption that sometimes characterized the young working population. In 1963 only 29 per cent of those aged 65 to 70 went away from home on holiday while 49 per cent of those aged 25–39 did so. The pensioners would have fitted-in well with the France of rentiers that had existed until the inflation of the 1914–18 war. A persistent element of French economic culture was the desire to obtain a secure, if modest, income and do nothing. Interest in retirement showed that this desire survived even in the climate of economic expansion. When the baker of the village studied by Lawrence Wylie retired and sold his shop he did not ask for a lump sum but for a guaranteed income of 2000 francs per year to be paid for the rest of his life.

11 Class Struggle

The Communist activist 'Colonel Fabien' initiated violent Resistance against the German Occupation in August 1941 when he shot a German officer in Barbès-Rochechouart metro station. Now there is another metro station named after 'Colonel Fabien' himself. Anyone who travels the short distance between these two points will cross Belleville and Montmartre, two quarters that are intimately associated with the history and struggles of the French working class. The journey goes through stations named after Stalingrad and Jean Jaurès. Zola's Nana was born in the Goutte d'Or just by Barbès-Rochechouart. The film *Hotel du Nord*, a brilliant evocation of working-class life in the 1930s, is set on the Canal Saint Martin, which runs parallel to the metro line. The *communards* fought their last battle close to the Place Colonel Fabien, which is now the headquarters of the *Parti Communiste Français*. However, members of the working class, whose history is so associated with this area, are less and less likely to live in it. The tenement blocks around Colonel Fabien are being redeveloped to accommodate ambitious professionals and few workers can afford to live here now. These changes owe something to the ambition of Jacques Chirac, the Gaullist mayor, to transform Paris into an exclusively bourgeois city, but they also reflect longer term changes. Ever since the early twentieth century, industry has been moving out of the capital city into the grim *banlieues* on its outskirts, and since 1960 it has also moved into rural areas.

All this raises an interesting paradox. On the one hand French workers have generated a powerful mythology. They have been seen, both by their admirers and by those who feared them, as a self-conscious class which was associated with an impressive tradition of protest and radicalism. The French Communist party, which was seen to be the representative of this class, established a heroic record of Resistance to Nazi Germany and thereafter attracted a large share of the vote in elections until the 1970s. On the other hand the French working class has gained a smaller share of the national wealth than that achieved by its less radical counterparts in Great Britain or West Germany and since the early 1960s it has seemed increasingly likely that the culture of the French working class, which is so well commemorated in the nomenclature of the Paris metro, will cease to have much impact in any other sphere of French life.

To understand this process it is necessary to go back to the decade after the Liberation. It was then that the working class was most prominent in French public life. In part this was a question of numbers. France was more industrialized than ever before and in 1954 the proportion of workers in the industrial population as a whole peaked at 87.2 per cent. French post-war industrial reconstruction concentrated on large-scale enterprises (particularly metallurgy and coal mining) which employed numerous workers (as opposed to managers and technicians).

French workers also achieved very high levels of class consciousness during this period. This consciousness was increased by industrial concentration: large plants encouraged workers to think of their interests in collective terms and facilitated union organization. Class consciousness was also linked to the fact that the proportion of skilled workers in the labour force as a whole increased to reach a historical peak of 46 per cent in 1954. In the 1930s only 168,000 workers had obtained a certificate of vocational skill; in the 1950s a million did so. Skilled workers tended to identify more closely with their work and hence with their class. This tendency was underwritten by the limited opportunities that those at the top of the working class, or their children, had to rise through through education: 85 per cent of the children of workers left school when they were 15 or younger. Those who had little chance to rise as individuals were likely to direct their energy to collective action.

In earlier periods, class consciousness had been undermined by the instability of industrial employment and by ethnic or gender differences among workers. In the 1940s and 1950s working-class employment became much more stable. This was partly because the legacy of the great depression and the Second World War had impeded technological innovation for some time. Annual turnover of workers in individual factories often dropped below 10 per cent in this period. A survey of 1969 showed that one third of workers aged between 35 and 49 had been employed by the same firm for more than 15 years; in the 1970s, 40 per cent of Renault workers had been with the company for more than 20 years. The working class also became homogeneous during this period. In spite of severe labour shortage, the proportion of workers who were women dropped from

36 to 31 per cent between 1931 and 1954 while the number of foreign-born workers dropped from 3 million to 1.7 million during the same period. Workers who were male and French, or at least established in France, were most likely to define themselves as members of the working class and most likely to take collective action to defend their position.

The image of the working class also changed in the 1940s. The First World War had been seen as a vindication of peasant France and an indictment of a defeatist and revolutionary proletariat. By contrast, the Second World War was seen as a working-class war. Desire to avoid *Service du Travail Obligatoire* ensured that many *maquisards* were young workers and Resistance networks had often worked closely with trade unions. Threequarters of the members of the main Resistance organizations in Valenciennes had been workers and over half of them had been metal workers. Interest in the working class reached a new peak during this period. Abbé Godin described working-class areas as the church's new 'missionary lands' and some 'worker priests' tried to combine their religious duties with work in factories. Bourgeois parties like the *Mouvement Républicain Populaire* and the *Rassemblement du Peuple Français* made vigorous – though not very successful – efforts to recruit working-class members.

The new prominence of the working class was accompanied by a new prominence for the *Parti Communiste Français*. Before the war the PCF had been the junior partner of the left and was consistently outstripped by the SFIO. After 1945 these positions were reversed. The PCF vote peaked, at 28.3 per cent of the electorate, in November 1946, by which stage it was the most popular party in France. After this date the Communist vote declined but it remained the main party of the left until the late 1970s, and it continued to gain votes at the expense of the SFIO until 1956 (see table 1). The same kind of increase could be seen in municipal elections: the party had 2000 mayors in 1946, compared to 297 in 1935. Most of all the party's membership increased in the immediate aftermath of the Second World War. In September 1938 there had been been 320,000 party members; by December 1947 907,785 party cards had been issued.

The Communist party was traditionally an *ouvrièriste* party: most of its voters, members, activists came from the working class. More unusual, both in the context of other French parties and of other European Communist parties, was the fact that most PCF leaders

Table 1 PCF and SFIO Votes in Legislative Elections (%)

	PCF	SFIO
1945	26.2	23.4
1946 (June)	26.0	21.1
1946 (November)	28.3	17.9
1951	26.9	14.6
1956	25.9	15.2
1958	19.2	15.7
1962	21.8	12.5
1967	22.5	18.9
1968	20.0	16.5

Source: R.W. Johnson, *The Long March of the French Left* (London: Macmillan, 1981), p. 137.

were of working-class origin. The party was proud of its intellectual recruits but it rarely gave them much power: in the 1960s even the head of the PCF school for *cadres* was an ex-steel worker. The PCF's links with the working class were strengthened by its preference for organization around cells based in the factories rather than in neighbourhoods – a preference that had been reinforced by the needs of clandestine action.

The Communist success in the early Fourth Republic gained it support outside the working class. It increased its membership dramatically in rural areas where the *maquis* had been successful. In Corrèze between 1937 and 1945 the number of PCF members increased from 2640 to 8152; in the Hautes-Alpes it increased from 250 to 2000. The party now had a genuinely national appeal and there were only three departments in France where it obtained less than 10 per cent of the vote in November 1946. In some respects this widening of the party's appeal was accompanied by a dilution of its working-class character: in 1946 there were only 8000 party cells in workplaces while there were 28,000 based on neighbourhoods.

The PCF's flirtation with groups outside the working class was brief. When the party's support dropped off from its 1946 peak, it lost members and supporters most rapidly in the non-industrial regions. By 1956 the PCF was firmly established again as the main working-class party: over 50 per cent of the PCF vote was working class while only 15 per cent of the SFIO vote came from this class. Furthermore, the party's relations with the working class in the non-electoral sphere were now tighter than ever. This was particularly visible in the trade unions. In 1945 the *Confédération Générale du Travail* (CGT) was still dominated by Socialists. However, the SFIO's links with industrial workers were weakened by the embour-geoisification of a party that was increasingly dominated by school-teachers and civil servants. In 1945 only 13 per cent of members of SFIO federal committees came from the working class while one third of them were civil servants; in the elections of October of that year only 21 of the SFIO candidates were industrial workers.

The Communist party exploited the weakness of its rival, its own Resistance prestige and the possibilities opened by purges of Pétainists. The bureau of the CGT was enlarged from eight to thir-teen members in September 1945; this change also increased the number of Communists from three to five and their influence was enhanced by the death of one of the non-Communist members and the sympathy of two others. Benoit Frachon, who became secretary of the CGT, was a loyal Communist and in 1956 the links between union and party were made explicit when he joined the bureau of the PCF. The domination of the PCF over the CGT was made even clearer in 1967 when Georges Séguy, a classic party hack, succeeded Benoit Frachon. Séguy was the son of a Communist, he had been a full-time trade union official since the age of 24, had served as a member of the party central committee since 1954, and seems to have owed his rise to party support rather than to any exceptional abilities. One Communist historian described him as a 'tranquil functionary operating in a family-type political party in which he spent his childhood and adolescence'.[1]

The working class was large, well-organized and class-conscious after the Second World War, but it did not prove good at defending its material interests. In 1952 real wages were 36 per cent lower than they had been in 1936. Later workers did begin to draw some benefits from the general prosperity of France, but they drew smaller benefits than any other group. The gulf between rich and poor increased con-siderably during the 'thirty glorious years' of post-war expansion. The ratio of the wealth of the poorest 10 per cent of French people to that of the richest 10 per cent had been 1 to 15.6 in 1949; by 1975 it was 1 to 28.3. The taxation system, which laid a heavy emphasis on sales tax, did little to redistribute wealth: the Americans threatened to suspend a proportion of Marshall Aid in 1949 as part of an, unsuccessful, attempt to make the French adopt a more equitable taxation policy. In 1962 only 6 per cent of overall household income went in income tax. The expansion of the state, which often worked to the advantage of workers in other European countries, tended to benefit more wealthy groups in France. Government-subsidized low cost housing (*habitations à loyer modéré* or HLMs) provides a good example of this. The distribution of such housing lay in the hands of committees which often favoured the bourgeoisie and a proportion of all HLMs were reserved for doctors and dentists. In 1970 the proportion of poor people living in housing of this kind was three times smaller than their proportion in the population as a whole.

The failure of the French working class can be explained in several terms. Firstly, it was a product of the fact that even in the 1950s the French proletariat remained small, by comparison with that of Britain or Germany. Workers could never hope to comprise an overall majority of the electorate, and they remained excluded from power by parties that drew their votes from the bourgeoisie and peasants. Political isolation often led the working classes to adopt an aggressive stance that then exacerbated this isolation.

Secondly, the distribution of the fruits of economic expansion is explained by the fact that the upper bourgeoisie proved so adept at dealing with the state. Members of this group had often been formed by their association with elite parts of the civil service (the *grands corps* and *grandes écoles*). The foundation of the *École Nationale d'Administration* in 1945 illustrated the survival of their power. The convergence of the state and large private sector companies was reflected in a similarity of attitudes between managers and civil servants during the Fourth Republic. During the Fifth Republic the state–large-scale business axis also came to take in a large part of the political elite. *Pantouflage*, the transfer of civil servants to highly paid business jobs, illustrated the closeness of relations between the spheres. The effects of all this could be seen most clearly in nationalized companies. In Britain nationalization was associated with an increase in the power and prosperity of the unionized working class. In France it was associated with a growth in the power and prosperity of the civil service–management elite: until recently the head of the French state oil company was required by law to have been a member of the inspectorate of finances. The elite managers who dominated French nationalized industries also tended to use such industries to pursue macroeconomic goals rather than to provide social benefits for their workers.

Thirdly, the power of the French Communist party often worked against the material interests of the working class. The party subordinated demands for higher wages, better conditions and shorter hours to its broad strategy, which in turn was often closely related to the interests of the Soviet Union. When in government the PCF refused to press for improvement in working-class living standards; when it was out of government its intransigent support for the Soviet Union helped to ensure that any demands that it did make would receive little sympathy from those in power. During the period of the provisional and tripartite governments, Communists held important posts – armament and industrial production – which might have been used to affect the lives of the working class. However, the party believed that it was the duty of the working class to increase productivity in order to help defeat Nazi Germany, thereby aiding Soviet Russia. Even after allied victory, Communist ministers continued to push for rapid industrial reconstruction and to denounce the 'economism' of trade union demands. At a private meeting in the northern coal fields, Maurice Thorez complained that the miners had 'still not understood the enormous responsibility that rests on their shoulders'.

The Communist party was also reluctant to support measures designed to ameliorate working-class conditions within the capitalist system: party ministers did much to prevent their Socialist colleagues from using nationalized industries as instruments of social justice. The departure of Communist ministers from government in 1947 liberated them from the constraints of ministerial responsibility and the party did then begin to support strikes and union pressure for pay increases. However, the party's preoccupation with the international divisions of the Cold War blunted its impact on social conditions within France. Communists liked to define their electorate as 'the 25 per cent against the American party', but most Frenchmen clearly regarded themselves as part of the '75 per cent against the Soviet party'. Hostility to communism was so great that by the early 1970s a survey showed that most children in France already disliked the leader of the PCF by the time that they were eight years old. The perception that the Communist party was merely a representative of the Soviet Union made it easier for employers to disregard and marginalize a Communist-dominated trade union movement. Cold War divisions also weakened the trade unions after the American-backed *Force Ouvrière* group broke away from the Communist-controlled CGT in 1948.

The decline in the intensity of the Cold War in France might have seemed to offer the Communist party some opportunity to reintegrate itself into national life. To some extent the party took advantage of this. It attempted to develop better relations with the Socialists and the left in general. Its short-term aim was always to create a united party of the left though the knowledge that its long-term aim was to dominate this party always limited the enthusiasm that Socialists showed for such an alliance.

However, the PCF, and the working-class movement as a whole, began to run into new problems. The stabilization of French politics after 1958 made it increasingly hard to see what the PCF could achieve. There was no foreseeable possibility of proletarian revolution: indeed, between 1958 and 1962, the PCF's leaders were obliged to present themselves as defenders of the republic against the threat of revolution from the right. In theory the party hoped that the unity of the left would bring it closer to power, but in practice direct elections for the presidency benefited those parts of the left that were best placed to gain centre votes, i.e. the non-Communist part. The PCF tacitly accepted this when it backed François Mitterrand in the second round of the 1965 presidential election. The PCF did, of course, exercise considerable power in certain spheres. It still dominated the main trade union confederation and it controlled local government in many areas – in 1966 about 20,000 majors were Communists. However, the very willingness of PCF members to fulfil such functions in a capitalist society sometimes seemed to mark an acceptance that they could only hope to serve as what Georges Lavau called a 'tribune party' within a system they could not overthrow.

The party also found it hard to devise an appropriate strategy to counter Gaullism. De Gaulle presided over a country in which capitalism, especially large-scale capitalism, did well and some of his entourage were closely linked to such capitalism, but standard terms of abuse – fascist, imperialist, American lackey – seemed inappropriate to the general. Henri Claude's book *Gaullisme et grand capital* illustrates some of the difficulties that party theorists had in explaining Gaullism.[2] Claude argued that big business looked to de Gaulle to preserve the empire: the book was published just before French withdrawal from Algeria. Other party theorists argued about whether Gaullism represented a particular strand of 'national' capitalism and whether the resignation of Antoine Pinay as finance minister, in 1960, should be seen as defection by capitalism in general from the regime or just an expression of discontent by small business. More

seriously, a section of the Communist electorate found elements in
Gaullism attractive, or at least preferable to the alternative. About
20 per cent of those who voted Communist in local or municipal
elections supported de Gaulle in presidential elections; about the
same number again supported de Gaulle in referenda.

The Communist party, and the labour movement generally, also
had difficulty adapting to economic changes during the 1960s. The
proportion of workers among all wage-earners dropped from 61 to
47.7 per cent between 1954 and 1975. The heavy industries that had
been associated with the employment of large numbers of skilled
workers began to decline. They were replaced either by highly sophisticated new industries (aeronautics and computers) that required
technicians rather than workers or by the manufacture of consumer
goods which needed an unskilled workforce. Technological change
was also associated with a move away from the old centres of French
industry. Often employers perceived such moves as a chance to break
the traditions of organization and protest that were associated with
certain regions. They were particularly prone to move to the west, a
traditionally right-wing and agricultural region where there was a
plentiful supply of labour and little history of union organization:
between 1962 and 1966, 37 per cent of new industrial jobs were
created in the west of France. By 1970, less than half of the 80,000
workers employed by Renault worked at the Boulogne Bilancourt
plant, which had been at the centre of the strikes of 1936 and 1947;
20 years later Boulogne Bilancourt had almost ceased production.

The homogenization of the French working class that had
occurred between 1945 and 1954 was reversed during the 1960s. The
proportion of women in the workforce increased from 33.4 to 38.7
per cent between 1962 and 1975. The number of immigrants in the
workforce rose from 1.7 million in 1954 to 4.1 million in 1975. All
these changes made it hard for a labour movement which had built
its organization around skilled male workers who were well established in traditional industries. Immigration posed particular problems. Immigrants in earlier periods had come largely from other
European countries and often from countries, such as Italy and
Spain, that had strong Communist traditions which had facilitated
their assimilation into the French working class. The immigrants of
the 1960s were often from Algeria and black Africa. Such immigrants
felt separate and vulnerable, their long-term ambitions often
remained focused on their country of origin and they rarely had previous experience of industrial work. The French labour movement

made little headway with such groups, French workers were often hostile to them and sometimes the Communist party itself began to flirt with racism.

The perceived strength of the industrial working class and the Communist party in the years immediately after the Second World War turned out to be a dangerous illusion. Even at their peak, the working classes never made up a majority of the French electorate and for this reason they could only hope to further their interests through alliances with other social groups. However, the Communist party, which became the principal representative of the working class, pursued a policy that was bound to exacerbate the isolation of those that it claimed to speak for. Furthermore, the fact that the labour movement structured itself to represent the homogeneous skilled, well-established heavy industrial working class of 1954 meant that it was badly adapted to deal with the changes brought about by technological change, industrial decentralization, deskilling, feminization and immigration during the following two decades.

12   Algeria

The Algerian war began on 1 November 1954 with attacks by Algerian nationalists on French citizens. The nationalists, grouped by the *Front de Libération Nationale* (FLN), wished to end the French rule of their country which had begun in 1830. Part of the French response to these events consisted of a rather half-hearted programme of reforms that were instituted in January 1955. The other part of the French response was repression. The French minister of the interior, François Mitterrand, ordered firm action against the rebels. In 1955 a state of emergency was instituted, reservists were called up and the general elections, scheduled for January 1956, were cancelled in Algeria. An FLN massacre of Europeans around Philippeville was followed by savage reprisals. In 1956, special powers were voted for Algeria. In September of that year, the FLN switched its attention from the countryside and launched what became known as 'the battle of Algiers' by bombing civilian targets in the city. At the beginning of 1957, colonel Massu, a hero of the Second World War, began to restore order in Algiers. He broke a general strike in February 1957, obtained information about the FLN with the aid of torture, and captured the main leader of rebellion in September. The FLN retreated once again to the countryside and the mountains, but in September 1957 the 'Morice Line' of barbed wire designed to cut off the FLN from their bases in Tunisia was completed.

The French campaign against the FLN continued after the fall of the Fourth Republic. General Challe replaced general Salan as commander-in-chief in Algeria in December 1958. Challe achieved much with a policy of *quadrillage* designed to divide up the country and isolate FLN units, but in April 1960 he too was removed from Algeria. Challe was removed because his loyalty to government policy was doubted, and because it was becoming increasingly obvious that the government intended to negotiate with the FLN and to agree to French withdrawal. Peace talks with the FLN were initiated at Melun in June 1960 and continued at Evian in May and June of 1961. Both these talks failed, but in March 1962 another round of talks at Evian achieved results and a ceasefire between

French forces and the FLN was declared on 19 March 1962. The French had lost a total of 17,456 soldiers during the war.

The struggle between French and nationalists was accompanied by two parallel struggles. The first, and most bloody, of these was that which took place as the FLN asserted its authority over other groups within Muslim society. 'Collaborators' and informers were killed; FLN agents collected money across Algeria and among Algerian immigrants in mainland France. Some commentators believe that total Muslim casualties ran into millions. The number of Algerian Muslims killed in mainland France alone had reached 3889 by January 1962.

The second struggle, and the one that concerns us here, took place among the French. It pitted those who wished to maintain *Algérie Française* against those who wanted to secure French withdrawal. The most extreme elements of both sides resorted to violence. The network led by Francis Jeanson acted as *porteurs de valise* transporting information and money on behalf of the FLN. On the other side, in January 1957 right-wingers attacked the office of general Salan whom, oddly in view of later events, they regarded as insufficiently committed to the defence of *Algérie Française*. Finally, when it became clear that French Algeria was to be abandoned, the *Organisation de l'Armée Secrète* (OAS) launched savage attacks designed to prevent, or avenge, what they saw as a betrayal. Conflicts between the OAS and the various French forces of order caused 563 deaths in February 1962 alone.

Algeria caused such divisions among the French for several reasons. The first of these was that Algeria, unlike Indo-China or the colonies of black Africa, contained a large population of European origin. There were 1 million European settlers, or *pieds noirs*, in Algeria. The *pieds noirs* were not a naturally right-wing group, some of them being descended from men who had been deported from France for involvement in revolutionary activities during the nineteenth century, and four out of ten deputies returned by Algerians in 1936 had been supporters of the Popular Front. However, the European population of Algeria had often come to seem right-wing for two reasons. Firstly, some of those who had Spanish origins had sympathized with Franco during the Spanish Civil War. Secondly, Algeria had been an area of Pétainist enthusiasm during the Second World War. As has been stressed above, Pétainism did not mean the same in Algeria and the mainland. The *pieds noirs* had never endured German occupation and they associated the Vichy period with Weygand's preparation for military revenge rather than with submission to the Germans. Furthermore, the nature of Algeria's liberation meant that the break between Gaullism and Pétainism seemed less intense there than in metropolitan France. The legacy of the Occupation created misunderstandings between Algeria and the mainland between 1954 and 1962. Military occupation, torture, the presence of German troops in the Foreign Legion and adoption of 'National Socialist' rhetoric by some defenders of *Algérie Française* all evoked painful memories among metropolitan Frenchmen and encouraged some former Resistance leaders to call for French withdrawal from Algeria. Memories of the occupation meant much less in Algeria.

Survival, or the survival of their way of life, dominated the minds of most Europeans in Algeria after 1954. Most of the *pieds noirs* had been born in Algeria, many of them had never seen mainland France, indeed some were descended from Italian, Spanish and Maltese immigrants. The majority of *pieds noirs* lived in cities (only 32,000 earned their living from agriculture), and most of them worked in comparatively humble jobs: 190,000 *pieds noirs* had clerical jobs, 92,000 were government employees, 90,000 were manual workers, 60,000 were shopkeepers and only 56,000 belonged to the managerial class. Life in Algeria could be agreeable for these people. They benefited from the low cost of living, the cheapness of servants and their access to beaches, sun and a distinctive Mediterranean rhythm of life captured in some of the writings of Camus (though few *pieds noirs* read Camus). These people had everything to lose if they were obliged to leave Algeria.

Traditionally, the *pieds noirs* electorate had been manipulated by a small number of wealthy wire-pullers – such as Alain de Sérigny or Lucien Bourgeaud – who controlled newspapers and party funds. During the late 1950s a new group of more demagogic leaders arose to represent the fear that was sweeping Algiers and Oran. Particularly important were Robert Martel, Jo Ortiz, Bernard Lefevre, Pierre Lagaillarde, Joseph Perez and Jean-Jacques Susini. Corruption, violence and excitable crowds, easy to bring together in the densely populated European quarters, provided them with the means by which they mobilized supporters. They made a particular appeal to groups that were already organized – students (Susini and Lagaillarde were both rather aged students), *anciens combattants*, and Poujadist commerçants (Susini, Lefevre and Ortiz had all been Poujadists and the movement claimed to have 15,000 European supporters in Algeria). Early in the Algerian war Martel founded the *Union des Français Nord-Africain*, and in November 1958 Perez founded the *Front National Français*, a paramilitary organization which began to stockpile arms. The *pieds noirs* intervened in politics directly on several occasions. On 6 February 1956 they confronted Mollet when he visited Algiers and shocked him into accepting the need to defend *Algérie Française* more vigorously. In 1958 they participated in the events that brought about the fall of the Fourth Republic, in 1960 groups, led by Lagaillarde and Ortiz, established barricades in Algiers and attempted to repeat the events of May 1958. De Gaulle faced out the protesters. However, 'barricades week' was important in two respects. Firstly, *pieds noirs* fired on French riot policemen for the first time, killing around 24 of them. Secondly, it was seen how reluctant sections of the French army, particularly the parachute regiments, were to act against the settlers.

Public opinion polls showed that the majority of the population of mainland France did not feel strongly committed to any position over Algeria, but large parts of the political elite were very engaged by the Algerian question. The politician whose views mattered most, Charles de Gaulle, was also the one whose views were least known. His public statements often seemed open to more than one interpretation. The general's withdrawal from public life in 1954 meant that, unlike almost every other French politician, he had not committed himself to any particular policy with regard to Algeria. He visited Algeria soon after his return to power in January 1958 and he greeted the Algiers crowd with the words '*Je vous ai compris*'. This was widely taken to mean that he sympathized with the continuation of the French presence – though he only used the words '*vive l'Algérie Française*' in one unguarded moment. On 23 October 1958 de Gaulle proposed a 'peace of the brave' to the FLN, but his offer elicited no response. In 1959 de Gaulle began to use the phrase 'auto-determination' – ambiguous words and ones that worried the most vigorous supporters of *Algérie Française*. In March 1960 de Gaulle visited officers in Algeria and talked in similar terms again. Finally in November 1961 de Gaulle talked of '*Algérie Algérienne*', a phrase that made clear his willingness to leave Algeria. De Gaulle's private actions and words are equally difficult to interpret. In 1959, he told Challe that his first duty was to win the military struggle against the FLN. In June 1960 the French were contacted by an FLN leader, Si Salah, who wished to discuss the possibility of making peace in the area of Algeria where the FLN was under his command. Not only did de Gaulle respond to Si Salah's initiative but, in one of the oddest episodes of his career, the general arranged for Si Salah and two of his colleagues to make a secret visit to the Elysée Palace. The negotiations came to nothing and Si Salah was subsequently killed by French soldiers.

De Gaulle himself claimed in his memoirs that the general lines of his policy were mapped out in his mind from the moment that he took power. This view was shared by de Gaulle's bitter enemies on the extreme right who believed that the general had conspired to bring down the French Empire. However, de Gaulle's associates and particularly his crucial aide on Algerian matters – Bernard Tricot – believed that things were less clear. Tricot suggested that de Gaulle had initially planned to maintain *Algérie Française* and that he had groped his way slowly and reluctantly to the solution that was eventually adopted. Two things are clear. Firstly, de Gaulle's celebrated 'certain idea of France' was always rather abstract. He did not have the intense attachment to specific regions that marked many leaders of the French right. He was ruthlessly unsentimental: when he was told that the inhabitants of Algeria were suffering, he replied 'well you will suffer then'. Secondly, de Gaulle always subordinated Algeria to the interests of metropolitan France. His greatest interest was aroused by the prospect that Algeria might provide France with material benefits, in the form of oil, and his decision to withdraw from Algeria was motivated by the belief that the war was costing France too much and impeding economic and military modernization.

Whatever de Gaulle's real intentions were, many of those who facilitated his return and the destruction of the Fourth Republic believed that de Gaulle would preserve *Algérie Française*. These people deeply resented what they believed to be de Gaulle's subsequent betrayal. Slowly men who had supported de Gaulle in 1958 turned against him. Dides, Jean-Marie le Pen and Tixier-Vignancour, all members of the extreme right who had been rather reluctant supporters of de Gaulle in the first place, condemned his speech on self-determination in September 1959. Jacques Soustelle was expelled from the Gaullist UNR on 25 April 1961. Some leaders of the pro-*Algérie-Française* group – such as general Juin, or the historian Raoul Girardet – did not denounce de Gaulle until after the referendum on Algerian independence in April 1962. Some supporters of *Algérie Française*, such as his prime minister Debré, remained loyal to the general in spite of the pain that his actions caused them.

Other French politicians took clearer stands on Algeria than de Gaulle. Initially the left did not oppose the French presence in Algeria. The Communist party did not regard Algeria as a major issue while Mendès-France, Mitterrand and Mollet all insisted that France should remain in Algeria. However, the measures taken by the French against the FLN began to generate opposition. In 1958 Henri Alleg, a Frenchman who had edited the Communist paper *L'Alger Républicain,* published *La Question* in which he detailed the torture to which he had been subjected by Massu's paras. Alleg's book became a clandestine bestseller, and other writers and witnesses soon produced evidence of French atrocities in Algeria. Opposition chrystallized around a newspaper, *Le Monde,* and three weekly journals, *Témoignage Chrétien, L'Express* and *France Observateur,* publications that Soustelle described as 'the big names in anti-French propaganda'. Two groups were particularly touched by the controversy. The first of these was made up of Resistance veterans, many of whom accused the French authorities of imitating the Gestapo. When Claude Bourdet was arrested in 1956 he told his interrogators that he had previously been taken to Fresnes prison 'by your predecessors'. In March 1957 Paul Teitgen resigned as secretary of the prefecture of police in Algiers and wrote that he had seen things 'that reminded me of the tortures that I suffered personally in the Gestapo cellars in Nancy'. The following month, Philippe Viannay sent back his Resistance decorations to the president of the Republic. A section of Catholic opinion, which had been moving to the left during the 1950s, was also particularly affected by the stories of French atrocities in Algeria.

The Algerian war came at a time when the left was already in turmoil. The Communist party had been discredited in the eyes of some intellectual sympathizers, such as Sartre, by the Soviet invasion of Hungary. The SFIO was discredited by its participation in conventional party politics and Mollet's support for colonialism added to this discredit. Opposition to French policy in Algeria provided a convenient rallying point for the left. On the one hand it allowed intellectuals like Sartre to move away from communism, without examining their relations to the Soviet Union and the Communist party. On the other hand it allowed bourgeois Resistance leaders like Viannay and Bourdet to move away from anti-communism without examining their own relations with the French class structure. Many of the people involved in these political realignments belonged to the self-enclosed world of Parisian intellectual life, but there were also changes in the structure of parties on the left: in April 1960 the *Parti Socialiste Unifié* (PSU) was formed to group left-wingers who did not feel happy in the established parties of the left.

On the other side of the political spectrum, Georges Bidault joined Tixier-Vignancour, from the extreme right, and Roger Duchet, from the Independents, to form the *Rassemblement pour l'Algérie Française*. The Algerian issue split parties of the right. Bidault effectively left the MRP in 1958; in the Independent grouping, Duchet quarrelled with his colleague André Mutter. The issue also cut across the old Vichy–Resistance split. Pétainists, such as Tixier-Vignancour and Duchet, were allied with Resistance leaders, such as Bidault and Soustelle, while former members of Pétain's *conseil national* such as Temple and Pinay accepted French withdrawal from Algeria. Ultimately Bidault and Soustelle broke away from legal politics and developed links with the terrorist OAS. They did so for a wide range of reasons. On one hand was Jacques Soustelle who believed that the solution to the Algerian problem was integration. He wanted Algerian structures of local government to be brought into the French system and full citizenship to be granted, eventually, to the whole Muslim population. At the other end of the spectrum were neo-fascists who did not believe in racial integration. Some, like Maurice Bardèche, did not even believe in *Algérie Française* but were willing to support the *Algérie Française* lobby because they saw it as an ally in their struggle against first the Fourth Republic and then de Gaulle.

The Algerian war spilled out of the realm of formal politics to divide almost every institution of bourgeois France. The *Fédération des Etudiants Nationalistes*, representing those in favour of *Algérie Française*, broke away from the *Union Nationale des Etudiants de France*, which was seen to be hostile to the French presence in Algeria, in 1960. The president of the Rennes Chamber of Commerce severed his associations with the city's university in protest at student hostility to military service. The French church was divided. On the one hand were those gathered around the journals *Témoignage Chrétien*, *Esprit* and *Bulletin*, who opposed French methods in Algeria. On the other hand, were a group of Catholics, gathered around organizations like *Cité Catholique* and reviews like *Verbe*, who regarded the Algerian war as a holy crusade to save Christian civilization from communism and Islam. Religious splits looked back to those of the Occupation, the church being one of the rare areas where divisions over Algeria almost exactly matched those over Vichy. They also anticipated the conflicts over Vatican II that would affect the church during the 1960s. Even the French boy scouts were influenced by the Algerian war – a group of scout leaders resigned in 1957 in protest against the censorship of references to torture from scout publications.

Some saw the debate over Algeria in metropolitan France as rooted in economic change. In 1956 Robert Cartier wrote an article in which he suggested that Empire was too costly a burden for a modern economy.[1] 'Cartierism' received little immediate and explicit support, but some alleged that a section of large-scale business in France no longer needed imperial markets and would have welcomed the diminished taxes that would come with withdrawal from Algeria. Often such views fitted in with an anti-semitic attack on *finance apatride* – a trait exemplified in Emmanuel de Beau de Loménie's book *L'Algérie trahie par l'argent*. There probably was an element of truth in the suggestion that large firms which sold sophisticated capital goods were primarily interested in selling to advanced economies – especially those of Europe – while those selling low technology products, such as textiles, benefited from a protected imperial market. However, it is not obvious that all the 'backward elements' of the French economy had an interest in defending *Algérie Française*. It is true that some – such as Pierre Poujade and Pierre Nicolle – who claimed to be spokesmen for small business were defenders of *Algérie Française*. However, there is little evidence that Nicolle ever represented anyone while Poujade's stance was partly a personal one, since his wife was a *pied noir*. In fact many small businessmen had every reason to oppose the Algerian war. The tax burden fell heavily on small shopkeepers while certain groups, such as winegrowers, suffered direct competition from Algerian production. Robert Bichet, a shrewd observer of politics in the Mayenne, suggested that most of those who voted Poujadist in 1956 opposed the Algerian war.

The most important group to oppose French withdrawal from Algeria was the army. Military activity, or the threat of it, was the key to the fall of the Fourth Republic in 1958, and the generals' putsch of 1961 seemed the most dangerous threat to the Fifth Republic. The motives of army officers did not always coincide with those of the rest of the *Algérie Française* lobby. Indeed the army were often on bad terms with the *pied noir* leaders. Many senior officers sincerely believed in racial integration and they regarded the Europeans in Algeria as exploitative racists. *Pied noir* leaders regarded the army as insufficiently committed to their cause: Lagaillarde refused a regular commission, saying that officers had physical courage but lacked 'civil courage'; Susini described the leaders of the generals' putsch as 'political adolescents'.

The behaviour of the French army over Algeria is partly to be understood in the context of new military theories. During the 1950s, the *Revue de Défense Nationale* had begun to feature articles on the theory of 'revolutionary' or 'subversive' warfare. This theory was based on the assumption that all contemporary conflicts were really part of a single struggle between the West and international communism. To win such conflicts, it was argued, the army needed to abandon conventional tactics and to gain the support of the local population. Revolutionary warfare had first been conceived in Indo-China by soldiers who sought to imitate the Maoist tactics of their Vietcong opponents. Officers attempted to put their new ideas into practice in Algeria by setting up *Sections d'Administration Spéciaux* (SAS). SAS officers were supposed to take over many of the functions that would normally be undertaken by civilian officials and to develop close contacts with villagers who might be tempted to join the rebel cause. Close contacts with local populations made officers ever more reluctant to countenance departure from Algeria, which they saw as a betrayal of local allies. Furthermore, the political interests that were encouraged by revolutionary warfare meant that officers were increasingly likely to blame the civilian government for their failure, to push for a total war that would mean unqualified support from the government, and finally to turn from combating revolution in Algeria to plotting revolution against the government in France.

Military theory alone does not explain the actions of the army. Revolutionary warfare was based on incoherent and poorly thought-out ideas, a fact pointed out by the pro-*Algérie Française* historian Raoul Girardet. Ideas that had been appropriate in Indo-China, where the French army confronted a Communist enemy and could ally with potentially friendly local Catholics, were quite inappropriate in a Muslim country where the driving force of the rebellion was nationalism not communism. The 'Centre of Higher Psychological Studies' which provided many officers with their ideas was not a centre of scholarly research, but a political office presided over by Georges Sauge, a former Communist who had become an extreme right-wing Catholic. The anti-republican ideas that were propagated by figures such as Sauge fitted in oddly with the republican assimilationist ideas with which many justified the continued French presence in Algeria.

There was much pseudo-scientific mumbo-jumbo in the theory of revolutionary warfare: Antoine Argoud, a leading exponent of the theory, subsequently became an enthusiastic graphologist.

The view of the Algerian war adopted by French officers was linked to a debate over the role of technology in warfare. The period after 1945 saw the development of missiles, jet aeroplanes and, most importantly, nuclear weapons, which transformed the technology of war. De Gaulle was particularly enthusiastic to see the French army adopt such new technologies, and France exploded her first nuclear bomb in February 1960. However, while warfare became more technologically orientated, the French army was becoming less so. In the past many officers had been educated at the *École Polytechnique* engineering school, and had thus acquired a high level of technological competence. After 1945 this changed. The army was seen as a less attractive career. The number of graduates of the *École Polytechnique* who accepted commissions dropped from 127 in 1938 to 10 in 1947: between 1950 and 1957 only 1 per cent of officers were graduates of the *École Polytechnique*. Military schools found it so hard to attract appropriate recruits that they were reduced to introducing courses in undemanding subjects such as history. Increasingly, non-commissioned officers who had distinguished themselves in the battlefield rather than the classroom were promoted to fill the gaps left by the departure of the social elites.

Those who had been promoted on the battlefield or served in combat regiments felt that their values – courage, loyalty, leadership – were despised in what they contemptuously labelled a 'push-button army'. Sociologists began to talk of 'military Poujadism' to describe the hostility of soldiers to new technology and particularly to nuclear weapons. However, new technology meant little in Algeria. Here jet fighter pilots were used for reconnaissance or for flying lumbering transport planes: only hand-to-hand combat could hope to defeat the FLN. Consequently Algeria became a centre of dispute over the nature of the French army. De Gaulle's desire to create a technologically modern army encouraged him to support withdrawal, while military Poujadists such as lieutenant Pierre Sergent and colonel Trinquier resisted withdrawal partly because they knew that Algeria was the last place in which their own skills would be valued.

The army's rebellion over Algeria cannot be explained entirely in terms of resistance to new technology. Some of the most militant officers were used to dealing with technological sophistication. Two of the four leaders of the generals' putsch, Challe and Jouhaud, came from the airforce, another, Zeller, was an artillery officer. Colonel Argoud, who became a leader of the OAS, was a graduate of the *École Polytechnique* who had spent his early years working on the theory of armoured warfare. Most strikingly, colonel Bastien-Thiry, who organized the attempt to assassinate general de Gaulle at Petit Clamart in 1962, was a *polytechnicien* who had worked designing missiles.

Another element leading to military rebellion in Algeria was the general status of the army in the period from 1945 to 1962. Traditionally, the French army had been the 'nation in arms'; this tradition had reached its height in the Third Republic and particularly in the aftermath of the First World War when the *poilus* or veterans had been presented as representatives of the ordinary virtues of peasant France. The Second World War disrupted this tradition. For the first time since the 1880s, not all young men underwent a unifying period of military service. Instead they suffered the fragmented and divisive experience of imprisonment, Resistance or compulsory labour service in Germany. Furthermore, the army's role in the Second World War was seen as unheroic: the army no longer seemed as representative of the nation. Post-war purges did more to alienate soldiers from the nation and vice versa. After the war, the army lost its role as the protector of France against the German menace. Now the French army seemed merely a small, and rather insignificant, element in a coalition arrayed against the Soviet Union under the aegis of the United States. The Indo-China war, which was fought by a small cohort of professional soldiers, exacerbated the sense that the old role of the army had broken down. Indo-Chinese veterans came to see themselves, not as representatives of the nation, but as heroic and isolated figures who expected nothing but betrayal from the home front.

The beginning of the Algerian war seemed to mark a reconciliation of army and society. The numbers of troops involved meant that this became a war of conscripts: 400,000 of them were sent to Algeria. However, in practice this was not seen as a necessary war for the defence of the *patrie*. Conscripts resented going to Algeria and they did not feel that the nation was grateful to them: a survey of those on leave found that the word they used most to describe their feelings at home was 'foreign'. Furthermore, conscripts were kept for garrison duties and routine work. The most dangerous fighting was undertaken by professional soldiers. There was great hostility between the two sorts of soldiers. Jean-Jacques Servan-Schreiber's account of his service as a lieutenant in Algeria records that one of the phrases that he heard most often was 'reservists are full of shit'.[2]

The mythology that grew up around the army in Algeria was different to that which had surrounded it in the Third Republic. In the 1930s, Pétain had been presented as a military hero because of his ordinariness: biographers had stressed his peasant origins and the unspectacular nature of his early career. By contrast Raoul Salan, a commander in Indo-China and later leader of the generals' putsch, was presented as a quite extraordinary man who read Mao, smoked opium and was nicknamed 'the Mandarin'. Writing on the army no longer concentrated on ordinary conscript soldiers, but on certain exceptional units. Critics of military atrocities focused on the Foreign Legion and stressed its heavy reliance on German, and by implication Nazi, troops. Admirers of the army concentrated on the highly trained parachute regiments. The neo-fascist Bardèche wrote of the 'myth of the paras'.[3]

The sense of isolation in the army was particularly strong among officers. If the army had been the nation in arms, the officers' corps had been the *haute bourgeoisie* in arms. Officers had been drawn from wealthy backgrounds, and educated alongside the rest of the social elite in institutions such as the *École Polytechnique*. After 1945, the army came to be seen as a less attractive career for the sons of good families. Military salaries were eroded by inflation. Soldiers felt excluded from the prosperity of post-war France. They resented the materialism which seemed to grip civilians. A character in Hubert Bassot's novel on army life, *Les Silencieux*, remarks: 'I care nothing for old age pensions as I am unlikely to reach the age to draw them, I have neither the time nor the possibility to obtain the advantages that have become the sole aim of my compatriots.'[4] Officers became increasingly dependent on the extra allowances and low prices that could be found by service in the Empire: a survey in 1959 showed that only one out of 395 officers had spent his entire career in the metropole; two thirds of the sample had spent less than six years of their careers in mainland France.

The change in the fortunes of the officer corps was made particularly painful by the contrast that it presented with other groups. Once, the officer corps had been intimately tied up with the rest of the ruling elite and particularly with the upper ranks of the civil service and industrial management: a graduate of the *École Polytechnique* might chose between a career in the artillery, the mining inspectorate, or the Schneider company. After 1945, the civil service and business elites drew closer together as both gained from France's economic success. The army, however, lost its links with both groups. In 1945 sons of senior civil servants had made up 21 per cent of officer recruits, by 1957 this figure had dropped to 14 per cent. General Zeller devoted a section of his memoirs to attacking the ministry of finances, the most elite section of the civil service.

The divergence between the army and the managerial elite in private industry was even more marked. Industry no longer regarded the army as a vital part of national life. Industrialists looked to the United States, rather than their own armed forces, for protection against communism: a survey of leading industrialists in the 1950s showed that the majority of them were unaware that France was represented at the Supreme Headquarters of the Allies in Europe. Perhaps more importantly, French firms no longer felt that former officers made particularly valuable managers: it may be significant that general Challe had been seeking a post with Pont-à-Mousson shortly before embarking on military rebellion. Officers resented the activities of large-scale capitalism, particularly when they believed that those activities were partly designed to dismantle the French Empire. A pamphlet circulated among right-wing officers described the *Conseil National du Patronat Français* as one of the 'agents of revolution' against which officers should struggle; *Patrie et Progrès*, a review aimed at army officers, was violently anti-capitalist.

The opposition of the army reached its peak in the spring of 1961 when four generals – Zeller, Challe, Salan and Jouhaud – attempted to launch a military putsch based in Algeria. The putsch created great nervousness among some Parisian politicians, but it was doomed because of some of the very changes that had led to dissatisfaction among officers in the first place. The presence of large numbers of conscripts in Algeria meant that de Gaulle was able to appeal over the heads of officers to the 'nation in arms' – an odd position for the most prominent proponent of the *armée de métier*. Furthermore, the army lacked the means to get to mainland France. The navy and, in spite of the involvement of Challe, the airforce did not support the putsch: transport planes flew back to mainland France before they could be commandeered by the paras. Furthermore, the young fighter jet pilots of the French airforce were the most technocratic and most Gaullist section of the French armed forces. Their world of technical achievement was very distant from the military traditions of the army rebels and they showed themselves willing to shoot down rebel aircraft.

In 1962, it seemed very unlikely to most people that French departure from Algeria would mean the end of the conflict that Algeria had engendered among the French. One million *pieds noirs* came to France in the space of a few months: most of them brought nothing with them but a couple of cheap suitcases and bitter memories. The French army was filled with men who resented the loss of Algeria, the loss of their comrades who had died defending it, and the purging of those who had sought to oppose withdrawal. One in every forty French people had served in the French army during the Algerian war, and, though these conscripts had never shared the political commitment of the professional soldiers, many of them had experienced extreme violence as victims, perpetrators or witnesses. Part of the French population never forgave de Gaulle for initiating withdrawal. There were around thirty attempts to assassinate the general during the next few years and he took to travelling with a cortege of bodyguards and doctors carrying flasks of his blood in case a transfusion was needed. Michel Debré remarked that it was a miracle that France survived the 1960s without civil war.

However, against all expectations, the Algerian war left few scars on French politics. The point can be emphasized with a brief comparison between the impact of Algeria on France and that of the Vietnam war on America. Military casualties in the two wars, as a proportion of total population, were about the same. But while Vietnam plays a central role in American politics and culture, Algeria is rarely mentioned in French public life. The first popular film on the Algerian war, *Mon Cher Frangin*, was not released until 1989, and Pontecorvo's *Battle of Algiers* is hardly ever shown in Paris. A survey of 1987 showed that a majority of French people regarded the Algerian war as a less important event than either of the two world wars or the student riots of 1968: even more strikingly, the survey showed that members of the generation that had lived through Algeria were less likely than their children to describe the war as an important event. The difference between French attitudes to Algeria and American attitudes to Vietnam was exposed by the presidential elections that occurred in both countries in 1988. The American campaign revolved around Vietnam: though none of the candidates had played any direct role in the war. Algeria was hardly mentioned in the French campaign although two of the candidates – Chirac and le Pen – had fought in the army there and a third – Mitterrand – had been intimately associated with the early stages of the war as minister of the interior.

In part, the different impacts of Vietnam and Algeria can be explained by the general histories of France and America. Vietnam tied in with the humiliations brought by Watergate and the oil crisis. By contrast France lost an empire and found a role. De Gaulle's foreign policy offered a sense of grandeur, while the Fifth Republic constitution brought a new degree of political stability. Most importantly, the economic growth of post-war France reached its apogee, and began to have a dramatic effect on living standards, during the 1960s.

The end of the Algerian war also speeded up economic change. The cost of maintaining an army in Algeria no longer fell on the French state, export industries turned away from imperial markets towards the more advanced, and ultimately more lucrative, markets of western Europe. Most importantly of all, the war relieved France's chronic labour shortage. Young men were freed by the shortening of military service, several hundred thousand economically active *pieds noirs* came to France, where they were soon joined by hundreds of thousands of Muslims who wished to escape the chaos of post-independence Algeria. The *pieds noirs* had a particularly dynamic influence on the French economy. Their lack of formal qualifications meant that many of them were unable to obtain the clerical employment that they had undertaken in Algeria. Instead they were forced to accept jobs as semi-skilled workers in the sectors where France lacked labour most. However, the decline in their social position made the *pieds noirs* exceptionally ambitious and energetic. People who had lost everything were often forced to take the kind of entrepreneurial risks that the French had traditionally avoided. In 1963 only 15 per cent of *rapatriés* in the Vaucluse were self-employed while 30 per cent were employed in the public sector; ten years later 30 per cent of them were self-employed while only 15 per cent worked in the public sector. Settlers from Algeria who moved to Corsica planted 15,000 hectares of vineyards and did much to revive agriculture. The fact that most *pieds noirs* settled in the south meant that they benefited from, and contributed to, the revival of formerly backward regions that had already begun. Like many groups that have undergone an artificial depression in their fortunes, the *pieds noirs* were particularly ambitious for their children, and they began to take a new interest in education. By the late 1980s, 158 children of *pieds noirs* had passed the fiendishly difficult examination for the *agrégation*. France's most prominent intellectual, Bernard Henry-Levy, is a *pied noir* as are the Attali brothers, archetypal members of the 'techno-cratic' business elite.

In political terms the *pieds noirs* remained bitter. They had been promised that the new Algerian government would pay compensation for property left in Algeria; this compensation was never paid, and the French government refused to underwrite the Algerian promise. *Pieds noirs* lobbied the French government for money and occasionally resorted to violent tactics to draw their cause to public attention. However, the political impact of such protest was limited. In part this was because the cause of *Algérie Française* had never commanded widespread public support in mainland France. The violence with which the OAS resisted French departure turned public indifference into outright hostility. Many Frenchmen came to associate the *pieds noirs* with terrorism, fascism and crime. Gaston Defferre, mayor of Marseilles where many *rapatriés* settled, equated the European settlers in Algeria with Pétainism. A survey in September 1962 showed that 32 per cent of Frenchmen believed that the aid given to *pieds noirs* was excessive. Before 1958, the *Algérie Française* lobby had been able to exercise power in spite of its lack of popular support because political parties were dominated by notables or militants who created a shield between politics and public opinion. The constitutional and political changes that accompanied the foundation of the Fifth Republic removed the shield of the Fourth Republic party system. Voters elected the president directly after 1962 and political parties were forced to respond directly to voter demands.

The only section of the political spectrum that nurtured the memory of *Algérie Française* was the extreme right. However, the very vehemence of the extreme right often condemned it to insignificance. Leaders of the *opposition nationale* became obsessively opposed to de Gaulle and everything that was associated with him. They denounced France's independent nuclear weapons programme and her attempts at rapprochement with the Communist bloc. Some right-wingers refused to serve in the 'Gaullist army'. Some even opposed the maintenance of Parisian monuments on the grounds that these were the responsibility of the Gaullist André Malraux. In the Fourth Republic, anti-communism had helped to reintegrate the extreme right into mainstream politics; in the Fifth Republic anti-Gaullism marginalized it. This was partly because the disciplined parties of the Fifth Republic did not offer the extreme right the kind of discrete links that had been possible with the loosely structured alliances of the Fourth Republic. It was also

because de Gaulle struck nationalist chords that had previously provided the extreme right with its most potent sources of popular
appeal. Indeed many voters who had normally voted for the extreme
right supported de Gaulle after 1958. During this period, the
extreme right really consisted of a number of leaders without a
natural following. The 5 per cent of the electorate that voted for
Tixier-Vignancour in 1965 was largely made up of former *pieds noirs*
(votes for him were heavily concentrated in the southern departments where the *pieds noirs* had settled). The alliance between *pieds
noirs* voters, who did not think of themselves as right-wing on most
issues, and extreme-right leaders was unstable and many *rapatriés*
were soon tempted away by politicians, like Mitterrand, who supported their demands for compensation. It was not until after the
death of de Gaulle that a large-scale party of the extreme right – the
Front National – was launched again in France and, though the
party was led by fanatical anti-Gaullists such as le Pen and Pierre
Sergent, a majority of Front National's voters said that they regarded
'the Gaullist experience' as a positive one.

The unpopularity of *Algérie Française* after 1962 had an effect on
the *pied noir* community itself. In Algeria, Europeans had lived in
tightly knit and concentrated communities; they had been supported by the army and by visiting politicians from the metropole.
Now they were scattered over France among a largely hostile population and denounced by politicians. It was a traumatic experience.
Many *pieds noirs* retreated into private life and business. However,
there was also a change in the nature of the *pieds noirs*. This was
partly a question of generations. The, often highly educated, children of the people who had left Algeria in 1962 began to rediscover
the particular identity of their community during the late 1980s –
though this rediscovery was accompanied by a recognition that
Algerie Française could not, and should not, be recreated. Books with
titles like *Pied noir et fier d'être* began to appear during the late 1980s.
Such books contained an element of apologia. They emphasized
that most of the European population in Algeria had not been
wealthy capitalists. The veterans of *Algérie Française* were also very
prone to distance themselves from the violence that was sometimes
associated with their community. This desire touched even the most
unlikely individuals. In 1976 a gang led by a veteran of the Foreign
Legion and the OAS tunnelled through the Nice sewers in order to
reach a bank vault. On the walls of the vault they painted the words
'Without arms or violence'.

13 The Foundations of the Fifth Republic

To loyal Gaullists, 1958 marks the birth of modern France. Before this date France had been plagued by political instability (no prime minister of the Fourth Republic had lasted much more than a year), weak governments, and a general sense of decline. After 1958 everything changed. There were only two prime ministers between 1958 and 1968. Furthermore, the president of the republic was not a figurehead but a ruler who imbued governments of the whole period from 1958 until 1969 with a sense of purpose. These changes were partly the product of a new constitution, introduced in September 1958. The constitution was drawn up fast by a small committee and it enshrined classic Gaullist principles, as stated in de Gaulle's Bayeux declaration ten years earlier. The powers of parliament were weakened and those of the president were strengthened. Ministers were now chosen by the president of the republic rather than by parliament, and ministers who had been members of parliament were obliged to resign their seats. The president had the right to dissolve parliament and, crucially, to call referenda. Deputies were now to be elected by *scrutin de liste*, i.e. election within single member constituencies, rather than by the complicated rules that had given small centre parties such advantages in the Fourth Republic.

The Fifth Republic constitution, however, was not solely responsible for the transformation of France. As late as 1962, Stanley Hoffmann entitled an essay on France 'Judgement Suspended'. The most important constitutional innovation of the new republic – the direct election of the president by the nation rather than by the 80,000 notables who had sanctioned de Gaulle's presidency in 1958 – was not instituted until 1962. Furthermore, the practical use to which the constitution was put varied over time. The first prime minister in the new system (Michel Debré) was an established and experienced politician: de Gaulle confined his interventions to foreign, military and Algerian policy. Debré was replaced in 1962 by Georges Pompidou who lacked independent authority, and de Gaulle then intervened more directly in domestic policy. His interventions became less frequent during the mid 1960s until the events of 1968 changed his relations with Pompidou whereupon de Gaulle appointed another prime minister (Couve de Murville) who could be seen as the creature and tool of the Elysée. In the 1980s, the 'cohabitation' between the Socialist president Mitterrand and the Gaullist prime minister Chirac was to expose the flexibility of the Fifth Republic constitution to an even greater extent.

The first 11 years of the Fifth Republic were clearly a period of Gaullist triumph, but Gaullism meant more than one thing. Firstly, there was the Gaullism of de Gaulle. His desire for a strong government and independent foreign policy dominated France during the 1960s. However, de Gaulle's desires counted for nothing on their own. The general's previous attempts to model a state on his 'certain idea of France' had failed. His success after 1958 was based on a wide variety of changes, the roots of which could be traced back to before 1958. Gaullism also meant the movement of those who defined their politics in terms of loyalty to the general. Among politicians de Gaulle evoked strong feelings on both sides. Men like Capitant, Terrenoire, and Guichard dedicated their whole life to following the general; men like Fabre-Luce dedicated much of their life to attacking him. At least 30 organizations grew up to represent various strands of Gaullism during the 1960s, the most important of these being the *Union pour la Nouvelle République* (UNR) which was founded to support the general's action in 1958. In order to preserve his image as a man above parties, de Gaulle refused to intervene in the life of the UNR. It was a disciplined body that was expected to accept alliance with other Gaullist parties and individuals at election time and to accept that it would be granted few rewards for its loyalty: ministers, and indeed prime ministers, were often chosen from outside its ranks.

The third strand of Gaullism was that of the electorate. Support for de Gaulle as an individual, measured in public opinion polls and presidential elections, was always different from support for the Gaullist party. De Gaulle appealed to the working class more, and the peasantry less, than the party that claimed to represent his ideas. However, support for de Gaulle was not simply a question of personality. Foreign leaders such as Eisenhower gained support by emphasizing their own private lives and characteristics. Some French politicians, such as Pinay, had made similar appeals. De Gaulle's public persona was coldly formal. There was no reference to his private or family life. Voters knew nothing of his tendency to talk in barrack room obscenity or of his touching affection for his mongol daughter Anne. De Gaulle's public statements, couched in language of classical elegance, conjured up an image based on public qualities of patriotism, strength and association with great moments in France's history.

Voters felt less strongly about Gaullism than professional politicians. Public opinion polls showed that large numbers of people were 'mainly satisfied' with de Gaulle but that only a small, and inconsistent, proportion of the electorate were wholly satisfied with his action. Furthermore, voters showed that they were capable of distinguishing between the various elements of de Gaulle's action, and many saw his rule as a means rather than an end. Particularly high satisfaction was registered with de Gaulle's capacity to deal with Algeria. In 1958, 83 per cent of respondents expressed faith in de Gaulle's ability to maintain discipline in the army, and his approval ratings peaked, at 74 per cent, immediately after barricades week. By contrast few people trusted de Gaulle on social matters: his approval ratings reached their nadir, at 42 per cent, during the miners' strike of 1963.

Great interest was aroused by the possibility that Gaullism might bring about a change in the party system. Before 1958, French political parties had fallen into one of two categories. The Radicals and Independents had been based around small groups of notables: individuals who derived power from their own social position in a particular area. The Socialist and Communist parties were based around a large number of dedicated militants who sought to implement a clearly defined ideology. The UNR fitted into neither of these categories. It had around 25,000 members in 1959 and 62,000 members in 1962. It aimed to be a party of elite rather than mass membership, but the elites to which it appealed were those of the centralized state rather than those who disposed of power at local level: the party never enjoyed much success in elections to municipal councils or departmental *conseils généraux*. Furthermore, the UNR insisted on a degree of discipline that the notables would never have tolerated. Jean Charlot suggested that the UNR was a 'voter orientated' party characterized by a direct appeal from the leader to the voters, an appeal which was based on general themes rather than on precisely defined ideologies. The shift towards 'voter orientated' parties was even more marked among some of de Gaulle's rivals. In the 1965 election both Lecanuet, the Christian Democrat centrist candidate, and Jean-Louis Tixier-Vignancour, the candidate of the *Algérie Française* lobby, built their campaigns on American models. Both avoided extreme ideological positions, and both ran their campaigns in an informal way that de Gaulle would have despised: Tixier-Vignancour even made a campaign tour of French beaches during the summer.

Some believed that France would move away from a multipolar party system in which numerous different groups appealed to segments of the electorate and towards a system in which two broad blocs would confront each other. There was an element of truth in these analyses. The UNR, and Gaullism in general, attracted a larger section of the population than any previous party in French history: Gaullists gained just over 42 per cent of seats in the general election of November 1958. The opposition responded to de Gaulle's popularity by seeking to achieve unity among themselves. Attempts were made to find a single candidate who could unite the left for the 1965 presidential election. After Gaston Defferre refused to accept this role, François Mitterrand put himself forward. Mitterrand attracted support from a loosely structured *Fédération de la Gauche Démocratique et Socialiste*, he was supported by the Communist party in the second round of the election and gained a respectable share of the vote (45.5 per cent). Mitterrand also began to present himself as a 'leader of the opposition' and even drew up a shadow cabinet.

If France was moving towards a two-party system, it was not very clear what defined those parties. In the past politics had been divided by attitudes to class, religion, empire and the constitution. Now France was a secularized country without colonies where most politicians seemed to have accepted the constitution. Broad attitudes to social and economic issues do seem to have divided the Gaullists from their opponents, but even here Gaullism, and anti-Gaullism, often cut across social divisions. Developments after 1965 also reflected the limits of the two-party system in France. The unity of the left remained precarious and subject to frequent splits between Communists and Socialists. The unity of the right was even more fragile. Giscard d'Estaing's Republican Independents continued to sum up their attitude to de Gaulle with the phrase 'yes but' and after de Gaulle's death they were often violently at odds with the Gaullists.

Changes in the political system were closely linked to broader social changes. One of the most important of these was the spread of television and radio. Third Republic politics had been built around newspapers, especially important local newspapers which had

reinforced the power of notables who controlled them. The hegemony of newsprint had been challenged after the war by the spread
of new means of communication and radio broadcasts were an
important tool for Mendès-France. In the first five years of the Fifth
Republic the number of television sets in France increased from 1 to
5 million. During the same period, 60 per cent of workers were estimated to listen to radio news broadcasts (though some displayed a
healthy scepticism about what they heard). Television and radio
underwrote Gaullism by allowing the president to make direct
appeals to the voters over the heads of politicians and political
parties. As a result of his wartime broadcasts on the BBC, de Gaulle
was the first politician in history whose national reputation had been
entirely built on broadcasting. Now French broadcasting was organized under firm state control in the form of the *Office de la Radio et
Télévision Française* (ORTF): Jean-Jacques Servan-Schreiber summed
up Gaullism as 'personal power plus monopoly control of television'.
Almost all of the crucial confrontations of de Gaulle's career
involved broadcasting. During barricades week and the generals'
putsch de Gaulle made impressive appeals for support on television,
and on the latter occasion his appeal was relayed to the young
Algerian conscripts by transistor radios. Emmanuel Le Roy-Ladurie
wrote that de Gaulle's television appearances had invested power in
the body of the ruler to an extent that had not been seen since the
middle ages. De Gaulle's assistant, Pierre le Blanc, remarked on the
extent to which the general – short-sighted and unable to go out
without being recognized – depended on television for his information on public opinion. It was appropriate that de Gaulle died watching television: the Fifth Republic that he created was built on ORTF
as much as the Third Republic had been built on the *Dépêche de
Toulouse*.

De Gaulle wished to draw support from outside party politics. He
had particular respect for those who had demonstrated their technical competence in the fiercely competitive French educational
system or in the *grands corps*. Couve de Murville, who served as
foreign secretary for ten years and then as prime minister, had been
an inspector of finances. Pelletier, who became minister of the interior, had served in the prefectural corps. Robert Janot, from the
conseil d'état, advised on constitutional matters. Such elites had always
existed, but they had acquired particular importance during the
period after 1945 as a result of the role that they had played in
economic management.

De Gaulle was also able to draw on certain new elites. Many groups, which had been too young to exercise much influence in the aftermath of the Liberation, reached important positions during the early years of the Fifth Republic. The most obvious of these groups was made up of graduates of the *École Nationale d'Administra-tion*, founded in 1945. In the private sector new elites trained up by *Catholic* bodies such as the *Centre des Jeunes Patrons* or the *Jeunesse Agri-cole Chrétienne* also began to obtain influence in mainstream organi-zations, and they were often sympathetic to the modernizing ethos of the Gaullist state. There was also a specifically Gaullist elite. During the Fourth Republic the *Rassemblement du Peuple Français* (RPF) had appealed to many very young men, such as Olivier Guichard, indeed the youth and experience of its activists helped to account for the movement's failure. However, the contacts formed by the RPF had persisted and Guichard was able to reactivate a network of supporters with a dozen phone calls.

Success in three areas was crucial to the general success of the Fifth Republic. The first and most important of these areas was Algeria. De Gaulle had been brought back to power to solve the Algerian war. The fact that he succeeded in doing so was partly due to his own decisions and partly due to a variety of other changes, described in the previous chapter, that allowed France to survive withdrawal without undergoing civil war. The second important area of Fifth Republic policy related to the economy. Antoine Dupont-Fauville remarked that France had reached an *impasse* by 1956: 'those in power avoided confronting social and economic prob-lems'.[1] De Gaulle's style presented a sharp contrast with that of his Fourth Republic predecessors. He seemed decisive and determined where they had seemed weak and vacillating. He effectively devalued French currency (a measure necessitated by the inflation of the Fourth Republic), but countered the psychological impact of this measure by declaring 1 new franc to be the equivalent of 100 old francs. In financial terms Rueff and his associates ran an orthodox policy which concentrated on restoring the balance of payments and removing economic controls.

However, the evidence that de Gaulle had much of an impact on the economic, rather than the financial, life of France is limited. De Gaulle disdained economic matters. He had supported the Monnet Plan's emphasis on heavy industry as a means to enhance national power and grandeur, but he probably did not understand, or even approve of, the rapid growth of a consumer economy in the 1960s.

Opinion polls taken in 1958 showed that only 42 per cent of French people expressed confidence in de Gaulle's capacities as an economic policymaker. The Fifth Republic was really the beneficiary of economic changes that had begun before 1958. Growing prosperity contributed to a certain sense of national well-being, allowed the government to buy off groups who might otherwise have caused political problems and helped to create the new affluent, urban, television-watching society in which Gaullism flourished.

The third keystone of de Gaulle's republic was the construction of a new role for France in the international arena. Independence was the key word in this project. France was to break away from an American-dominated bloc and to show herself capable of guaranteeing her own security. France exploded her first atomic bomb in February 1960, and in March 1966 she withdrew her forces from NATO's joint command. De Gaulle visited the Soviet Union, he recognized Communist China in January 1964, and he developed relations with East European nations such as Romania. He sought to create a special role for France as a leader of Third World states that were not aligned with either East or West. He made particular efforts to obtain rapprochement with the Arab world, and he condemned Israel after the six day war in 1967. He also sought to maintain good relations with the French-speaking states of black Africa. Culture became an important part of French *rayonnement* and substantial subsidies were given to the education of young men from the Third World in France, international broadcasting in French and the activities of French cultural missions around the world. Finally, de Gaulle adopted a sceptical attitude towards the European Economic Community, much to the annoyance of his Christian Democrat allies. He stressed, in a press conference of May 1962, that the EEC could only be an association of independent states – a '*Europe des patries*' – never a state in its own right. De Gaulle was willing to use aggressive techniques to get his own way in Europe. He boycotted EEC meetings in order to impose the Common Agricultural Policy, and in January 1963 he vetoed the application of the United Kingdom (which might have challenged French hegemony) to join the EEC.

There are three different, but not mutually exclusive, ways in which to interpret de Gaulle's foreign policy. Firstly, it can be argued that de Gaulle merely implemented the 'certain idea of France' which had remained consistent throughout his life. Such an interpretation would present de Gaulle as being, in foreign policy at least, the last Maurrassian. He continued to define his politics exclusively in terms of nationalism long after most of the right had begun to talk in terms of defending the interests of a wider 'occident' or western bloc. De Gaulle had always been distrustful of international bodies and he believed that nations were guided by self-interest, not by ideology. The Soviet Union was simply the latest incarnation of Russia and as such it shared many interests with France; equally, the United States threatened French interests even though the two countries happened to share the same kind of social organization.

Secondly, it can be argued that de Gaulle's policies were guided by realism. They were not simply the implementation of eternal principles, but a response to the specific circumstances of the 1960s. Decolonization, the breech between Russia and China, and the decline of Cold War hostility all offered opportunities for French diplomacy that had not existed in, say, the late 1940s. Furthermore, de Gaulle responded to changes in international conditions. A man brought up to regard Germany as the hereditary enemy of France fostered good relations with Konrad Adenauer, signed a Franco-German treaty of cooperation in January 1963, and called for German reunification. De Gaulle's policies were also a response to developments in French internal politics: they fitted in with a current of neutralism that had been developing in public opinion since the early 1950s.

Finally, it can be argued that de Gaulle's policies were really more to do with mythology and image than with the exercise of power. The aim of such policies was to create symbols of French greatness that could be used to mobilize and unite the French people. De Gaulle had begun his career in foreign policy during the war when he had no money, no army to speak of, and not even an unquestionable claim to popular support. During this period, de Gaulle had learned the importance of gesture and illusion. His actions during the 1960s were also based on illusion. The French nuclear bomb was really too small to count for anything, it was contemptuously described as a *bombinette*. Some commentators were uncertain if a single one of the Mirage jets that were charged with delivering the bombs could actually reach Moscow. Far from France being independent of the United States, her nuclear weapons were only really effective because of a tacit alliance that persisted with NATO. French soldiers knew that the western allies would never really tolerate an attack on France, and some of them admitted that the French atom bomb was mainly useful as a 'tripwire' that would provoke all-out nuclear war between the superpowers in the event of an attack by Soviet conventional forces.

France's foreign policy in the 1960s only worked because the Cold War had thawed sufficiently to allow western nations to take independent initiatives without having thawed so much that America could be entirely indifferent to the fate of her former clients. The dramatic impact of gestures such as the recognition of Communist China hinged on the very fact that America, and the atlanticist lobby in France, still disapproved of them. In a world of genuinely independent states, France would have been insignificant, but as the spoilt and naughty child of a still powerful western alliance she could attract a degree of attention that was disproportionate to her real influence. De Gaulle's German and European policies were also based on the continuing division of Europe: he could afford to call for German reunification and for the creation of a Europe stretching 'from the Atlantic to the Urals' because he knew that they would not be allowed to occur. A unified Germany at the heart of a large and undivided Europe would have exposed the absurdity of Gaullist pretensions to grandeur. The illusory nature of Gaullist foreign policy was revealed by the Four-Power Conference held in Paris in 1960. The discussions achieved nothing because relations between the powers were soured by the fact that an American spyplane was shot down over the Soviet Union as the conference began. These events threw the British prime minister, Harold Macmillan, into deep depression, but de Gaulle remained gleefully happy: for his purposes, what mattered was that France had been recognized as a 'great power', not that anything concrete should be achieved.

14 The End of the Beginning: 1968–1969

One book on the events of 1968 was entitled *The Beginning of the End.*[1] Such works interpreted the student riots of that year as marking the breakdown of the bourgeois order. In fact the events in France did not shake either the capitalist economy or the Communist party, the two main targets of the protesters. Nor did the protest shake the political regime in France; indeed, if anything, the events showed how secure the foundations of the Fifth Republic had become. The only victim of the events was Charles de Gaulle, and his eventual departure showed that the political system no longer needed to be held together by loyalty to a single heroic individual.

On one level the student protests of 1968 were part of an international movement that embraced people from Berkeley, to the London School of Economics, to Tokyo University. A general sense of hostility to the consumerism and prosperity of the decade had grown up among the young, who were such conspicuous beneficiaries of this prosperity. More specifically, a political sympathy for the people of the Third World had grown up and this was particularly stimulated by the Tet offensive that the Vietcong launched against South Vietnamese and American forces at the beginning of 1968. On a second level, student protest was part of a movement that was specific to continental Europe. Most European universities accepted any student who was capable of meeting undemanding entrance requirements. The prosperity of the 1960s had increased the numbers of students whose families were capable of supporting them through university. However, university facilities had not expanded to meet the requirements of this enlarged intake, and job opportunities for graduates did not always match the hopes of fond petit-bourgeois parents who had saved hard to give a cherished child an education. The number of students in French universities had increased from 200,000 to 500,000 between 1960 and 1968. Universities were hierarchical institutions in which 'mandarins' such as Roland Mousnier treated both students and their junior colleagues with disdain. Expansion during the 1960s created a rapid increase in the numbers of lecturers on temporary contracts: in 1956 tenured professors had made up 56 per cent of university teaching staff, by 1963 this figure had dropped to 33 per cent. Junior lecturers felt powerless, insecure and unrecognized. The university teachers' union (the *Syndicat National de l'Enseignement Supérieur*) expressed sympathy for the protesting students.

The demands of French students were varied and often contradictory. A small group of activists were concerned with explicitly political matters from the start. This group controlled the *Union Nationale des Etudiants de France*. The activists were often older than the majority of students, and their politics had been formed by the Algerian war. They were particularly hostile to the *Parti Communiste Français* which they saw as having failed to adjust to changing circumstances and particularly to the role of Third World struggle. Some activists joined the *Parti Socialiste Unifié* (PSU), others joined a variety of small left-wing groups during the 1960s. Some looked to Mao's China as an alternative to the Soviet Union, some looked to the Trotskyite Fourth International or to anarchism. Some declared themselves to be 'situationalists'. Situationalists differed from the conventional left because they believed that consumption rather than production was the key to modern capitalism and because their rebellion often took playful, almost surrealistic, forms. The student *groupuscules* were ridden with mutual hostility. Those from the PSU denounced the Communist party for being Stalinist while Maoists denounced it for having betrayed Stalinism. The Trotskyites were split into two factions. Disciples of the Marxist philosopher Althusser split with the Communist party in 1966 before turning against Althusser himself. The venerable *Fédération Anarchiste* was regarded as authoritarian by the 'neo-anarchists' who grouped around the journal *Noir et Rouge*.

The activists were isolated from the bulk of the student community. At the end of the Algerian war, the UNEF had mobilized 100,000 out of 220,000 students; in 1968 only 45,000 out of half a million students were members of the union. Ordinary students were likely to be concerned by issues that touched their daily lives rather than by grand ideological concerns. The gulf between ordinary students and activists was exacerbated by the fact that many of the latter had been educated at the *École Normale Supérieure* (ENS). The atmosphere in this prestigious institution was very different from that in universities. It was highly academic – Régis Debray records that he redoubled his efforts to learn Latin and Greek so that he might, as the top graduate in his year at the ENS, have the opportunity to refuse to shake de Gaulle's hand. The grievances of ordinary students meant little to *normaliens*. University students were concerned by oversized classes and by the poor quality of teaching; the ENS had hardly increased its intake over the past century, teachers there were young and classes were small. University students were worried by unemployment; *normaliens* were more or less guaranteed a job in a *lycée* or university and, as late as 1988, Henri Weber remarked that none of his friends had even considered the prospect of unemployment. University students feared the prospect of selective exams that Christian Fouchet, the education minister, had threatened to introduce; most *normaliens* would have found it hard to conceive of a world without competitive exams.

Even among ordinary students, the discontent of 1968 was often rooted in apparently contradictory feelings. Commentators disagreed on whether students were protesting about modern consumer capitalism, or seeking to enter it. Conservatives, such as Raymond Aron, saw the events of 1968 as a 'modernization crisis' provoked by the failure of universities to adjust to new demands. Authors who sympathized with the protest movement believed that the students were seeking to reject modernity, or at least the modernity of consumer capitalism. In some respects both sets of commentators were right. Different groups of students were radicalized by different grievances. Edgar Morin pointed out such a difference among sociology students. Some resented the fact that the introduction of questionnaires and numerical methods into their subject during the 1950s had made it into a tool of capitalism rather than a means of criticizing capitalism. Others resented the fact that overproduction of sociology graduates reduced their chances of obtaining a job. Often contradictory motives may have co-existed within the mind of a single student: the deliberate irrationality of the protest movement may have sprung partly from the need to gloss over such contradictions.

Student discontent erupted several times in the 1960s – most notably when a group of situationalists took over the students' union at Strasbourg University in 1966. However, these disturbances were successfully contained until March 1968 when discontent touched the University of Paris at Nanterre. Initial protests were caused by a dispute over the rights of male students to visit female dormitories, but soon became generalized under the leadership of Daniel Cohn-Bendit – a half-German sociology student and activist. The dean of Nanterre responded to a strike and occupation by closing the campus. This measure shifted attention to the Sorbonne at the centre of the Paris Latin Quarter. The closure of the Sorbonne provoked riots, and on the night of May 10, students erected barricades in Paris. The government responded to this development by sending in the CRS (riot police). The CRS became the major villains of 1968. The Parisian bourgeois were shocked by what they saw as the violence of the riot police. Students chanted 'CRS/SS'. André Quattochi described the CRS as 'peasants made into watchdogs'. The CRS themselves were bitterly conscious of the contempt in which they were held and seem to have come close to striking themselves around May 13.

On May 13 the protest movement began to spread from the students to sections of the working class. Strikes began at Renault, the epicentre of labour protest since 1936, and spread. By May 22 there were 9 million workers on strike in France and hundreds of factories had been occupied. This was unexpected. Links between the working class and the students were weaker than in Britain, where a significant minority of students came from proletarian backgrounds, or Italy, where intellectuals exercised great influence in the Communist party. Trade union leaders had even assured the leader of the main employers' association that 'the summer will be quiet' and that it would be possible for him to go into hospital for an operation. The most important unions were grouped in the *Confédération Générale du Travail* (CGT), which was dominated by the Communist party, and Communist leaders were hostile to the student protests which were led by professed enemies of the party.

The working-class discontent that exploded in 1968 was rooted partly in economics – the depression that had begun in 1967 had driven unemployment up to half a million (an number unprecedented since before the war). However, there were also more complicated reasons for discontent. Some workers felt that neither the growing prosperity of France nor the efforts of the *Confédération Générale du Travail* to gain them a greater share of that prosperity in the form of higher wages could satisfy their real desires. The CGT had come to seem as much a part of the industrial relations system as the employers' organizations. It seemed reluctant to take measures that would really challenge the existing order or change the lives of workers. Infuriated CGT officials such as Pierre le Brun or André Barjonet resigned from their posts in protest at the movement's refusal to change or respond to the student protests. Workers also became hostile to the CGT; in May 1968 strikers at St Ouen refused to allow CGT officials into occupied factories. Some workers felt an alienation from the tedium and humiliation of industrial work that could not easily be expressed: strikers at the St Nazaire shipyards in May 1968 refused to draw up a list of demands. Others looked to new kinds of demands that touched on issues such as worker participation.

The *Confédération Française des Travailleurs Chrétiens* (CFTC), the second largest union confederation in France with 750,000 members, seemed particularly well qualified to deal with such matters. The CFTC had once been a Christian association and, even when it abandoned its religious links, it continued to be interested in aspects of labour relations that related to dignity and independence. The CFTC had particular appeal to the white-collar professions which had expanded during the 1960s: the journalists at ORTF and air traffic controllers went on strike in 1968. Striking workers were joined by other social groups who had normally been separate from the labour organization. Peasants had clashed with police in Redon in Brittany in March 1968, and on May 18 the leader of the, usually conservative, farmers' organization (the FNSEA) broke with his national leaders to call for occupation of land. Immigrant workers, normally too vulnerable and frightened to take action that might draw attention to themselves and largely disdained by the CGT, also became involved in strikes.

Protest spread to the most unexpected areas of French life: dissident employers occupied the buildings of the *Conseil National du Patronat Français*, soccer players occupied their grounds and raised placards saying '*le football aux footballeurs*', the Cannes film festival broke down as directors like Jean-Luc Godard walked out, teachers in *lycées* awarded full marks to all students in the *baccalauréat* examination. Louis Malle's film *Milou en mai* captures the extent to which even a bourgeois family of middle-aged provincials could feel that the drama in the Sorbonne touched their own lives. Social crisis eventually produced a political crisis. The Communist party called for de Gaulle's replacement. More significantly the leaders of the non-Communist left (the politicians who seemed closest to the mood of the protesters) began to make their moves. A meeting at the Charléty stadium, organized by the UNEF and the *Parti Socialiste Unifié*, brought together thousands of people including Mendès-France. Soon both Mendès-France and Mitterrand had announced, in terms that echoed de Gaulle's statement of 1958, that they were available to form a government.

The participation of the left in the protests against de Gaulle in 1968 often leads to the assumption that the extreme right must have supported de Gaulle. This was not always the case. The extreme right had its own tradition of student rioting and sections of the universities – particularly the law faculty at Assas in Paris – remained right-wing strongholds. There were several reasons why the extreme right often sympathized with the student protesters. Some saw the protests as motivated by straightforward, and justified, demands of bourgeois children for better campus facilities and job opportunities. This was the view expressed by the former Pétainist Bernard Fay in the conservative journal *Ecrits de Paris*. Others sympathized with the more radical student demands. The new left of Cohn-Bendit and the CFTC bore some resemblances to the old Maurrassian right. Both condemned centralization, materialism, and both were at odds with the Communist party. A left-wing student who attended a meeting addressed by Georges Sauges, the right-wing Catholic who had acted as a guru to activist officers in Algeria, recalled: 'I think that it was all quite sincere. For them [the right] the consumer society is something to be rejected.'[2] Pierre Pujo wrote that *Action Française* had 'gone further' than the students in its criticisms of the established order.[3] Philippe Ariès, a historian and veteran of *Action Française*, recalls turning on the radio in May 1968 and realizing that the words used by the students were the words that had inspired his own royalist youth: 'What a surprise. Under the flood of speeches and graffiti, we found the familiar themes of our reactionary youth. Suspicion of the centralizing state, attachment to real freedoms and to small intermediate communities, to the region and its language.'[4] In some respects, 1968 permanently changed the spectrum of French politics. Regionalism and ruralism, which had always been identified with the anti-Jacobin right, became features of a new ecologically orientated left. Demonstrations in Brittany and the west, which had been the homeland of the French right since the 1790s, were particularly important.

Most importantly of all, the right's attitude to 1968 was influenced by the memory of Algeria and by its bitter hatred of de Gaulle. Men who had supported the OAS were willing to go to any length to attack de Gaulle. The leader of the *Association Fédérale des Rapatriés d'Algérie et d'Outre-Mer* wrote: 'Faced with the systematic repression of the police,which has been substituted for all dialogue, we declare our solidarity with the students.'[5] Pierre Sergent, the former parachute captain and OAS commander, said 'my instinct is to be on the barricades ... I did not wait for M. Cohn-Bendit to denounce the consumer society.'[6]

Not all supporters of the extreme right adopted such uncompromising positions. Alongside those who joined the students were those who remained neutral and those who fought against both left-wing students and the 'Gaullist forces of order'. There were also right-wingers who rallied behind the regime. The most prominent of these was Jean-Louis Tixier-Vignancour who had challenged de Gaulle for the presidency in 1965, but who joined the demonstration in favour of order on 30 May 1968. Some right-wingers rallied behind the regime when protests spread from universities to the working class and thus seemed to threaten the rights of property. The attempt by Mitterrand and Pierre Mendès-France to substitute themselves for the existing government exposed divisions on the extreme right. Some right-wingers prefered government of the left to de Gaulle. The Pétain apologist Jacques Isorni expressed his support for a government led by François Mitterrand – the two men had been closely linked during the conservative phase of Mitterrand's career in the Fourth Republic. More surprisingly, Alfred Fabre-Luce announced that he would prefer a government led by Pierre Mendès-France, against whom he had made anti-semitic attacks in 1954, to that of de Gaulle. Tixier-Vignancour had preferred Mitterrand to de Gaulle in the second round of the 1965 presidential election. However, in 1967, Mitterrand and the Communist party had signed a *declaration commun* and Tixier had formed a *Front National Anti-communiste*. The division between the Tixier-Vignancour faction and other elements of the extreme right was a division between those who had subordinated anti-Gaullism to anti-communism and those who subordinated anti-communism to anti-Gaullism.

De Gaulle's own relationship to the events of 1968 marked a break in his career. Strangely, the 78-year-old stiffly formal politician and soldier had many things in common with the protesters. All the major episodes of his life had involved rebellion against the established order, he despised the values of bourgeois prosperity and consumption, he had never worked in private business or shown any interest in money, and he had done more than any individual in western Europe to lessen the power of the United States. De Gaulle had even seriously contemplated moving the president's official residence from the stuffy upper-class eighth *arrondissement* to the Left Bank. The possible similarities were recognized by de Gaulle's police chief who said, in an astonishing book,[7] that de Gaulle had missed the opportunity to make himself the 'Mao of France' (that is to put himself at the head of revolutionary youth). Many student leaders such as Serge July and Régis Debray acquired a retrospective admiration for de Gaulle. However, in May 1968, de Gaulle played little role in the thoughts of the students or workers. Students' leaders were concerned with broad social forces, not with individuals. Régis Debray was later to write: 'we did not talk of de Gaulle, but of the Gaullist power. That of the banks, trusts and monopolies, our faceless enemies.' De Gaulle, who had often been loved or hated, was now ignored. The Elysée Palace was never attacked and de Gaulle was left unmolested when he laid a wreath on the Tomb of the Unknown Soldier on May 7. De Gaulle had often been hated, but May 1968 was the first time that he had been despised.

De Gaulle himself seemed to be caught off guard by the events of 1968. He was out of the country from May 14 to May 18, on a state visit to Romania. The decision to reopen the Sorbonne was taken by his prime minister Pompidou acting on his own. On May 24 de Gaulle made a television broadcast in which he promised to hold a referendum on the, rather vaguely defined, issue of 'participation'. However, unlike previous broadcasts at moments of crisis, this one failed to produce the desired effect. It was followed by serious rioting in many cities. At the end of May de Gaulle left France again in odd circumstances: he flew to the French army base at Baden Baden in West Germany to see general Massu. There is debate about the reasons for this voyage. Massu himself believed that de Gaulle had despaired and that only his urgings had persuaded the president to return to the fray. Others suggest that de Gaulle wished to test the loyalty of the army, which was still bitter about the legacy of the Algerian war, before he risked confronting the protests in France. Perhaps de Gaulle himself did not foresee what he would do, but was motivated by certain instincts: the desire to make a dramatic gesture and to ensure that he preserved his freedom of manoeuvre.

On his return from Baden Baden, de Gaulle announced that he would defer the referendum, which would have been difficult to organize in circumstances of such confusion. Instead, legislative elections would be held at the end of June. These elections proved a triumph for Gaullism: in a parliament of 487, the UNR had 300 seats and its allies had a further 58. However, the triumph for Gaullism did not mean a triumph for de Gaulle. The general had not risen to the occasion as he had done during previous threats to the regime. In the past he had addressed the nation in striking, carefully prepared, speeches of classical French, in May 1968 he resorted to the platitudes and vulgarity of a retired officer: 'reforme oui, le chienlit non.' For the first time in his life, de Gaulle seemed like a conventional conservative, whose only responses to challenge were surrender or repression. He himself remarked of his actions 'c'était du Pétain, ce n'était pas du de Gaulle'. Furthermore, the events seem to have made him dependent on agencies that he had previously controlled – such as the army and organized Gaullism.

Only after the events did de Gaulle recover his taste for political innovation, and when he did so he felt uncomfortable with those who had supported him. He is said to have remarked when faced with the new parliament 'Here is a PSF [right-wing] chamber with which I will make a PSU [left-wing] policy', but this change came too late. During the events de Gaulle had seemed to owe his survival to a part of the extreme right. Many believed that the amnesty granted to OAS leaders was the price that had been paid for the support of Tixier, or the army, in May. Furthermore, Pompidou, once de Gaulle's cipher, had shown himself to be a real leader. Pompidou was now seen as the dauphin and he became the focus of loyalty for many Gaullists. Pompidou was particularly popular among conservatives who believed that he had tried to restrain de Gaulle's vengeful feelings against the *Algérie Française* lobby. De Gaulle tried to regain the initiative by dismissing Pompidou and appointing Couve de Murville, a loyal functionary, as prime minister. This produced short-term results, in the form of a victory in the parliamentary elections of 1968, but de Gaulle then used a referendum on the vague notion of participation as a vote of confidence on his own presidency. When the results of this vote were not satisfactory he resigned. A year later he was dead.

In so much as they had coherent demands, the protesters of 1968 were largely successful. The students prevented the introduction of selection in universities and succeeded in making life on campus more bearable – though they could do nothing about the overcrowding of universities. The workers were granted pay increases, a one hour reduction in the working week, and a few concessions to the 'qualitative' demands that had provoked the strikes. However, people whose slogan had been 'be realistic, ask for the impossible' can hardly have regarded such limited concessions as a success. Consumer capitalism survived the events of May 1968 unscathed. Some argue that the hedonism and libertarianism of 1968 facilitated the development of consumerism: when students attacked the headquarters of the Club Med, the company responded by offering them free holidays. Students who had participated in the events often went on to work in marketing or personnel. The memories of 1968 helped to create a generation that was particularly conscious of fashions, fascinated by America and interested in novelty of every kind. Some student leaders discovered entrepreneurial talents. Henri Weber ploughed the proceeds of the book that he wrote on the events of 1968 into setting up an anarchist journal. Later he was commissioned to write a semi official history of the *Conseil National du Patronat Français*. In 1985 one of the most prominent *soixante huitards*, Serge July, founded a new newspaper, *Libération*, that became the emblem of chic and prosperous Parisians in the 1980s. The message of 1968 had become so diffuse that it fitted in with the very values that 1968 had been devoted to attacking. In 1988 Daniel Cohn-Bendit was in a restaurant interviewing an old friend, now a journalist on *Libération*, about the events of 1968. Their conversation was interrupted by a young woman at a neighbouring table. She explained that she worked in marketing and that she had only been 14 in 1968, but that she understood their conversation because 'she had smoked a joint in the car on her way to the restaurant'.

In political terms, 1968, which seemed for a time to shake the regime, finished up by showing how strong the Fifth Republic had become. The events were particularly important in three respects. Firstly, they reflected the continued power of the bourgeoisie. The student protests attracted widespread support from the French middle classes. The students themselves were overwhelmingly middle class (only 2.5 per cent of them came from proletarian families) and, as Aron bitterly remarked, many parents believed that throwing stones at the police was a safer diversion for their sons than driving fast cars on the motorway. Working-class strikes were a different matter, and it was after such strikes that public enthusiasm for the regime began to return. France's rulers learned the lesson of 1968. In December 1986, France was gripped by another wave of students' protest and workers' strikes. The government of the Gaullist Chirac, who had been a member of Pompidou's cabinet in 1968, conceded to the student demands, but it refused to make any concessions to the workers.

Secondly, the events of 1968 reflected the decreasing role of violence in French politics: no one was killed during the riots. Raymond Aron attributed this to the fact that the protesters espoused a 'purely verbal violence'.[8] Edgar Morin attributed it to the spirit of generosity that pervaded the protests.[9] Even more striking than the students' restraint from violence was that of the government. De Gaulle's ministers refrained from waking him up on the night of 10–11 May partly because they feared that he might order that the Sorbonne be evacuated by force. In part this hostility to violence was due to the fact that the government did not wish to spill blood, especially the blood of bourgeois students. Some ministers may also have suspected that the army, which was still bitter over Algeria, would be reluctant to return to its barracks if it was used to restore order. The government was helped to avoid violence by the existence of the *Compagnies Républicaines de Sécurité* (CRS). The CRS had been founded in 1945 and transformed into loyal servants of the bourgeois state by the purge of Communists from their ranks in 1947. Before this, riots had often been dealt with by soldiers. Frightened young conscripts with bolt action rifles were bad at holding their nerve when faced with hostile crowds and this had often produced massacres. The CRS, by contrast, were tough but also disciplined, well-trained and equipped with techniques (such as tear gas) that allowed them to disarm opponents. The CRS were obliged to account to the minister of the interior for every live round that they fired in action. They knew that violence against certain groups – such as Algerians or, in 1961, *pieds noirs* – would be tolerated by the government. They also knew that violence against groups that were politically important would not be tolerated. The CRS had handled Poujadism and peasant protest without causing bloodshed, and they ensured that most students in 1968 suffered nothing more than a whiff of tear gas.

Thirdly, the events of 1968 showed that the Fifth Republic constitution would last. Until this time, it had still seemed possible that the new traits in French politics that had emerged since 1958 might be dependent on the intervention of a single man. The role of Pompidou and his associates in May 1968 demonstrated the arrival of a 'Gaullism' that was independent of de Gaulle. The behaviour of the Communist party in 1968 demonstrated that it had become a part of the system rather than a movement dedicated to the overthrow of the system. The rallying of part of the extreme right to the regime, if not to de Gaulle as an individual, demonstrated that the scars of Algeria and Vichy would eventually be healed.

15   Conclusions

How did France change between 1934 and 1970 and how lasting were these changes? In political terms France has achieved a degree of stability that would have seemed surprising to those brought up during the 1930s. This stabilization has three dimensions. The first of these is the decline in political violence. The second relates to constitutional change. The Fifth Republic has survived the death of its founder and outlived all but one of the regimes that have governed France since 1789. Constitutional practice has been slightly altered by events such as the cohabition of right-wing prime ministers with a Socialist president, but the constitution itself has remained almost unchanged. Few people now argue in favour of significant constitutional change. Indeed François Mitterrand was president of the republic, which he had once criticized so bitterly, for 14 years. The third form that stabilization has taken in France relates to the party system. During the 1960s some commentators believed that France was moving toward an Anglo-Saxon two-party system. This has not happened. The right remains divided between the Gaullist *Rassemblement pour la République* and the Centrist *Union pour la Démocratie Française*, a division that was exacerbated by the personal animosity between Jacques Chirac and Valéry Giscard d'Estaing. The left also remains divided between the *Parti Socialiste* and the *Parti Communiste Français* and the former of these groups is further split by numerous factional rivalries. However, French party politics have not returned to the kaleidoscope of small parties that dominated the Third and Fourth Republics; nor do divisions within left and right generate the same short-lived governments that were so common before 1958.

The growth of political stability cannot be explained in purely political terms. It was also linked to social and economic changes: the new political style of the Fifth Republic had as much to do with rising standards of living, and particularly with the spread of television, as it did with constitutional formulae or new party structure. This raises the question of France's economic transformation during the period from 1934 and 1970. The changes wrought by the *trente glorieuses* still affect France. Economic growth has continued, although at much lower levels than those that it achieved before the oil crisis of the mid 1970s, and France continues to be regarded as one of the economic successes of Europe. To some extent the radical economic change of the post-war period has generated its own momentum. An underdeveloped economy before 1945 helped to sustain a certain kind of social structure which, in turn, impeded economic change. The rapid growth of 1948 to 1975 created a society that was more willing to accept large-scale industry and encouraged individuals to take a more relaxed view of economic risk.

How were the fruits of economic growth divided? Broadly this question can be answered by dividing France into winners, survivors and losers. The winners were the upper reaches of the French bourgeoisie. For much of the period from 1934 to 1970 this class seemed to be threatened. Hostility to big business was found across almost the entire political spectrum and, after 1936, France had one of the largest Communist parties in western Europe. The bourgeoisie also seemed to be compromised by its involvement with the Vichy government. However, far from losing power or prestige the upper bourgeoisie have become more prosperous and powerful in post-war France. This book has argued that this prosperity can be explained in several ways. Firstly, the upper bourgeoisie was a small and tightly knit group formed by common education in *grandes écoles*, service in the *corps d'état*, and a network of social relations. This group stuck together and often succeeded in protecting its own during times of political trouble: this tendency was particularly important under Vichy and during the Liberation. Secondly, the training of the French bourgeoisie encouraged them to be pragmatic and flexible, at least with reference to their own interests. Almost all graduates of the *École Polytechnique* abandoned military careers after 1945, in spite of the fact that it was still, theoretically, a military school. Later graduates of the same school moved out of the heavy industrial sectors with which they had been closely associated and sought careers in aeronautics and electronics. Members of the *grands corps* repeatedly used new developments such as the rise of town-planning or economic *dirigisme* to further their own interests.

The upper reaches of the bourgeoisie were particularly well placed to exploit the post-war expansion of the state because they had a tradition of close relations with the administration and because many of them began their careers in the civil service. Post-war economic growth also increased the number of very large

industrial companies in France and the management of these companies often converged with the upper reaches of the French civil
service to create a new kind of elite. No institution incarnated the
hegemony of this state–big business elite more than the *École
Nationale d'Administration* (ENA) which was founded in 1945. ENA
was initially designed to provide a meritocratic means of recruitment
into the French civil service. In practice it remained the preserve of
the children of upper level civil servants and the *bourgeoisie des
affaires*. As time has gone on, the *énarques* have expanded their power
in a variety of ways. Increasing numbers of them indulged in
pantouflage that took them to highly paid positions in the private
sector: a survey in the 1970s showed that many students at *grandes
écoles* regarded a brief period of state service as a good preparation
for a lucrative career in a large company. During the Fifth Republic,
increasing numbers of top-flight administrators also began to enter
the political arena and to hold ministerial office. The power of this
elite seemed to reach a peak during the presidency of Valéry Giscard
d'Estaing, when the president himself and over half of all members
of ministerial cabinets were *énarques*. Mitterrand's first government
seemed to represent a setback for big business and the upper civil
service. The number of former civil servants who held ministerial
office or who worked in ministerial entourages was reduced. An
attempt was also made to force nationalized industries, traditionally
a fiefdom of the *grands corps*, to take more account of 'social interests'. However, this period proved to be short-lived. Laurent Fabius,
an *énarque* who became minister of industry and later prime minister, encouraged a return to the previous status quo. The Mitterrand
government does not seem to have damaged the economic interests
of the established elite and it did not even exclude them from political power for very long. If anything in French politics is certain, it is
that François Mitterrand will be the last president for many years
who is not an *énarque*.

The survivors of French economic growth were the small businessmen and peasants who had made up such an important part of
Third Republic society. It was widely assumed that these groups were
allergic to modernity. Jean Touchard interpreted the Poujadist
rebellion of the mid 1950s as the death throes of this group; Pierre
Birnbaum argued that the advent of the Fifth Republic marked the
passing of power from small-scale to big business; Communist theorists interpreted the resignation of Antoine Pinay from de Gaulle's
cabinet in 1960 as a final protest on behalf of the archaic groups that

he was seen to represent. It is true that the number of peasants and small businessmen in France has declined during the past half century. It is also true that many of the peasants who left the land to enter factories became the most under-privileged section of the proletariat. However, the peasantry and small businessmen have never been afflicted by the total extinction that so many regarded as their inevitable fate. The reasons for this are partly economic. France is a 'dualist' economy which requires a large sector of small subcontractors to service its large industrial companies, general prosperity has also helped shopkeepers because the French remain attached to the particular service that such shops provide. Sometimes small producers have been able to benefit from technological development and some new technologies – electrical power, motor cars, cheap personal computers – have actually made it easier to decentralize production.

Most importantly, the small business and peasant sector has been protected by its political power. Governments have consistently needed the votes of these groups particularly because few post-war governments have been able to expect much support from the industrial working class. It is true that the political importance of the peasantry and *petite bourgeoisie* declined during the early Fifth Republic because the political system gave fewer advantages to the small centre parties for which they voted and because de Gaulle attracted some support from the working class. However, Suzanne Berger has argued that the government's dependence on the 'backward' sector of the economy increased during the late 1960s as the appeal that Gaullism had once made to the working class diminished.[1] 'This dependence ensured that the government maintained some of the tax-breaks, subsidies and regulations that protected small economic units. Economic growth and European integration often provided the state with new resources from which to provide this kind of protection. During the 1960s, the French state opened up a new form of support for its agriculture by devising the Common Agricultural Policy and during the early 1970s Jean Royer was appointed to the Pompidou cabinet with the specific brief of protecting small business.

The biggest losers of post-war economic growth were the industrial working classes. Their living standards increased more slowly than those of other groups, and the enormous apparent power that the labour movement possessed in the aftermath of the Second World War never translated into concrete economic benefits. In the

1980s, low working-class standards of living were still reflected in very tangible ways. A worker of 35 could expect to live for six years less than a teacher of the same age; the average worker was almost 2 centimetres shorter than his bourgeois counterpart. In part this was because of the very success of the groups described above. An upper bourgeoisie with traditions of good access to the administration and petit-bourgois–peasant bloc with traditions of good access to the French parliament, simply squeezed the proletariat out. It was also because the working class was changing in ways that made it smaller, less powerful and less likely to seek its salvation in collective action. At the top, workers escaped from their class into salaried non-manual positions. At the bottom, after 1975, increasing numbers of workers fell into unemployment, a situation of which the French had little experience. Those who entered the industrial workforce tended to be former peasants or non-European immigrants who lacked much sense of class consciousness. The proportion of the French population who defined themselves as working class dropped from 26 per cent to 22 per cent between 1975 and 1982.

This book has argued that working-class weakness also owed something to the organization of the proletariat itself. The working class seemed strong because of a brief convergence of economic and political circumstances. On the economic level, the great depression, the war economy and the Monnet Plan produced industrial concentration, an emphasis on heavy industry, and a freezing of technical change. They also produced homogenization of a workforce that was increasingly male, skilled and well established. On the political level, the Popular Front and, especially, Communist entry into the Resistance in 1941 produced a very strong Communist party that was closely linked to the main trade union confederation. However, both these circumstances were temporary. Working-class strength was broken by economic growth that occurred outside the old heavy industries, and by the large-scale entry, or return, of women, immigrants, and rural workers into the factories. Communist strength was weakened by destalinization, the invasion of Hungary, and the success of de Gaulle. Furthermore, the link between the industrial working class and the PCF was so strong that each exacerbated the other's decline. The PCF's *ouvrièrism* prevented it from adapting to new circumstances with the skill that was shown by its Italian counterpart, while the Communist-controlled labour movement's aggressive stance and preoccupation with the Soviet Union exacerbated the isolation and impotence of the working class.

Why end in 1970? To some extent the answer to this question lies in the fact that the changes described above had worked their effects by this date. It also lies in the fact that French history seems more fragmented after 1970. New political movements – such as feminism and ecology – did not fit neatly into the established categories of French politics. France's large immigrant population no longer seemed to be sure that assimilation into French culture was either possible or desirable. The growing power of the regions challenged the centralized state and even that quintessential Fifth Republic agent of national integration, *Organization Radio et Télévision Française,* was broken up into its constituent parts in 1974. Judged in an international context, such developments may not seem so important: France is still, in most respects, a more centralized state and a more unified culture than any other European country. It is in the context of earlier French history that the absence of a single national culture seems so strange. From the beginning of the Third Republic, French leaders have emphatically asserted the importance of a common political culture that revolved around loyalty to the Republic, national unity, patriotism and a certain conception of French history. During the period between the Popular Front and the Liberation this sense of common political culture became even more highly developed. The Communist party abandoned its inter-nationalism to accept the *patrie* while most of the extreme right abandoned its Maurrassian royalism to accept the Republic.

All this presents a paradox. The assertion of French national culture was at its most intense at a time of national weakness and division. Violent political conflict might be carried out between groups that appealed to the same political traditions – both the die-hard defenders of *Algérie Française* and the Frenchmen who aided the FLN genuinely believed that they were defending the 'Republic'. Curiously, the fact that France is now free from violent political divi-sion or foreign threat makes it less necessary for the French to assert their common national history. The change can be seen by examining the anniversaries of the French Revolution. The centen-ary, celebrated in the aftermath of the Boulanger affair, emphasized the defence of the Republic. The one hundred and fiftieth anniver-sary, celebrated on the eve of the Second World War, emphasized patriotism. The bicentenary, celebrated in 1989, emphasized nothing in particular: it was a muted and confused affair that was overshadowed by much more dramatic events in eastern Europe and Peking.

Some people recognized that national unity had to be asserted vigorously precisely because it was so remote from reality: on the opening pages of his memoirs, Charles de Gaulle wrote: 'All of my life, I have had a certain idea of France...I imagine her like the princess in the fairy-tales or the Madonna in the frescos destined for an exceptional destiny...If she is touched by mediocrity, I sense an absurd anomaly which can be attributed to the French, but not to the essence of France.'[2] Some French people now might argue that the 'essence of France' is the absurd anomaly. They would argue that the idea of a single unified history which can take in the range and diversity of experience of individual French people is a myth. The most important change wrought by the events of 1934 to 1970 may have been to create circumstances in which the French people no longer need the myth of a unified national history. This is not, however, something that the writer of a historical textbook can afford to dispense with.

Notes

Unless otherwise stated, books cited in Notes and Bibliography are published in London or Paris.

Chapter 1.   Background

1. Stanley Hoffman, 'Paradoxes of the French political community', in Stanley Hoffman (ed.), *France: Change and Tradition* (1963) pp. 1–112.

Chapter 2.   *'Inaction française'*

1. Lucien Rebatet, *Les décombres* (1942).
2. Cited in Stanley Hoffman, *Le mouvement Poujade* (1956) p. 227.
3. René Rémond, *Les droites en France* (1982) pp. 218–23.
4. Francisque Gay, *Dans les flammes et dans le sang. Les crimes contre les églises et les prêtres en Espagne* (1936).

Chapter 3.   Strange Defeat

1. Jean-Paul Sartre, *War Diaries. Notebooks from a Phoney War November 1939–March 1940* (1984) p. 356.

Chapter 4.   Vichy

1. Robert Paxton, *Vichy France. Old Guard and New Order 1940–1944* (New York, 1982) p. 139.
2. Marc Ferro, *Pétain* (1987) p. v.
3. Charles Rist, *Une saison gâtée. Journal de la guerre et de l'occupation 1939–1945* (1983), and Pierre Nicolle, *Cinquante mois d'armistice, Vichy 2 juillet 1940–26 août 1944: journal d'un témoin*, 2 vols (1947).

4. René Benjamin, *Les sept étoiles de France* (1942); *Le maréchal et son peuple* (1942); *Le grand homme seul* (1943).
5. Benjamin, *Le maréchal et son peuple*, p. 1.
6. Henri Du Moulin de Labarthète, *Le temps des illusions: souvenirs (juillet 1940–avril 1942)* (Geneva, 1946) p. 91.
7. Benjamin, *Le maréchal et son peuple*, p. 6.
8. Louis Girard, *Montoire. Verdun diplomatique* (1948).
9. Lucien Romier cited in Benjamin, *Le maréchal et son peuple*, p. 6.
10. Ibid., p. 5.
11. Emile Laure, *Pétain* (1941) p. 29.
12. Alfred Fabre Luce cited by Pierre Assouline in *Le Nouvel Observateur*, 21–27 September 1989.
13. Jules Roy, *Le Nouvel Observateur*, 21–27 September 1989.
14. Benjamin, *Le grand homme seul*, p. 10.
15. Laure, *Pétain*, p. 421.
16. Yves Bouthillier, *Le drame de Vichy*, 2 vols (1950) I, p. 209.
17. Nicolle, *Cinquante mois d'armistice*.
18. Emmanuel Berl helped write the first and second speeches that Pétain delivered as head of state. However, he did not meet Pétain and he was later to admit that 'I stressed his bucolism more than anyone, and more than the Marshal himself'. See Emmanuel Berl, *La Fin de la 111ème République* (1968) pp. 13, 178.
19. Gordon Wright, *Rural Revolution in France. The Peasantry in the Twentieth Century* (Stanford, CA, 1964) p. 224.
20. Cited in Richard F. Kuisel, *Capitalism and the State in Modern France. Renovation and Economic Management in the Twentieth Century* (Cambridge, 1983) p. 131.
21. Roger Martin, *Patron de droit divine* (1984) pp. 34–5.
22. Edgar Faure, *Mémoires*. I: *Avoir toujours raison ... c'est un grand tort* (1982) p. 176.

Chapter 6.   Rebuilding Bourgeois France: 1944–1951

1. Henry Charbonneau, *Le roman noir de la droite française* (1969).
2. Philippe Viannay, *Du bon usage de la France* (1988) pp. 152–4.
3. Cited in Roger Faligot and Rémi Kauffer, *Les résistants. De la guerre de l'ombre aux allées du pouvoir 1944–1989* (1989) p. 52.
4. Michel Debré, *Trois républiques pour une France. Memoires* II: *1946–1958. Agir* (1988) p. 33.
5. Kenneth Pendar, *Adventure in Diplomacy* (New York, 1945).

Chapter 7.   The Fall of the Fourth Republic: 1951–1958

1. François Mitterand, *Aux frontières de l'Union Française* (1953).

Chapter 8.   *Trente glorieuses*

1. Michel Crozier (ed.), *L'Administration face aux problèmes du changement* (special issue of *Sociologie du Travail,* 1966).
2. Jean-Jacques Servan-Schreiber, *Le défi Américain* (1967).
3. Cited in Maurice Larkin, *France since the Popular Front. Government and People 1936–1986* (Oxford, 1988) p. 185.
4. Roger Martin, *Patron de droit divine* (1984).
5. Edgar Morin, *Commune en France. La métamorphose de Plodémet* (1967).
6. Ibid., p. 73.
7. Lawrence Wylie, *Village in the Vaucluse* (Cambridge, MA, 1957) p. 32.
8. Morin, *Commune en France,* p. 107.

Chapter 9.   The Second Sex

1. Huguette Bouchardeau, *Pas d'histoire, les femmes* (1977).
2. Eugen Weber, *Peasants into Frenchmen: the Modernization of Rural France 1870–1914* (Stanford, CA, 1976).
3. Martine Segalen, *Love and Power in the Peasant Family* (1983).
4. Morin, *Commune en France,* p. 164.
5. Daniel Bertaux and Isabelle Bertaux-Wiame, 'Artisanal Bakery in France: How it Lives and Why it Survives', in Frank Bechofer and Brian Elliot (eds), *The Petite Bourgeoisie. Comparative Studies of the Uneasy Stratum* (1981) pp. 155–81, p. 166.
6. Dominique Wolton, cited in Bouchardeau, *Pas d'histoire,* p. 137.

Chapter 10.   Generation Gaps

1. Jean-Louis Servan-Schreiber, *A mi vie. L'entrée en quarantaine,* cited in Luc Boltanski, *The Making of a Class. The Cadres in French Society* (Cambridge, 1987) p. 103.

2. Claude Nicolet, *Pierre Mendès-France ou le métier de Cassandre* (1959) p. 37.
3. Françoise Giroud, *La nouvelle vague* (1958) p. 328.

Chapter 11. Class Struggle

1. Annie Kreigel, *The French Communists. Profile of a People* (1968) p. 168.
2. Henri Claude, *Gaullisme et grand capital* (1960).

Chapter 12. Algeria

1. In *Paris Match*, 1 September 1956; cited in Nathalie Riz, 'La force du cartiérisme' in Jean-Pierre Rioux (ed.), *La guerre d'Algérie et les français* (1990) pp. 328–36.
2. Jean-Jacques Servan-Schreiber, *Lieutenant in Algeria* (1958) p. 85.
3. *Defense de l'Occident*, November 1958.
4. Cited in Paul Marie de la Gorce, *The French Army. A Military Political History* (1963) p. 355.

Chapter 13. The Foundations of the Fifth Republic

1. Antoine Dupont-Fauville, 'La situation de l'économie française avant 1958', in Institut Charles de Gaulle, *De Gaulle en son siècle. 3: Moderniser la France* (1982) pp. 48–50.

Chapter 14. The End of the Beginning: 1968–1969

1. André Quattrochi and Tom Nairn, *The Beginning of the End* (1968).
2. 'Vincent' cited by 'Y.L.' in 'The May Movement at the Lycée Pasteur, Neuilly', in Charles Posner (ed.), *Reflections on the Revolution in France: 1968* (1968) pp. 128–53.
3. Cited in René Chiroux, *L'extrême droite sous la Ve République* (1974) p. 151.
4. Philippe Ariès, *Un historien du dimanche* (1980) p. 184.

5. Cited in William B. Cohen, 'The Legacy of Empire: the Algerian Connection', *Journal of Contemporary History*, 15 (1980) 97–123.
6. *Rivarol*, 20 June 1968.
7. M. Grimaud, *En mai fais ce que qu'il te plait* (1977).
8. Raymond Aron, *La révolution introuvable* (1968).
9. E. Morin, C. Letort and C. Castoris, *Mai 68: la brèche, suivi de vingt ans après* (Brussels, 1988).

Chapter 15. Conclusion

1. S. Berger and M.J. Piorre, *Dualism and Discontinuity in Industrial Societies* (Cambridge, 1980).
2. Charles de Gaulle, *Memoires de guerre. L'appel 1940–1942* (1980) p. 8.

Bibliography

General accounts

James Mcmillan's *Twentieth century France. Politics and Society 1899–1991* (1985 and 1992) is solid. Maurice Larkin, *France since the Popular Front 1936–1986* (1988) contains good tables on France's social and economic development. Theodore Zeldin's *France 1848–1945* (2 vols, 1973 and 1977) contains flashes of brilliance. On elections see François Goguel, *Géographie des élections françaises sous la troisième république et la quatrième république* (1970). Peter Morris, David Bell and Douglas Johnson (eds), *A Biographical Dictionary of French Political Leaders since1870* (Hemel Hempstead, 1989) defines 'political leaders' broadly. Two superb biographies of de Gaulle have much to say about many aspects of French history since the 1930s. Andrew Shennan, *De Gaulle* (1993) is a concise and balanced summary of academic research. Jean Lacouture, *De Gaulle* (3 vols, 1984) is a long, immensely detailed, work full of the insights and intuitions of a journalist who has spent half a lifetime observing the general. Documents relating to de Gaulle have been published in de Gaulle, *Discours et messages* (5 vols, 1970) and *Lettres, notes et carnets* (12 vols, 1980–8). René Rémond's *Les droites en France* (1982) was a seminal book but is rather schematic. Stanley Hoffmann (ed.), *In Search of France* (New York, 1965), contains a number of interesting essays. Hoffmann's own contributions to this work and to *Decline or Renewal? France since the 1930s* (New York, 1974) have been very influential. The essays in Roland Barthes, *Mythologies* (1957) explore subjects ranging from steak and chips to Poujadism. Raoul Girardet, *Mythes et mythologies politiques* (1986) concentrates on more conventional political analysis. Georges Vedel (ed.), *La dépolitisation, mythe ou réalité* (1962) deals with several aspects of an important subject. Discerning judges assure me that Tony Judt's *Marxism and the French: Studies in Labour and Politics in France 1830–1881* (Oxford, 1986) has many virtues, though I have never been able to see what these are. A number of politically *engagé* French historians have written their memoirs. Philippe Ariès, *Un historien du dimanche* (1980) and Annie Kriegel *Ce que j'ai cru comprendre* (1991) make an interesting comparison. Emmanuel Le Roy-Ladurie,

Paris–Montpellier PC–PSU 1945–1963 (1981) is good on the intellectual left. The essays by Maurice Agulhon and Raoul Girardet in Pierre Nora (ed.) *Essais d'ego-histoire* (1987) are revealing. Eugen Weber's *My France* (Cambridge, MA, 1991) is characteristically stimulating. Julian Jackson and Roderick Kedward are both preparing general histories of France since 1914, Nick Atkins and Robert Gildea are preparing books on France since 1945, Kevin Passmore is writing a study of the Third Republic.

Journals

The *Revue Française de Science Politique* and the *Revue Française de Sociologie* both contain some useful studies. The *Revue d'Histoire de la Deuxième Guerre Mondiale* devoted much space to studies of Vichy France. *Vingtième Siècle. Revue d'histoire* runs short accessible articles with good photographs. *Modern and Contemporary France* concentrates mainly on the twentieth century.

Economic history

For a general survey, see J.J. Carré, P. Dubois and E. Malinvaud, *French Economic Growth* (1976). On the continued survival of small-scale production see Suzanne Berger and M. J. Piorre, *Dualism and Discontinuity in Industrial Societies* (Cambridge, 1980). On the French attachment to 'sound money' see Kenneth Mouré, *Managing the Franc Poincaré. Economic Understanding and Political Constraint in French Monetary Policy, 1928–1936* (Cambridge, 1991). On the economic role of the state see Patrick Fridenson and André Straus (eds), *Le capitalisme français* (1987); Peter Hall, *Governing the Economy: the Politics of State Intervention in Britain and France* (Cambridge, 1986); Jean Monnet, *Mémoires* (New York, 1978); Alan Milward, *The Reconstruction of Western Europe 1945–51* (1984); Richard Kuisel, *Capitalism and the State in Modern France* (Cambridge, 1981); Michel Margairaz, *L'Etat, les finances et l'économie. Histoire d'une conversion 1932–1952* (2 vols, 1992), and François Bloch-Lainé and Jean Bouvier, *La France restaurée 1944–1954 – Dialogue sur le choix d'une modernisation* (1986). Robert Frost, *Alternating Currents. Nationalized Power in France 1946–1970* (Cornell, NY, 1991) describes the political debates around and within EDF. On the development of consumerism, see M. Perrot, *Le mode de vie des familles bourgeoises* (1961). Janine Morice, *La demande d'automobiles en France. Théorie, histoire, répartition, géographie* (1957) describes the geographical distribution of motor cars in a series of baffling statistical tables.

Society   •

The counterpart of the 'stalemate society' works on the Third Republic are the 'transformation of society' works on France since 1945. The most typical of these is Jean Fourastié, *Les trente glorieuses ou la révolution invisible de 1946 à 1970* (1979). On the peasantry see Gordon Wright, *Rural Revolution in France. The Peasantry in the Twentieth Century* (Stanford, CA, 1964), and Jacques Fauvet and Henri Mendras (eds), *Les paysans et la politique en France contemporaine* (1958). On artisans see Steven Zdateny, *The Politics of Survival: Artisans in Twentieth Century France* (Oxford, 1990). F. Gresle, *L'univers de la boutique* (Lille, 1981) is an exhaustive study of small shopkeepers in the north. The career of the self-appointed spokesman of small business is examined in Sylvie Guillaume, *La Confédération Générale des Petites et Moyennes Entreprises. Son histoire, son combat, un autre syndicalisme patronal 1944–1978* (1978). On the working class, Roger Magraw's *History of the French Working Class*, vol. 2: *Workers and the Bourgeois Republic 1871–1939* (1992) crosses its chronological borders to discuss the post-war labour movement. Jane Marceau, *Class and Status in France. Economic Change and Social Immobility 1945–1975* (Oxford, 1977) is good on the persistence of social inequality during the *trente glorieuses*. Gerard Noiriel's *Workers in French Society in the Nineteenth and Twentieth Centuries* (New York, 1990) advances an ambitious general interpretation. Gary Cross has recently published two important books: *A Quest for time: the Reduction of Work in Britain and France 1840–1940* (Berkeley, CA, 1989), and *Immigrant Workers in Industrial France: the Making of a New Labouring Class* (Philadelphia, 1983). Tyler Stoval, 'French communism and suburban development. The rise of the Red Belt', *Journal of Contemporary History*, 24 (1989), 437–60 argues that Communist strength in the *banlieues* was built on neighbourhood as much as workplace. On the upper classes see Pierre Birnbaum, *La classe dirigeante française* (1978) and *Les sommets de l'état. Essai sur l'élite du pouvoir en France* (1977), Alain Girard, *La Réussite sociale en France* (1961), and Ezra Suleiman, *Elites in French Society: the Politics of Survival* (1978). The culture of the French civil service is examined in Pierre Lalumière, *L'inspection des finances*

(1959) and J.-C. Thoenig, *L'ère des technocrates. Le cas des ponts et chaussées* (1973). On big business see Maurice Levy-Leboyer (ed.), *Le patronat de la seconde industrialisation* (1979). Jean-Noel Jeanneney's essays in *L'argent caché. Milieux d'affaires et pouvoir politique dans la France du XXe siècle* (1980) examine a number of business interventions in politics. Henry Ehrmann, *Organized Business in France* (Princeton, NJ, 1957) concentrates on the Fourth Republic but has some interesting comments on the 1930s and the Vichy period. Henri Weber, *Le parti des patrons. Le CNPF (1946–1986)* (1986) contains useful biographies of individual business leaders. P. Bernoux, *Les nouveaux patrons. Le centre des jeunes dirigeants d'entreprise* (1974) looks at one business group. François Jacquin, *Les cadres de l'industrie et du commerce en France* (1955) is a solid empirical study of industrial managers. Luc Boltanski, *The Making of a Class: Cadres in French Society* (1987) is more wide-ranging and theoretical. On women, Huguette Bouchardeau's *Pas d'histoire, les femmes* (1977) is an important, if rather dated, book with a good chronological table. Simone de Beauvoir, *Le deuxième sexe* (1949) is interesting on many issues. On de Beauvoir's own life see among many other biographies, Dierdre Bair, *Simone de Beauvoir* (1990). Claire Duchen, *Women's Rights and Women's Lives in France 1944–1968* (1994) is good on the development of the idea of the housewife. The best works on women's voting behaviour were published during the 1950s. Maurice Duverger, *The Political Role of Women* (1955) deals with women in a number of countries. Mattei Dogan and Jacques Narbonne, *Les françaises face à la politique. Comportement politique et condition sociale* (1955) is a wide-ranging work that deals with many issues other than politics. Antony Copley's *Sexual Moralities in France 1780–1980. New Ideas on the Family, Divorce and Homosexuality* (1989 and 1992) is disappointing. J. Girard, *Le mouvement homosexual en France 1945–1980* (1981) is better. On youth, see François Giroud, *La nouvelle vague* (1958). On old age, see Simone de Beauvoir, *La vieillesse* (1970). There are many excellent local studies of post-war France. Jacques Lagroye, *Société et politique. J. Chaban-Delmas à Bordeaux* (1973) is good on notables, business influence and the role of the church. Pierre Clément and N. Xydias, *Vienne sur le Rhône* (1955) and Charles Bettelheim and Suzanne Frère, *Une ville française moyenne: Auxerre en 1950* (1950) both contain detailed statistics on large towns. L. Bernot and R. Blacard, *Nouville. Un village français* (1953), Edgar Morin, *Commune en France. La métamorphose de Plodémet* (1967), Lawrence Wylie, *Village in the Vaucluse* (Cambridge, MA, 1957) and *Village in Anjou* (Cambridge MA, 1964) are founded on a more anecdotal approach to small villages. Michel Lagrée, *Religion et cultures en Bretagne (1850–1950)* (1992) traces social change over a longer timescale.

Memoirs

In addition to the works cited with relation to specific subjects, the following memoirs may prove particularly interesting. Georges Bidault, *Resistance: the Political Autobiography of Georges Bidault* (1967) is good on the the MRP, and the campaign to defend *Algérie Française*. François Bloch-Lainé, *Profession fonctionnaire* (1976) is a shrewd book by an archetypal member of the Parisian *noblesse de robe*. François Brigneau, *Mon après guerre* (1985) describes the life and times of an *opposition nationale* journalist. It begins with his release from prison in 1945 and ends in March 1963 with him weeping on the morning of Bastein Thiry's execution. Roger Martin, *Patron de droit divine* (1984) is good on the *École Polytechnique*, Vichy economic organization, the civil service and the culture of big business. Michel Debré, *Mémoires* (3 vols, 1984–8) is good on local politics, radicalism and all aspects of Gaullism. Edgar Faure, *Mémoires*. I: *Avoir toujours raison c'est un grand tort* (1982) and II: *Si tel doit être mon destin ce soir* (1983) are wonderful books full of local and personal detail that reveal much about the reasons for the survival of radicalism after 1945. Olivier Guichard, *Un chemin tranquille* (1975) is good on the RPF and de Gaulle's return to power. Roger Duchet, *La République épinglée* (1978), contains a brief history of the CNIP and some poisonous portraits of post-war politicians. René Paira, *Affaires d'Alsace* (1990) describes the particular problems facing a prefect in the eastern provinces. Louis Franck, *697 ministres. Souvenirs d'un directeur général des prix. 1947–1962* (1990) has some good sketches of leading figures from politics and the administration. Roger Peyrefitte, *Propos secrets* (1977) reveals, among many other things, which Fourth Republic minister seduced the sentry outside his bedroom door while on a state visit to Indo-China.

The 1930s

D.W. Brogan's *The Development of modern France (1870–1939)* (1940) provides a good narrative account of the 1930s. See also Philippe Bernard and Henri Dubief, *The Decline of the Third Republic 1914–1938*

(Cambridge, 1985). Julian Jackson, *The Politics of Depression in France* (Cambridge, 1985) describes the failure of political parties to devise new strategies to deal with economic crisis. There is an enormous literature on the leagues and on French fascism. Rémond, *Les droites en France*, denies that there was a significant fascist movement in France. Zeev Sternhell, *Ni droite ni gauche. L'idéologie fasciste en France* (1983) argues that fascism originated on the left and that it came to pervade much of French political culture. Sternhell's arguments have been very unpopular with French historians. Jacques Julliard reviews Sternhell in 'Sur un fascisme imaginaire: à propos de Zeev Sternhell', *Annales*, 4 (1984) 849–61. Robert Wohl surveys the debate in 'French Fascism, both right and left. Reflections on the Sternhell controversy', *Journal of Modern History*, 63 (1991) 91–8. A searching critique of the assumptions behind much French writing on fascism is provided in Michel Dobry, 'Février 1934 et la découverte de l'allergie de la société française a la Révolution fasciste,' *Revue Française de Sociologie*, 3/4, xxx (1989) 511–33. Philippe Burin describes the migrations of three left-wingers to fascism in *La dérive fasciste. Doriot, Déat, Bergery 1933–1945* (1986). Robert Soucy, 'French fascism and the *Croix de Feu:* a dissenting interpretation', *Journal of Contemporary History*, 26, 1 (January, 1991) 159–88 argues that fascism in France was a movement of the right. Similar arguments are advanced by William Irvine in 'Fascism in France: the strange case of the *Croix de Feu,' Journal of Modern History*, 63 (1991) 271–95. Kevin Passmore's thesis on 'The right and the extreme right in the Rhône, 1928 to 1940' (Phd, Warwick University, 1992) is one of the rare contributions to this debate that combines theoretical rigour with detailed research. The particular situation of Alsace is discussed in Philip Bankwitz, *Alsatian Autonomist Leaders 1919–1947* (Kansas, 1978); Francis Arzalier, *Les Perdants. La dérive fasciste des mouvements autonomists et indépendantistes au XXe siècle* (1990); Samuel H. Goodfellow, 'Fascism in Alsace, 1918–1945' (Phd, Indiana University, 1992), C. Baechler, *Le parti catholique Alsacien 1890–1939* (1983), and F.-G. Dreyfus, *La vie politique en Alsace 1919–1939* (1969). On the democratic right see W.D. Irvine, *French Conservatism in Crisis. The Republican Federation in the 1930s* (Baton Rouge, LA, 1975). On the Communist party, see Edward Mortimer, *The Rise of the French Communist Party* (1974). The best work on the Popular Front is Julian Jackson's *The Popular Front in France: Defending Democracy 1934–1938* (Cambridge, 1988). R. Rémond and R. Renouvin (eds), *Léon Blum chef du gouvernement 1936–1937* (1967) is also good. Adrian Rossiter, 'Popular Front economic policy and the Matignon agreements', *Historical Journal*, 30 (1987) 663–84, is good on the pre-election intentions of the Popular Front leaders. Attempts to place the French experience in international perspective include Helen Graham and Paul Preston (eds), *The Popular Front in Europe* (1987) and Martin Alexander and Helen Graham, *The French and Spanish Popular Fronts. Comparative Perspectives* (Cambridge, 1989). On the reaction against the Popular Front, see Guy Bourdé, *La défaite du Front Populaire* (1977), René Rémond and Janine Bourdin (eds), *Edouard Daladier chef du gouvernement avril 1938–septembre 1939* (1977). René Rémond and Janine Bourdin (eds), *La France et les Français en 1938–1939* (1978) describes French society under the Daladier government. On business reorganization in the wake of the Popular Front see Ingo Kolboom, *La revanche des patrons. Le patronat français face au front populaire* (1983).

The Defeat

Charles Micaud's *The French Right and Nazi Germany 1933–1939: a Study of Public Opinion* (New York, 1972) argues that sympathy for fascist Italy alienated a part of the right from French foreign policy. Antony Kemp, *The Maginot Line: Myth and Reality* (1981) describes the context in which French fortifications were constructed. Robert Young, *In Command of France: French Policy and Military Planning 1933–1940* (Cambridge, MA, 1978) argues that the defeat was not inevitable. Robert Frankenstein, *Le prix du réarmement français, 1935–1939* (1982) examines the financial basis of French policy. Martin Alexander's detailed study, *The Republic in Danger. Maurice Gamelin and the Politics of French Defence, 1933–1940* (Cambridge, 1993) shows that Gamelin was good at almost everything except winning battles. Philip Bankwitz, *Maxime Weygand and Civil–Military Relations in modern France* (1968) deals with Gamelin's rival. Marc Bloch's *L'étrange défaite* (1946) was based on the personal experience of the author as the oldest captain in the French army and written before his entry into the Resistance. The Assemblée Nationale carried out an exhaustive series of interviews with individuals involved in events leading to the defeat and armistice: Assemblée Nationale, *Première législature, session de 1947, rapport fait au nom de la commission chargée d'enquêter sur les événéments en France de 1933 à 1945* (11 vols). Paul Reynaud's memoirs relating to the period are defiantly entitled *La France a sauvé l'Europe* (2 vols, 1947).

Vichy

Robert Paxton's *Vichy France. Old Guard and New Order 1940–1944* (New York, 1972) is the best book on Vichy, and in many ways the best book on twentieth-century France. Some of Paxton's arguments should be considered in the light of John Sweets, 'Hold that pendulum! Redefining fascism, collaborationism and Resistance in France', *French Historical Studies*, 15 (1988) 731–58. Jean Pierre Azéma, *From Munich to the Liberation 1938–1944* (Cambridge, 1984) is a solid narrative. It is interesting to compare the two large collective works on Vichy: René Rémond (ed.), *Le gouvernement de Vichy 1940–1942* (1973), and Jean-Pierre Azéma and François Bédarida, *Vichy et les français* (1992). H.R. Kedward, 'Patriots and patriotism in Vichy France', *Transactions of the Royal Historical Society*, 32 (1982) 175–92 examines the reasons for the popularity of the Vichy government. Andrew Shennan, *Rethinking France* (Oxford, 1989) concentrates on the intellectual foundations of the projects of both Vichy and the Resistance. Nick Atkins describes the, largely unsuccessful, attempts to restore the influence of the church in 'The challenge to laïcité: church, state and schools in Vichy France 1940–1944', *Historical Journal*, 35 (1992) 151–69. On public opinion under Vichy, see Pierre Laborie, *L'opinion française sous Vichy* (1990); Roger Austen, 'Surveillance and intelligence under the Vichy regime: the service du contrôle technique 1939–1945', *Intelligence and National Security*, Vol. 1, no. 1 (1986), and 'Propaganda and public opinion in Vichy France: Hérault 1940-1944', *The European Studies Review*, 13, 4 (1983). Much of the best work on Vichy has been produced in the form of local studies. See particularly, Paul Abrahams, 'Haute -Savoie at war 1939–1945' (Phd, University of Cambridge, 1992); Pierre Laborie, *Résistants, vichyssoises et autres, l'évolution de l'opinion et des comportements dans le Lot de 1939 à 1944* (1980); Monique Luirard, *La région stéphanoise dans la guerre et dans la paix 1936–1951* (Saint-Etienne, 1980). John Sweets, *Choices in Vichy France. The French under Nazi Occupation* (Oxford, 1986), and *The Politics of Resistance, 1940–1944* (Dekalb: Northern Illinois University Press, 1976) are both based on research in the Auvergne. On the *zone interdite* see the special issue of the *Revue du Nord* (1975). On prisoners of war see Yves Durand, *La captivité. Histoire des prisonniers de guerre français 1939–1945* (1980), and Sarah Fishman, 'Grand delusion: the unintended consequences of Vichy France's propaganda on prisoners of war', *Journal of Contemporary History*, 26, 2 (April 1991) 229–54. On

youth see W.D. Halls, *The Youth of Vichy France* (Oxford, 1981), and
Roger Austin, 'The Chantiers de la Jeunesse in Languedoc, 1940–44'
French Historical Studies, 13 (1983) 106–26. On the arts see Jean-
Pierre Rioux (ed.), *La vie culturelle sous Vichy* (1990). On Jewish
policy see Michael Marrus and Robert Paxton, *Vichy France and the
Jews* (New York, 1981). On social and economic life under Vichy see
A.S. Milward, *The New Order and the French Economy* (Oxford, 1970);
Isabelle Boussard, *Vichy et la corporation paysanne* (1980), and Richard
F. Kuisel, 'The legend of Vichy synarchy', *French Historical Studies*, 6
(1970) 365–98. The best biography of Pétain for the period before
1940 is Richard Griffiths, *Marshal Pétain* (1970 and 1994); the best
biography for the period after 1940 is Marc Ferro, *Pétain* (1987). On
Laval see Geoffrey Warner, *Pierre Laval and the Eclipse of France*
(1968). On collaborationism see the special issue of the *Revue d'histoire de la deuxième guerre mondiale* (July 1973); Pascal Ory, *Les collabo-
rateurs 1940–1945* (1976), and Bertram Gordon, *Collaborationism in
France during the Second World War* (Ithaca, NY). Paul Jankowski,
*Communism and Collaborationism: Simon Sabiani and Politics in
Marseilles 1919–1944* (New Haven, CT, 1989), is thin. On the *milice*
see Jean Delpierre de Bayac, *Histoire de la milice* (1969). Richard
Cobb, *French and Germans, Germans and French: a Personal Interpretation
of France under Two Occupations 1914–1918/1940–1944* (Hanover,
New England, 1983) reveals much about Richard Cobb. Pierre
Nicolle's diary, *Cinquante mois d'armistice, Vichy, 2 juillet 1940–26 août
1944: journal d'un témoin* (2 vols, 1947), is written by a Pétainist with
links to small business; Charles Rist, *Une saison gâtée. Journal de la
guerre et de l'occupation 1939–1945* (ed. Jean-Noel Jeanneney, 1983) is
written by an opponent of Vichy with links to big business.
Emmanuel Berl spent little time in Vichy France, but did stay long
enough to write one of Pétain's most important speeches. His *La fin
de la IIIe République* (1968) is useful as are the memoirs of another
unlikely associate of Pétain, Henri Lémery, *D'une république à l'autre*
(1964). The Hoover Institute's *France during the German Occupation*
(3 vols, Stanford, CA, 1959) contains interviews collected by Laval's
family. Not surprisingly, these interviews tend to be favourable to
Laval, but many of them are informative. Henri du Moulin de
Labarthète, *Le temps des illusions: souvenirs (juillet 1940–avril 1942)*
(Geneva, 1947) is a suprisingly detached book by a member of
Pétain's inner circle. See also Yves Bouthillier, *Le drame de Vichy* (2
vols, 1950), René Belin, *Du secrétariat de la CGT au gouvernement de
Vichy* (1978); Benoist Méchin, *De la défaite au désastre* (2 vols, 1984);

Marcel Peyrouton, *Du service public à la prison commune* (1950), Pierre Pucheu, *Ma vie* (1948). Gérard Miller, *Le Pousse-au-jouir du maréchal Pétain* (1975), is an examination of Pétainist language. Those who wish to understand Pétain's appeal should read some of the hagiographic works devoted to him. Gustave Hervé, *C'est Pétain qu'il nous faut* (1935) helped to build up the marshal's reputation and associated it with republicanism. Emmanuel Laure's *Pétain* (1941) was written at the height of Pétain's popularity. René Benjamin, *Le maréchal et son peuple* (1941) includes many accounts of Pétain's conversations. The same author's *Le grand homme seul* (1943) is the expression of a more embattled and unpopular Pétainism. On the legacy of Vichy see Henri Rousso, *The Vichy Syndrome 1944–198–*(Cambridge MA, 1991).

The early role of the Communist party in the Resistance has been the subject of much controversy, which is reviewed in J.C. Simmonds, 'The French Communist party and the beginnings of the Resistance: September 1939–June 1941', *European Studies Review*, 11 (1981) 517–42. Jean-Pierre Azéma, Antoine Prost and Jean-Pierre Rioux (eds), *Les communistes français de Munich à Chateaubriant (1938–1941)* (1987) stresses the local variation in Communist reactions. Roger Bourderon and Yvan Avakoumovitch, *Detruire le PCF. 40/44 Archives de l'Etat français et de l'occupant hitlérien* (1988) shows that the Germans certainly *believed* the Communist party to be their most dangerous enemy. See also S. Courtois, *Le PCF dans la guerre* (1980), and Jean-Pierre Azéma, Antoine Prost and Jean-Pierre Rioux (eds), *Le PCF des années sombres 1939–1941* (1986).

On the *maquis* see H.R. Kedward, *Resistance in Vichy France. A Study of Ideas and Motivations in the Southern Zone* (Oxford, 1978), and H.R. Kedward, *In Search of the Maquis. Rural Resistance in southern France 1942–1944* (Oxford, 1993). Some of the essays in H.R. Kedward and R. Austen, *Vichy France and the Resistance: Culture and Ideology* (Brighton, 1985) are weak. The role of the right in the Resistance has been neglected. Daniel Cordier, *Jean Moulin. L'inconnu du Panthéon*, Vol. 2: *Le choix d'un destin* (1980) casts some light on the views of Henri Frenay. Alain Griotteray, *1940: La droite était au rendezvous. Qui furent les premiers résistants?* (1985) is partisan, but useful. A number of Resistance leaders have written their memoirs. See Henri Frenay, *The Night Will End* (1976), and Philippe Viannay, *Nous sommes les rebelles* (1945). De Gaulle's *Mémoires de guerre* (3 vols, 1954–9) have been translated into English under the titles *Call to Honour 1940–1942* (1959), *Unity 1942–1944* (1959) and *Salvation 1944–1946* (1960). On de Gaulle in London see the excellent F. Kersaudy, *Churchill and de Gaulle* (1982), and Jean Lacouture, *De Gaulle, le rebelle* (1984). For an amusingly hostile view of de Gaulle from an English perspective see Edward Spears, *Assignment to Catastrophe* (2 vols, 1964). For hostile views from (anti-Vichy) French perspectives see Robert Mengin, *No Laurels for de Gaulle* (1967), Emile Muselier, *De Gaulle contre le Gaullisme* (1946), and Henri de Kérillis, *De Gaulle dictateur. Une grande mystification de l'histoire* (Montreal, 1945). Pierre Péan, *Une jeunesse française. François Mitterrand 1934–1947* (1994) captures the political complexity of a period that allowed one man to have met Pétain, de Gaulle and the comte de Paris by the time that he was 30.

Liberation

The collection of papers published by the Comité d'Histoire de la Deuxiéme Geurre Mondiale as *La Libération de la France* (1974) is comprehensive. Herbert Lottman, *The People's Anger, Justice and Revenge in post-Liberation France* (1982) is more recent but weaker than Peter Novick, *The Resistance versus Vichy: the Purge of Collaborators in Liberated France* (New York, 1968). For some idea of the impact that purges had on those who underwent them see Alfred Fabre-Luce, *Vingt-cinq années de liberté. II. L'épreuve 1939–1946* (1963), *Au nom des silencieux* (Bruges, 1945), and Henry Charbonneau, *Le roman noir de la droite française* (1969); several of the Pétainist memoirs cited above finish with descriptions of prison life. Abbé Jean Popot, *J'étais aumônier à Fresnes* (1962) is also useful on this subject. Two lawyers who made their names defending Pétainists and went on to play important roles in the French right have written accounts of this period: see J.-L. Tixier-Vignancour, *J'ai choisi la défense* (1976), and J. Isorni, *Ainsi passent les républiques* (Paris, 1959). On the *opposition nationale* that was created by post-war purges, and reinforced by the abandonment of Algeria, see two books by individuals who knew the milieu from the inside: François Duprat, *Les Mouvements de l'extrême droite en France depuis 1944.* (1972), and Francis Bergeron and Philippe Vilgier, *De le Pen à le Pen. Une histoire des nationaux et des nationalistes sous la Ve Republique* (1989). René Chiroux, *L'extrême droite sous la Ve République* (1974) is a meticulous and well-organized guide to this confusing world. Joseph Algazy, *La tentation neo fasciste en France, 1944–1965* (1984), and *L'extrême droite en France 1965–1984* (1989) contain some interesting details and photographs.

Fourth Republic politics

MacRae, *Parliament, Parties and Society in France 1946–1958* (London and New York, 1967), undertakes some rather confusing statistical studies. Philip Williams, *Politics in Post-war France. Parties and the Constitution in the Fourth Republic* (1954) is the standard account in English. Jacques Fauvet's *La Ve République* (1959) is based on his work as a correspondent for *Le Monde*. Georgette Elgey, *La république des illusions (1945–1951)* (1965) and *La république des contradictions (1951–1954)* (1968) draws on interviews conducted with leading politicians. Vincent Auriol, *Journal du septennat (1947–1953)* (7 vols, 1970–80) recounts numerous conversations between the president of the republic and leaders of political parties: it has a good index. On radicalism see William de Tarr, *The French Radical Party from Herriot to Mendès-France* (Oxford, 1961). There is a substantial literature on the MRP, largely written by militants or sympathizers. See: E.F. Callot, *Le Mouvement Républicaine Populaire. Un parti politique de la démocratie chrétienne en France. Origine, structure, doctrine, programme et action politique* (1978) and *L'action et l'oeuvre politique du Mouvement Républicain Populaire* (1986); Robert Bichet, *La démocratie chrétienne en France* (Besançon, 1980); Bruno Béthouart, *Le MRP dans le Nord–Pas-de-Calais 1944–1947* (1984) and Ronald Irving, *Christian Democracy in France* (1971). On the SFIO see B.D. Graham, *French Socialists in Tripartisme* (1965). The same author has recently returned to the SFIO with *Choice and the Democratic Order. The French Socialist Party 1937–1950* (Cambridge, 1994). On the RPF see (in addition to the numerous general works on Gaullism) C. Purtschet, *Le Rassemblement du Peuple Français 1947–1953* (1965); Patrick Guiol, *L'impasse sociale du gaullisme. Le RPF et l'Action Ouvrière* (1985) is wider than its title suggests. Jean Charlot, *Le Gaullisme d'opposition, 1946–1958* (1983) is good on the UDSR and the MRP as well as the RPF. Irwin Wall, *French Communism in the Era of Stalin* (Westport, CT, 1983) is a provocative and original book. Annie Lacroix Riz, *Le choix de Marianne: les relations franco-américaines, 1944–1948* (1985), looks at France and the United States. Irwin Wall's *American Influence in France 1944–1954* (Cambridge, 1991) tackles the same subject with the benefit of American archives and a more sceptical attitude. Specific aspects of American influence are examined by Richard Kuisel, 'L'américain way of life et les missions françaises de productivité', *Vingtième Siècle. Revue d'histoire*, 17 (1988) 21–38; Gérard Bossuat, *La France, l'aide américaine et la construction européene 1944–1954* (2 vols, 1992);

Anthony Carew, *Labour under the Marshall Plan. The Politics of Productivity and the Marketing of Management Science* (Manchester, 1987). On Fourth Republic conservatism see Sylvie Gauillaume, *Antoine Pinay ou la confiance en politique* (1984), and Malcolm Anderson, *Conservative Politics in France* (1974). On Poujadism see Dominique Borne, *Petits-bourgeois en révolte? Le mouvement Poujade* (1977); Stanley Hoffmann, *Le mouvement Poujade* (1956). Jean Touchard, 'Bibliographie et chronologie du poujadisme', *Revue française de Science Politique*, 6,1 (1956), and J. Campbell 'Le mouvement Poujade', *Parliamentary Affairs*, 10 (1957) (in English). The neo-fascist Maurice Bardèche and his associates prepared a special issue of *Défense de l'Occident* (1956) entitled *Poujadisme*, which gives good biographical information on Poujadist deputies. Steven Zdateny, *The Politics of Survival*, looks at Poujadist success in the *chambres des métiers*. Annie Collovald, 'Les Poujadistes, ou l'échec en politique', *Revue d'Histoire Moderne et Contemporaine*, 36 (1989), 113–33 describes the fate of the Poujadist group in parliament. Roger Eatwell, 'Poujadism', in P. Cerny (ed.), *Social Movement and Protest in France* (1982) argues that the movement had achieved many of its aims before the elections of 1956. Poujade's first autobiography, *J'ai choisi le combat* (1956) is interesting; his second autobiography *A l'heure de la colère* (1977) reflects his drift to the right. Pierre Mendès-France, *Choisir. Conversations avec Jean Bothorel* (1974) should be read in conjunction with François Béderida and Jean-Pierre Rioux, *Pierre Mendès-France et le mendèsisme. L'experience gouvernementale (1954–1955) et sa postérité* (1985).

Decolonization

On the early stages of French decolonization see P.C. Sorum, *Intellectuals and Decolonization in France* (North Carolina, 1977), D.B. Marshall, *The French Colonial Myth and Constitution Making in the Fourth Republic* (New Haven, CT, 1973), and Grégoire Madjarian, *La question coloniale et la politique du Parti Communiste Français, 1944–1947* (1977). On Indo-China see Ronald Irving, *The First Indo-China War* (1975). On the political importance of Africa see Edward Mortimer, *France and the Africans, 1940–1960: a Political History* (1969). Philip Williams, *Wars, Plots and Scandals in Post-war France* (Cambridge, 1970) contains a variety of articles on aspects of French decolonization. Jacques Marseille, *Empire colonial et capitalisme français: histoire d'un divorce* (1984) is an important book.

Algeria

The events leading to the fall of the Fourth Republic are described in Merry and Serge Bromberger, *Les treize complots du treize mai*, (1959). Alistair Horne, *A Savage War of Peace: Algeria: 1954–1962* (1977) is long and detailed. John Talbot, *The War Without a Name. France in Algeria, 1954–1962* (1981) is good. De Gaulle's own account of this period, *Mémoires d'espoir. Le renouveau 1958–1962* (1969) should be read in the light of remarks made by his own aide Bernard Tricot in *Les sentiers de la paix. Algérie 1958–1962* (1972). Raoul Girardet, M. Boujou and J.P. Thomas, *La crise militaire française, 1945–1962. Aspects sociologiques* (1964) brilliantly describes the marginalization that drove some officers to rebellion in 1961. Jean Planchais, *Une histoire politique de l'armée. II: 1940–1967, de de Gaulle à de Gaulle (1967)* is also very good. John S. Ambler, *The French Army in Politics 1945–1962* (Ohio, 1966) criticizes interpretations based on 'military Poujadism'. See also G. Kelly, *Lost soldiers: the French Army and Empire in Crisis, 1947–1962* (Cambridge, MA, 1965). On 'psychological' warfare see Bernard Trinquier, *Modern Warfare: a French View of Counterinsurgency (1964)*, and Raoul Girardet, 'Réflexions critiques sur la doctrine militaire française de la guerre subversive', in *Revue de l'Academie des Sciences Morales et Politiques* (1961). Several of the officers involved in Algeria have published their memoirs. See especially André Zeller, *Soldats perdus* (1977), and Maurice Challe, *Notre révolte* (1968). Jean-Jacques Servan-Schrieber's *Lieutenant in Algeria* (1958) describes the experience of a, rather exceptional, reserve officer. H. Hamon and P. Rotman, *Les porteurs de valise* (1983), looks at those Frenchmen who aided the FLN. Henri Alleg, a Communist journalist who was tortured by Massu's paras, describes his experiences in *La Question* (1958). J-P. Rioux (ed.), *La guerre d'Algérie et les Français* (1990) contains many informative articles. Jean-Pierre Rioux and Jean-François Sirenelli (eds), *La guerre d'Algérie et les intellectuels français* (1988), and François Bédarida and Etienne Fouilloux, *La guerre d'Algérie et les chrétiens* (1988) are also useful. Daniel Leconte, *Les pieds noirs. Histoire et portrait d'une communauté* (1978) is an excellent and sympathetic book by a journalist whose own family returned from Algeria. On the OAS and its aftermath see Paul Henissart, *Wolves in the City. The Death of French Algeria* (New York, 1971); Alexander Harrison, *Challenging de Gaulle, the OAS and Counterrevolution in Algeria 1954–1962* (New York, 1989); A. Heggoy, *Insurgency and Counterinsurgency in Algeria* (Indiana, 1972), P. Nora,

L'OAS parle (1964), and Claude Paillat, *La liquidation* (1972). On the political legacy of Algeria see W.B. Cohen, 'The legacy of Empire: the Algerian Connection', *Journal of Contemporary History*, 15 (1980), D. Tucker, 'The new look of the French extreme right', *Western Political Quarterly*, 21 (1968), and T.A. Smith, 'Algeria and the French modérés: the politics of immoderation?' *Western Political Quarterly*, 18 (1965) 86–116.

Gaullism

On the general nature of Gaullism see Jean Charlot, *The Gaullist Phenomenon. The Gaullist Movement in the Fifth Republic* (1971), and Jean Touchard, *Le Gaullisme 1940–1969* (1978). On de Gaulle's entourage see Institut Charles de Gaulle, *De Gaulle et ses premiers ministres 1959–1969* (1990), and G. Pilleul (ed.), *L'entourage et de Gaulle* (1979). Many members of this entourage contributed to *De Gaulle en son siècle. Actes des journées internationales tenues à l'Unesco Paris, 19–24 novembre 1990* (6 vols, 1992). Most of the contributions to this work are excruciatingly dull. Numerous associates of de Gaulle have published their memoirs. See especially Léon Noel, *Comprendre de Gaulle* (1972), Alain de Boisseau, *Pour servir le Général, 1946–1970* (1982), Christian Fouchet, *Mémoires d'hier et de demain 1: Au service de général de Gaulle* and *2: Les lauriers sont coupés* (1971–73). Pierre Blanc, *De Gaulle au soir de sa vie* (1990) is a revealing book by the civil servant who helped de Gaulle to research his memoirs in 1969 and 1970. On the political impact of television see Jean-Pierre Guichard, *De Gaulle et les mass media. L'image du général* (1985), and René Rémond and Claude Neuschwander, 'Télévision et comportement politique', *Revue Française de Science Politique* 13, 2 (June 1963). François Mitterrand criticizes the Bonapartist nature of the Fifth Republic constitution in *Le coup d'état permanent* (1964). The literature of right-wing anti-Gaullism is immense. Some works of this kind verge on hysteria, but some understand facets of de Gaulle that remain hidden to liberal commentators. Alfred Fabre-Luce devoted much of his career to studying de Gaulle and wrote a book to coincide with every major episode in the general's life. See especially *Gaulle deux* (1958); *The Trial of Charles de Gaulle* (1963), published in English with an introduction by Dorothy Pickles; *Le Général en Sorbonne* (1968); and *De Gaulle l'anniversaire* (1971). De Gaulle's view of France in the world is described in Philip Cerny, *The Politics of*

Grandeur. Ideological Aspects of de Gaulle's Foreign Policy (Cambridge, 1980). Philip Gordon, *A Certain Idea of France. French Security Policy and the Gaullist Legacy* (Princeton, NJ, 1993) explores some of the contradictions in de Gaulle's approach.

Communism

In addition to the works cited above, there are several general histories of the *Parti Communiste Français.* Philippe Robrieux, *Histoire intérieure du parti communiste* (4 vols, 1980–4) is detailed. George Lavau, *A quoi sert le Parti Communiste Français* (1981) developed the influential thesis that the PCF acted as a 'tribune' party. This thesis is also discussed in Jean Jacques Becker, *Le parti communiste veut-il prendre le pouvoir prendre le pouvoir* (1981). Annie Kreigel's *The French Communists. Profile of a People* (London and Chicago, 1968) describes the social basis of the party. Kreigel modestly refrains from discussing her own role in maintaining Stalinist orthodoxy during the Fourth Republic. Pierre Juquin, *Autocritiques* (1985) provides the viewpoint of a former PCF official who has broken with the party line, but not with the party. Anglo-Saxon historians have taken French Communist intellectuals almost as seriously as those intellectuals took themselves. On this subject see Tony Judt, *Past Imperfect. French Intellectuals 1944–1956* (Berkeley, CA, 1992), Sadur Hazareesingh, *Intellectuals and the French Communist Party* (Oxford, 1991). M. Adereth, *The French Communist Party: a Critical History 1920–1984* (Manchester, 1984) makes one wonder what might constitute an uncritical history.

1968

David Caute, *The Year of the Barricades '68* (1988) is a pedestrian account of the events of 1968 throughout the world. The best general study of 1968 in France is Julian Jackson, 'De Gaulle and May 1968' in Hugh Gough and John Horne (eds), *De Gaulle and the Twentieth Century* (1994). Jacques Capdevielle and René Mouriaux, *Mai 68. L'entre-deux de la modernité* (1988) has a good bibliography. See also Roger Absalom, *France: the May Events 1968* (1971), B. Brown, *Protest in Paris: Anatomy of a Revolt* (Princeton, NJ, 1974), Richard Johnson, *The French Communist Party versus the Students:*

Revolutionary Politics in May-June 1968 (New Haven, CT, 1972), and Drost and I. Eichelberg, *Mai 1968. Une crise de la civilisation française: anthologie critique de documents politique et littéraraires* (Frankfurt, 1986). A large number of near contemporaneous accounts were produced by participants in 1968. Some of these were gathered together in Charles Posner (ed.), *Reflections on the Revolution in France: 1968* (1970). See also Daniel Cohn-Bendit, *Obsolete Communism: the Left-wing Alternative* (1969). Philippe Beneton and Jean Touchard surveyed various views in 'Les interpretations de la crise de mai–juin 1968', in *Revue Française de Science Politique* (1970) 504–16. The works published by participants to mark the twentieth anniversary of May 1968 are usually more interesting, and more accessible, than those published at the time. See especially Henri Weber, *Vingt ans après. Que rest-t-il de 68* (1988), and Daniel Cohn-Bendit, *Nous l'avons tant aimé la révolution* (1986). E. Morin, C. Lefort, and C. Castoris, *Mai 68: la brèche, suivi de vingt ans après* (Brussels, 1988) contains assessments written at the time as well as more recent analysis. For a study of the careers of activists before and after May 1968 see H. Hamon and P. Rotman, *Génération* I: *Les années de rêve* (1987), and II: *Les années de poudre* (1988). Alain Tourraine, *Le mouvement du mai ou le communisme utopique* (1968) is an account by an academic sociologist at Nanterre who was sympathetic to the students. Michel Crozier, *The Stalled Society* (1970) is an account by an academic who was unsympathetic to the students; Raymond Aron, *The Elusive Revolution* (1969) is by an academic who was violently hostile to the students. For a view of events from the other side of the barricades see R. Marcellin, *L'importune vérité. Dix ans après mai 1968 un ministre de l'intérieur parle* (1978), and the very odd book by a police chief who supported many of the students' demands: M. Grimaud, *En mai fais ce qu'il te plaît* (1977). On de Gaulle's actions and motives in 1968 see Julian Jackson 'De saulle and May 1968' and F. Goguel, 'Charles de Gaulle, du 24 au 29 mai 1968', *Espoir*, XLVI (1984) 3–14. General Jacques Massu, who was de Gaulle's host during his brief visit to Germany, gives his version of events in *Baden 68, souvenirs d'une fidelité gaulliste* (1983). Georges Pompidou's account is given in *Pour rétablir une vérité* (1982). Edouard Balladur was a member of Pompidou's cabinet in 1968, but his *l'Arbre de mai, chronique alternée* (1979) says more about its author than the events that it describes. On the workers see G. Adam, 'Etude statistique des grèves de mai et juin 1968', *Revue Française de Science Politique* (Feb, 1970) 105–119; J.-D. Reynaud, S. Dassa, J. Dassa and P. Maclouf, 'Les événments de mai et juin 1968 et le système français de rélations professionnelles,' *Sociologie du Travail* (Jan–Mar 1971) 77; G. Durand, 'Ouvriers et techniciens en mai 1968', in P. Dubois, *Grèves revendicatives ou grèves politiques?* (1971); M. Bellas, 'Ambiguités des négotiations de Grenelle', *Projet*, 27 (July-August, 1968) 809–13, and CGT, *Le bilan social de l'année 1968* (1968). The role of the anti-Gaullist right in the events of 1968 is discussed in the works by Duprat, Chiroux and Ariès cited above.

Films

Three films have exercised an important influence on the perception of recent French history. *The Sorrow and the Pity* was made by Marcel Ophuls in 1971. This film was produced for French television but banned by the head of ORTF, himself a resistance veteran, who argued that 'the French still need their myths'. John Sweets remarked that his own book on Clermond-Ferrand (*Choices in Vichy France*) was partly designed to counteract the message of *The Sorrow and the Pity*. In fact, the picture that the film presents, one of a nation where opposition to Vichy came from only a marginal minority, is one that, as Ophuls himself admitted, had as much to do with the conflicts of 1968 as with those of the Vichy period.

Louis Malle's *Lacombe Lucien* (1974), provides an interesting contrast to *Le Chagrin et la Pitié*. Ophuls' film is a wide-ranging documentary that implies that collaboration was a bourgeois vice. *Lacombe Lucien* is a fictional narrative centred on a young peasant who joins the *milice* almost by accident. *Lacombe Lucien* has influenced Kedward's view of the *maquis* and one historian argues that Malle's vision is closer to the truth than that presented in most written acounts: Jankowski 'In defence of fiction. Resistance, collaboration and "Lacombe Lucien"', *Journal of Modern History*, 63 (1991), 457–82.

Pontecorvo's *The Battle of Algiers* has also influenced historians: one of the chapters in Alastair Horne's work *A Savage War of Peace* on the Algerian war is almost entirely derived from this film. However, as suggested in chapter 11, the most revealing aspect of this film is the limited attention that it has received within France. The film was made by an Italian and is hardly ever shown in Paris. The treatment of the Algerian war in French cinema has been taken up by Michael Dine in *Images of the Algerian War. French Fiction and Film 1954–1962* (Oxford, 1994).

Care should be taken when using film as a historical source. The most 'significant' films were not always the most popular. Julian Jackson points out that the 15 biggest box office hits of 1936 had no obvious relation to the Popular Front. Often the best films were made by directors who refused to be bound by the need to transmit an obvious message. Such a refusal is obvious in Lacombe Lucien, but it is also visible in *The Battle of Algiers* and *The Sorrow and The Pity* (both of which display a sympathy bordering on fascination for the characters who represent the political 'enemy'). The conflict between artistic and political needs was seen clearly in the three years that followed the Popular Front. Jean Renoir's *La Vie est à nous* (a grotesquely bad film in which actors from the Comédie Française impersonate the French proletariat) exemplified the film-maker as propagandist. Renoir argued that cinema should instill its audience with optimism, patriotism and anti-fascist unity. Marcel Carné represented a cinema that laid greater emphasis on the merit of an individual film than on its political impact. Renoir described the pessimism of Carné's *Quai des Brumes* as fascist.

Often the most revealing films are those that do not contain any explicit political message at all. Louis Malle's *Ascenseur pour l'Echafaud* (1958) is a murder story but it contains three interesting characters: the large-scale capitalist who is linked to the exploitation of Algeria, the hero/anti-hero whose military career has distanced him from society, and the German who talks of his compatriots in the Foreign Legion. All these characters say something about the growing gulf perceived between the army and the nation during the Algerian war. Tavernier's *La vie et rien d'autre* shows how widespread and long-lasting were the myths of the First World War 'marchands des canons'. Sometimes the title credits cast a new and interesting light on films. Who would guess that Marcel Carné's *Les Enfants du Paradis* was made in the last months of the Occupation if the credits did not thank those who 'worked on the film in clandestinity'? Who would guess that the wounded man in Patrick Leconte's *Le Parfum d'Yvonne* is a member of the OAS if it were not for the titles? Perhaps the French film-maker whose work most defies social or political categorization is Eric Rohmer. His films display a fascination with eroticism, romantic love and an unorthodox version of religious faith; his only explicitly political film (*L'arbre, le maire et la médiathèque* [1993]) describes a world in which political tradition, even the Vendée, cannot be used as a guide for current behaviour.

Chronology: France 1934–1970

1934

6 Feb.	Anti-parliamentary riots
7 Feb.	Resignation of Daladier government
12 Feb.	General strike
22 Feb.	Doumergue granted power to govern by decree law
27 July	Socialists and Communists agree on pact for joint action
8 Nov.	Resignation of Doumergue government

1935

18 Jan.	Gamelin replaces Weygand as commander-in-chief
14 July	Demonstration by *Rassemblement Populaire*
16 July	Laval introduces deflationary policy
6 Dec.	Suppression of paramilitary organizations

1936

12 Jan.	Manfesto of *Rassemblement Populaire*
24 Jan.	Resignation of Laval government
25 March	Unification of Socialist and Communist trade unions
5 May	Election victory of Popular Front
7 June	Matignon agreement
12 June	Introduction of collective agreements, paid holidays and 40-hour week
18 June	Suppression of leagues
21 June	Creation of *Parti Social Français* (successor to *Croix de Feu*)
27 Sept.	Devaluation of franc

1937

13 Feb.	Blum 'pause' begins
22 June	Resignation of Blum government

1938

10 March	Resignation of Chautemps government
24 March	Strikes
8 April	Resignation of Blum government
12 April	Daladier government gains almost unanimous support from parliament
4 Oct.	Parliament approves Munich agreement
1 Nov.	Reynaud replaces Marchandeau as minister of finances
12 Nov.	Publication of Reynaud decree laws
30 Nov.	General strike by CGT

1939

28 July	Family code enacted
29 July	Chamber of Deputies prorogued by decree
25 Aug.	*l'Humanité* seized
1 Sept.	General mobilization
2 Sept.	Parliament votes war credits
3 Sept.	France declares war on Germany
26 Sept.	Dissolution of Communist party
4 Oct.	Thorez (Communist leader) deserts from army
8 Oct.	Arrest of PCF deputies

1940

20 Jan.	Parliament votes to disqualify Communist deputies
20 March	Daladier resigns and is replaced by Reyanud
13 May	German forces cross Meuse
18 May	Ministerial reshuffle brings in Pétain as deputy prime minister
19 May	Weygand replaces Gamelin as commander-in-chief

5 June	Ministerial reshuffle brings in de Gaulle as undersecretary of state for war
10 June	Government leaves Paris
16 June	Reynaud resigns and is replaced by Pétain
17 June	Pétain enquires about conditions of an armistice. De Gaulle flies to London
19 June	Communist enquiries about possibility of publishing *l'Humanité* in German-occupied Paris
23 June	Laval enters government. Armistice signed
2 July	Parliament convoked to Vichy
9–12 July	Parliament decides to revise constitutional laws, and grants full powers to Pétain who issues acts founding French state and nominates Laval as his heir apparent
August	Rejection of Déat's plan to create single party
16 Aug.	Creation of Organization committees to run industry
29 Aug.	Creation of *Légion Française des Combattants*
6 Sept.	Most parliamentarians ejected from government
7 Sept.	Weygand made delegate general in North Africa
10 Sept.	Creation of *Office Centrale de Répartition des Produits Industriels*
23–25 Sept.	Unsuccessful mission by Gaullists to rally Dakar
27 Sept.	Germans promulgate decree on Jews in occupied zone
3 Oct.	Statute of Jews in Vichy zone
22 Oct.	Meeting between Hitler and Laval
24 Oct.	Meeting between Hitler and Pétain at Montoire
27 Oct.	De Gaulle creates council of imperial defence in Brazzaville
11 Nov.	Anti-German demonstrations by students
13 Dec.	Laval dismissed and briefly arrested
14 Dec.	Flandin becomes minister of foreign affairs

1941

22 Jan.	Creation of National Council
1 Feb.	Déat and Deloncle found *Rassemblement National Populaire*
9 Feb.	Flandin resigns; Darlan is appointed deputy prime minister and minister of foreign affairs
10 Feb.	Darlan become heir apparent to Pétain
29 March	Xavier Vallat becomes commissioner for Jewish affairs

8 June	Gaullist forces enter Syria
15 May	Creation of Front National Resistance organization
May–June	Strike in northern coal fields
18 July	Pucheu becomes minister of the interior
21 Aug.	First assassination of German soldier
4 Oct.	Promulgation of labour charter
20 Nov.	Weygand recalled from Africa
12 Nov.	Creation of *service d'ordre légionnaire*

1942

1 Jan.	Jean Moulin parachuted into France
19 Feb.	Beginning of Riom trial
3 March	Muselier leaves French National Committee in London
15 April	Riom trial suspended
17 April	Darlan resigns
18 April	Laval returns to Vichy as 'head of government'
22 June	Laval announces his 'sincere desire for German victory'
14 July	Free France become Fighting France
16–17 July	Large-scale deportations of Jews from Paris
4 Sept.	*Service du Travail Obligatoire* programme set up
8 Nov.	Americans land in Algeria
9 Nov.	Giraud arrives in Algeria
11 Nov.	Germans take southern zone
12 Nov.	Weygand arrested by Germans
13 Dec.	Americans strike deal with Darlan in Algiers
24 Dec.	Darlan assassinated

1943

19 Jan.	Peyrouton becomes governor of Algeria
30 Jan.	Creation of *milice*
16 Feb.	*Service du Travail Obligatoire* deportations begin
14 March	Giraud, under the influence of Jean Monnet, makes speech in favour of republican institutions
25 March	Catroux arrives in Algeria
15 May	In the name of the Resistance, Moulin declares loyalty to de Gaulle

27 May	*Conseil National de la Résistance* is founded
30 May	De Gaulle arrives in Algeria
July	Death of Jean Moulin
3 Sept.	Announcement that those who have served Vichy will stand trial
8 Sept.	Germans occupy zone formerly held by Italians
2 Oct.	De Gaulle gains exclusive political authority among Fighting French
5 Oct.	Corsica liberated
13 Nov.	Pétain ceases to exercise his functions

1944

1 Jan.	Darnand appointed secretary of state for order
6 Jan.	Henriot appointed secretary of state for information
16 March	Déat is appointed minster of labour
21 April	*Comité Français de Libération National* declares itself to be a provisional government
26 April	Pétain visits Paris
4 June	De Gaulle returns to Great Britain
6 June	Allied landings in Normandy
13 June	Darnand becomes minister of the interior
28 June	Henriot is assassinated
11 July	United States recognizes the de facto authority of the provisional government
20 Aug.	Pétain leaves Vichy
25 Aug.	De Gaulle visits Paris
23 Sept.	FFI incorporated into regular army
23 Oct.	Allies give formal recognition to provisional government
26 Nov.	Foundation of MRP
14 Dec.	Ordinance establishing nationalized coal mines
18 Dec.	First issue of *Le Monde*
26 Dec.	Ordinance establishing *indignité nationale* as punishment

1945

1–5 Jan.	Defence of Strasbourg
16 Jan.	Nationalization of Renault

6 Feb.	Execution of Brassilach
5 April	Resignation of Mendès-France after argument over financial policy
8 May	German surrender
13 May	Municipal elections
22 June	Creation of the *École Nationale d'Administration*
August	Pétain tried and condemned to death (commuted to life imprisonment)
4–15 Sept.	Trial and execution of Laval
21 Oct.	Referendum on constitution and legislative elections
21 Nov.	Formation of de Gaulle's government
2 Dec.	Nationalization of Bank of France and deposit banks
21 Dec.	Creation of the *Commissariat Général du Plan*
22 Dec.	Creation of *Parti Républicain de la Liberté*

1946

20 Jan.	Resignation of de Gaulle
24 Jan.	Tripartite alliance of MRP, SFIO and PCF
8 April	Nationalization of gas and electricity
5 May	No vote in referendum on constitution
28 May	Blum–Byrnes agreements on American loans to France
2 June	Legislative elections
12 June	Creation of the *Conseil National du Patronat Français*
27 July	Palais Royal conference between employers and trade unions
13 Oct.	Referendum accepts new constitution
27 Nov.	Adoption of the Monnet Plan
8 Dec.	Elections to council of the republic

1947

16 Jan.	Parliament elects Auriol as president of the republic. Resignation of Blum government
28 Jan.	Ramadier government
7 April	Foundation of the RPF
25 April	Strike at Renault
4 May	Communist ministers dismissed from Ramadier government

10 June	Start of wave of strikes
17 June	France accepts Marshall Aid
26 Oct.	Municipal elections
15 Nov.	Miners' strike begins
19 Nov.	Resignation of Ramadier government
22 Nov.	Schuman government
19 Dec.	Creation of *Force Ouvrière*

1948

5 Jan.	Deflationary Mayer plan launched
19 July	Resignation of Schuman government
24 July	Marie government
27 Aug.	Resignation of Marie government
31 Aug.	Schuman government
11 Sept.	Queuille government
7 Nov.	Elections to council of the republic
13–29 Nov.	General strike in Paris region

1949

6 Oct.	Resignation of Queuille government
29 Oct.	Bidault government

1950

11 Feb.	Adoption of minimum legal wage
9 May	Schuman announces Coal and Steel Plan
24 June	Resignation of Bidault government
30 June	Queuille government
4 July	Resignation of Queuille government
13 July	Pleven government
12 Sept.	Foundation of *Paix et Liberté*

1951

15 Feb.	Foundation of *Centre National des Indépendants et Paysans*

28 Feb.	Resignation of Pleven government
13 March	Queuille government
17 June	Legislative elections
10 July	Resignation of Queuille government
16 July	Death of Pétain
8 Aug.	Pleven government
14 Oct.	Cantonal elections
13 Dec.	Parliament ratifies Schuman Plan

1952

7 Jan.	Resignation of Pleven government
22 Jan.	Faure government
29 Feb.	Resignation of Faure government
6 March	Pinay government
23 Dec.	Resignation of Pinay government

1953

7 Jan.	Mayer government
10 Feb.	European Coal and Steel Community begins operating
13 March	Amnesty law relating to crimes committed under Vichy
3 May	Municipal elections
6 May	De Gaulle ceases to play role in RPF
14 May	First number of *L'Express*
21 May	Resignation of Mayer government
26 June	Laniel government
22 July	Birth of Poujadism in Saint-Céré
7 Aug.	Public sector strike
23 Dec.	Parliament elects Coty as president of the republic

1954

10 April	Value added tax introduced
12 June	Resignation of Laniel government
18 June	Mendès-France government
20 July	Geneva settlement

1–7 Aug.   Ceasefire in Indo-China
1 Nov.   Beginning of rebellion in Algeria

1955

5 Jan.   Programme of reforms in Algeria
25 Jan.   Soustelle appointed governor of Algeria
6 Feb.   Resignation of Mendès-France
25 Feb.   Faure government
2 April   State of emergency in Algeria
24 Aug.   Call up of reservists to Algeria
29 Nov.   Resignation of Faure government
12 Dec.   Adjournment of elections in Algeria

1956

2 Jan.   Legislative elections
5 Feb.   Mollet government
5 Nov.   Franco-British raid on Suez

1957

7 Jan.   Massu appointed to restore order in Algiers
25 March   Treaty of Rome
21 May   Resignation of Mollet government
12 June   Bourgès-Manoury government
30 Sept.   Resignation of Bourgès-Manoury government
5 Nov.   Gaillard government

1958

15 April   Resignation of Gaillard government
13 May   Pflimlin government
15 May   Salan cries 'Vive de Gaulle' to crowd in Algiers forum
24 May   Forces from Algeria take over Corsica
28 May   Pflimlin resigns
1 June   De Gaulle invested

2 June	De Gaulle voted full powers
4–7 June	De Gaulle visits Algeria
28 Sept.	Referendum on new constitution
23 Oct.	De Gaulle offers *paix de braves* to FLN. UNR created
30 Nov.	Legislative elections
21 Dec.	De Gaulle becomes first president of the Fifth Republic
28 Dec.	Creation of new franc (and effective devaluation)

1959

6 Jan.	School-leaving age raised to 16 – with delayed effect
9 Jan.	Debré becomes prime minister
15 Sept.	De Gaulle talks of 'auto-determination' for Algeria

1960

13 Jan.	Pinay resigns as finance minister and is replaced by Baumgartner
19 Jan.	Massu removed from Algiers
24 Jan.	Barricades week begins in Algiers
5 Feb.	Partisans of *Algérie Française*, notably Soustelle, leave government
13 Feb.	Explosion of first French atomic bomb
March	De Gaulle visits officers in Algeria
3 April	Creation of *Parti Socialiste Unifié*
4 Nov.	De Gaulle talks of 'Algerian Algeria'

1961

8 Jan.	Referendum on self-determinination for Algeria
22–25 April	Generals' putsch

1962

18 March	Evian agreement
19 March	Ceasefire in Algeria

23 March	Riots and massacre of *piedsnoirs* in Bab-el-Oued
8 April	Referendum approves Evian accords
14 April	Debré replaces Pompidou as prime minister
15 May	De Gaulle rejects European integration
1 July	Algeria gains independence
28 Oct.	Referendum approves election of president by universal suffrage
25 Nov.	Legislative elections

1963

14 Jan.	De Gaulle vetoes Britain's entry to Common Market
27 Jan.	Treaty of Franco-German cooperation
March–April	Miners' strike

1964

27 Jan.	France recognizes Communist China

1965

10 Sept.	Creation of *Fédération de la Gauche Démocratique et Socialiste* (FGDS)
19 Dec.	De Gaulle defeats Mitterrand by a narrow margin in the second round of the presidential election

1966

4 March	France withdraws from NATO integrated command
20 Dec.	Electoral pact between Communists and FGDS

1967

12 March	Legislative elections
19 Nov.	Neuwirth law authorizes contraception

1968

22 March	Occupation of faculty at Nanterre
3 May	Disturbances in Latin Quarter
10–11 May	Night of the barricades
13 May	Students and workers demonstrate together
27 May	Grenelle agreements between unions and employers. Meeting of non-Communist left at Charléty stadium
28 May	Mitterrand calls for de Gaulle to resign
29 May	De Gaulle flies to Baden-Baden
30 May	Demonstration by those in favour of order
16 June	Sorbonne evacuated
30 June	Legislative elections bring victory for the right
10 July	Couve de Murville replaces Pompidou as prime minister

1969

27 April	Referendum produces majority against participation
28 April	De Gaulle resigns

1970

9 Nov.	De Gaulle dies

Index